TOWARD
THE MEIJI
REVOLUTION

JAPAN LIBRARY

TOWARD THE MEIJI REVOLUTION

The Search for "Civilization" in Nineteenth-Century Japan

KARUBE TADASHI

Translated by David Noble

Japan Publishing Industry Foundation for Culture

NOTE ON ROMANIZATION

This book follows the Hepburn system of romanization. Except for place names found on international maps, long vowels are indicated by macrons. The tradition of placing the family name first has been followed for Japanese, Chinese, and Korean names.

Toward the Meiji Revolution: The Search for "Civilization" in Nineteenth-Century Japan by Karube Tadashi. Translated by David Noble.

Published by
Japan Publishing Industry Foundation for Culture (JPIC)
3-12-3 Kanda-Jinbocho, Chiyoda-ku, Tokyo 101-0051, Japan

First English edition: March 2019

© 2017 by Karube Tadashi
English translation © 2019 by Japan Publishing Industry Foundation for Culture

All rights reserved.

This book is a translation of *"Ishin kakumei" e no michi: "Bunmei" o motometa jūkyū seiki Nihon* (SHINCHOSHA Publishing Co., Ltd. 2017).
English publishing rights arranged with SHINCHOSHA Publishing Co., Ltd.

Book design: Miki Kazuhiko, Ampersand Works

Printed in Japan
ISBN 978-4-86658-059-3
http://www.jpic.or.jp/japanlibrary/

CONTENTS

Preface to the English Edition

The year 2018 marks the 150th anniversary of the collapse of the Tokugawa shogunate and the establishment of a new, modern government in Japan in 1868. The anniversary has inspired a variety of books, academic symposiums, novels, and television dramas on the theme of the Meiji Revolution (also known as the Meiji Restoration). Many readers no doubt saw the original Japanese edition of this book, published in 2017, as part of this larger social phenomenon.

Yet instead of focusing on the new government created by Satsuma and Chōshū samurai, some historians have centered their narrative on the "losers"—the Tokugawa regime and the domains of northeastern Japan that remained loyal to it. And a small number of historians have published work critical of the political transformation of 1868, seeing it as the point of departure for Japan's subsequent imperialist expansion.

I believe that neither side of this argument adequately explains the significance of the regime change of 1868, because both are too narrowly focused upon it. Certainly the transfer of the center of Japan's political framework from the Tokugawa family to the imperial house was a major event, but arguably, in terms of broader social revolution, of greater importance was the abolition of the domains and establishment of a centralized prefectural system (*haihan chiken*) four years later in 1871. This point was made by the influential writer and educator Fukuzawa Yukichi as early as 1875 and remains a persuasive assessment, even in light of current historical scholarship.

Moreover, neither the transfer of political power in 1868 nor the social revolution of 1871 was suddenly initiated in response to the encroachment of the United States and the other Western powers from 1853 onward, as was once widely believed. The Meiji Revolution was possible only as an extension of major shifts in society and thought taking place in the preceding era. During the course of the nineteenth century, the Japanese experienced a number of significant social transformations and engaged in a variety of efforts to understand foreign cultures. The magnitude of the changes that this wrought upon Japanese society is perhaps unique in human history. I believe that the investigation of the Japanese experience of the nineteenth century presents valuable lessons for the present era of globalization—not only in Japan but everywhere in the world. That is the aim of this book.

I would like to take this opportunity to express my gratitude to the Office of the Prime Minister and the Japan Publishing Industry Foundation for Culture (JPIC) for making this English edition possible. Special thanks as well to David Noble, for his superb translation, following upon that of my earlier book, *Maruyama Masao and the Fate of Liberalism in Twentieth-Century Japan* (I-House Press, 2008). I am also grateful to Sanbe Naota, my original editor, and to Shinchōsha for permission to publish this translation.

Karube Tadashi
Tokyo, December 2018

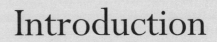

Reading "The Clash of Civilizations?" in 2017

After the opening of Japan to diplomatic relations and international trade with the West in the 1850s, Japanese society began to undergo a massive transformation. The Japanese came to describe their collective experience as an encounter with "civilization and enlightenment" (*bunmei kaika*). This encounter did not follow a smooth, predetermined course. People were faced with a variety of events and issues that challenged them to examine everything from politics and economics to their views of history, and even their concepts of life and death. Records of their efforts to understand the dramatic changes they were experiencing can be found in the copious archives of nineteenth-century Japanese intellectual history—the primary focus of this book.

In the latter half of the Tokugawa period (1603–1868), Japan faced many crossroads suggesting possible alternative paths for subsequent history as society gradually advanced toward its encounter with "civilization"— which could also be described as an encounter with the unknown. This book attempts to share with the reader a bird's-eye view of this process of encounter. And from this perspective, I hope to provide an alternative narrative to the conventional success stories of Japan's modernization.

We will later touch upon the issue of whether the Japanese word *bunmei* and the Western word "civilization" actually signify the same thing. But in any case, at the time of the opening of Japan, it was widely believed in both Japan and the West that there was only one path for the entire human race as it progressed toward "civilization."

Of course "civilization" is a Western concept, one that the sociologist Norbert Elias characterized as an expression of "European self-awareness" from the eighteenth century onward.[1] It was also used to legitimate Western colonialism. Here we should take care to observe that nineteenth-century

Japanese accepted the Western nations as the vanguard of "civilization." Today, this concept is widely criticized, but the Japanese of that era took this Western term of self-praise, translated it with an existing word in their own language—*bunmei*—and did not question its value or validity.

At the same time, a different use of the term "civilization" was beginning to make an appearance in the West. From about the middle of the nineteenth century, we see the gradual diffusion of a plural concept of "civilizations" unique to specific cultural spheres—thus, Western or Islamic or Hindu civilizations—in place of the idea of progress toward a single, universal "civilization." In the twentieth century this plural concept of civilizations dominated, and cultural relativism—avoiding discussion of the superiority or inferiority of different civilizations, and according equal value to all—made its appearance. The historian Fernand Braudel articulated this shift toward pluralism beginning in the 1960s. In *Grammaire des civilisations*, a high school textbook that he published in 1987, Braudel encourages intellectuals in the developed nations to criticize Eurocentrism and to acknowledge the value of diverse civilizations.

Yet in an essay published in the influential journal *Foreign Affairs* in 1993, Samuel P. Huntington, a leading American political scientist, poses the question whether a clash of civilizations might prove to be one of the principal sources of conflict in global politics in the years to come.[2] With the end of the Cold War, liberal democracy had spread to the former communist bloc, and the world seemed headed toward peace under an American hegemony. Huntington's essay threw cold water on such optimism, drawing attention throughout the world and inspiring much critical reaction.

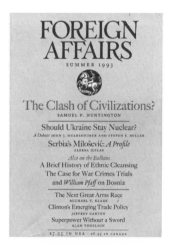

The issue of *Foreign Affairs* (Summer 1993) featuring "The Clash of Civilizations?" by Samuel P. Huntington.

According to Huntington, from the nineteenth century to World War I, conflict in the world was in essence a conflict between nation-states, while from World War II to the end of the Cold War, ideological conflict

Samuel P. Huntington
(1927–2008).

between the two superpowers shaped world politics. These were primarily conflicts within Western civilization, but with the end of the Cold War, conflicts between Western and non-Western civilizations would become a leading cause of warfare—in particular, the challenge to Western civilization presented by the Confucian[3] and Islamic states. Huntington predicted that, as the development of arms export routes from China to Pakistan and from North Korea to Syria and Iran would suggest, a "Confucian-Islamic military connection" would eventually come into being and pose a threat to the nations of the West, led by the United States.

As critiques by the German political scientist Dieter Senghaas[4] and the British historian Niall Ferguson[5] observe, historical studies previous to the publication of Huntington's essay, as well as developments since that time, show that global conflicts have usually occurred internally, within a particular civilization, whereas conflicts between different civilizations have been relatively rare. Huntington argued that the Gulf War of 1991 heralded the beginning of a clash between civilizations. He may have overestimated the gravity of the conflict between Christians and Muslims in Eastern Europe as well as the rise of Chinese military power. Conversely, his concern did not extend to the outbreak of domestic terrorist incidents by Islamic radicals in the developed nations or to Russia's territorial expansion under the aegis of bolstering elements of Slavic civilization. Or at least in hindsight that seems to be the case.

But an even more fundamental problem is the vagueness of the criteria that Huntington used to classify the various civilizations under consideration. He writes that civilizations are defined by "common objective elements such as language, history, religion, customs, institutions, and by the subjective self-identification of people." But if we look at this in terms of the three civilizations (Islamic, Confucian, and Western) that he cites as the principal actors in present and future conflicts, then it is clear that religion—if we adopt a definition of religion that can embrace both Confucianism and faith in transcendent, monotheistic deities—is posited as the nucleus of the concept of "civilization." This approach calls to mind the religious wars of the past, and tends to lead to the conclusion that the clash of civilizations is inevitable.

The vagueness of the concept of civilization in Huntington's essay was pointed out soon after its publication by the Japanese critic Yamazaki Masakazu.[6] If civilizations according to Huntington's classification were to be the source of global conflict from this time forward, then it would seem natural for Christianity and Islam, whose teachings are actually quite similar, to ally with one another in a conflict with Confucianism. Yamazaki also argued that since such highly developed systems of belief and organizations of believers are conscious, artificial creations, they could be propagated widely, transcending normal cultural boundaries. And since they are different in nature from customs and mores, which are bound more intimately to immediate human experience, they are capable of accepting and adapting to different cultures and potentially harmonizing with them. Religions distributed over broad geographic areas already possess, as a result of conscious human engagement, the potential for reform oriented toward coexistence with other faiths.

Huntington was probably aware of such criticism. In *The Clash of Civilizations and the Remaking of World Order*, a revised and expanded book-length version of his earlier essay, the final section is a discussion entitled "The Future of Civilizations."[7] Here he presents a dark vision of the future of international politics, one that attracted considerable attention at the time of publication: a world war between the United States and China, pitting a coalition of Western states against a coalition of Sinic and Islamic states.

The point of this scenario was not to advocate preparation for armed conflict with China and the Islamic nations. The narrative involves a dispute between China and Vietnam over territorial issues in the South China Sea that would develop into a military confrontation in 2010, with American intervention on the side of Vietnam expanding the conflict into a global war. To prevent such a worst-case scenario from occurring, Huntington argues that the "core states" of each civilization should develop an "abstention rule" regarding nonintervention in the internal conflicts of nations or groups within the spheres of other civilizations, as well as a "joint mediation rule" in the event of armed conflict on the fault lines between civilizations.

According to Huntington, we must abandon the assumption that Western civilization possesses a universality shared with the entire human race. Acknowledging the reality that the world is made up of multiple cultures, we should abstain from intervention in the internal conflicts of other civilizations with appeals to universal justice. Clearly, even when speaking of the "core states" of the different civilizations, it is really only the United States that he has in mind. He is saying, let's stop being the world's policeman, sending troops overseas to resolve the disputes of other nations. So the last word from this political scientist warning of the danger of the clash of civilizations is not a call for the United States to sally forth to bravely solve the world's problems, but a proposal that it refrain from involvement in foreign conflicts and the internal disputes of other regions in order to assure the stable coexistence of the world's civilizations.

In Huntington's hypothetical scenario for 2010, the correct response for the U.S. was to leave the conflict in East Asia alone—even if that meant large numbers of civilian deaths as a result of wartime atrocities, the conquest of Vietnam by China, and the establishment of a puppet regime. His "joint mediation rule" would also not seem to function when the civilization being negotiated with has no established "core state," as is the case with Islamic civilization. But in any case, refraining from intervention seems to be Huntington's proposal for "the remaking of world order."

Michael Ignatieff, a Canadian historian of political thought who at the time was working as a journalist in the United Kingdom, delivered a sharp criticism of Huntington's approach in a book review in the *New York Times* in 1996.[8] He writes, "The question is whether there remain certain human interests that all civilizations had better endorse for our common survival. Genocide is genocide, famine is famine, and a world where civilizations no longer intervene to save strangers from these universal threats is one that not even Samuel P. Huntington would feel safe in."

Even if we acknowledge that civilizations may possess different value systems, there exist certain universal evils that humanity cannot ignore. When they arise, do we not have the responsibility, Ignatieff asks, to transcend our cultural differences and actively oppose such evils? He also points to the double standard implied by Huntington's claim to acknowledge global cultural diversity while at the same time warning against and rejecting the impact of multiculturalism and cultural relativism in the United States.

From our present vantage, what relevance do the arguments set forth in Huntington's article and book still possess? Economic and cultural globalization have spawned reactions in the form of a rising tide of fundamentalist religious forces and movements to return to traditional culture in many parts of the non-Western world. Huntington's thoughts on the rise of fundamentalism have certainly captured global developments from the 1990s to the present. And then there is his assertion that the United States should abstain from interventions abroad and focus on setting its own house in order. According to Huntington, the spread of multiculturalism should not be encouraged; cohesion around the core values of traditional Western culture should be reaffirmed. It is this latter point that seems to have had the most predictive accuracy in light of the election of Donald Trump as president of the United States.

The trap of *wakon yōsai* ("Japanese spirit, Western technique")

There is a reason why, at the beginning of this chapter, I spoke of "nineteenth-century Japan" rather than "late Tokugawa and Meiji Japan." The regime change of 1868 that contemporaries called "the collapse" (*gakai*) or "the renewal" (*go-isshin*) was certainly a major political transformation, even viewed in terms of Japanese history as a whole. The encounter with "civilization" paved the way for this transformation at a fundamental level, while the transformation itself propelled Japan ever more swiftly toward "civilization." But if we focus exclusively on the discontinuity represented by 1868, we risk overlooking what we might call the structural changes in society and thought that were already in progress before that time. The reason I have defined my scope as the nineteenth century—spanning both the late Tokugawa and early to mid-Meiji—is that I want to trace the changes that occurred during the course of this *longue durée*.

The common understanding (as represented in middle school and high school textbooks and the like) of Japan's modernization places its starting point in 1868, commencing the narrative of "modernity" there, and treating the period prior as "early modern"—with an emphasis on discontinuity frequently accompanied by a stereotypical treatment of modernization itself. Huntington's writings on "the clash of civilizations" are not focused on Japan, but they do display a similarly stereotypical view of Japanese modernization.

As noted earlier, Huntington sees the world as "multicivilizational," with different civilizations occupying major regions of the globe, rooted in the traditions of those regions. In his 1996 book he lists nine such civilizations (Western, Orthodox, Islamic, African, Latin American, Sinic, Hindu, Buddhist, and Japanese). Huntington predicted that in the post–Cold War world order, nations would divide into groups aligned according to these civilizational affiliations, and that these groups would come into conflict with one another.

The reality of intense conflicts within the Islamic world, as well as doubts as to whether Latin America should be regarded as a discrete culture, invites counterarguments to Huntington's classification system. But I would like to focus here on his categorization of Japan as a discrete civilization, which he explains in terms of its approach toward modernization, unique among the nations of the non-Western world. Huntington defines modernization through indices such as industrialization, urbanization, and improvements in, for example, education and social mobility. From the mid-nineteenth century onward, as non-Western states were presented with the challenge of modernizing to catch up with the West, the majority either chose to import and assimilate Western culture for the purpose of modernization, like Kemal Atatürk's republic of Turkey, or else rejected modernization as the product of an alien culture.

In contrast, in Huntington's assessment, Japan is the only non-Western civilization to succeed at becoming modern without becoming Western—an isolated example among the nations that might otherwise be its peers. He is

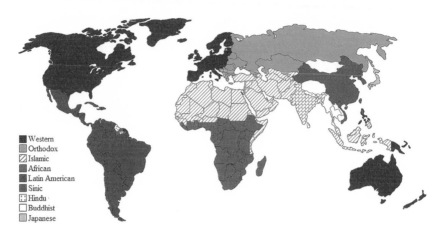

Western
Orthodox
Islamic
African
Latin American
Sinic
Hindu
Buddhist
Japanese

A map from Huntington's 1996 book *The Clash of Civilizations and the Remaking of World Order.*

not necessarily praising this uniqueness, since in his scenario of a U.S.-China conflict in *The Clash of Civilizations and the Remaking of World Order* Japan ends up betraying the U.S. and Western civilization and falling under Chinese hegemony. While Japan may appear to be Westernized, Huntington draws attention to its durable non-Western core. In chapter 5 of his book, Huntington describes the course of Japan's modernization:

> With the Meiji Restoration a dynamic group of reformers came to power in Japan, studied and borrowed Western techniques, practices, and institutions, and started the process of Japanese modernization. They did this in such a way, however, as to preserve the essentials of traditional Japanese culture, which in many respects contributed to modernization and which made it possible for Japan to invoke, reformulate, and build on the elements of that culture to arouse support for and justify its imperialism in the 1930s and 1940s.[9]

The unique aspect of Japanese modernization touched on here is characterized in chapter 3 of *The Clash of Civilizations* as *wakon yōsai*, translated as "Japanese spirit, Western technique." In the Meiji period, Japan's modernization was driven by government bureaucrats schooled in Western learning. They were assiduous in importing the fruits of Western culture in practical areas such as technology and social institutions, but in terms of moral and spiritual culture they strove to maintain a traditional ethos, an effort embodied in the Imperial Rescript on Education (1890). This strategy was useful in balancing modernization with the stability of the social order by avoiding the wholesale Westernization of society and preserving the traditional mores of the general populace. But the maintenance of a traditional morality rooted in loyalty to the emperor and filial piety supported the slogans of "national polity" (*kokutai*) and "Japanese spirit" in the crisis years of the 1930s and early 1940s and helped mobilize the nation for war and legitimate an oppressive military regime. Or so we might summarize the passage just quoted, adding further detail from opinions widely expressed in previous scholarship on modern Japanese history.

This perspective on modern Japanese history had been espoused by Marxist Japanese intellectuals since the 1920s. After World War II, it became part of the discourse of "postwar democracy" and spread widely, among not only the intelligentsia but also the general public. Huntington's information no doubt derived from the writings of English-speaking Japan experts who had been schooled in this approach to modern Japanese history. At present, there are few, if any, specialists in Japanese history who espouse this historical vision of Japan's modernization. Yet it is a narrative we still frequently see in historical writing by nonspecialists and in film and television.

At least in terms of the issues addressed in this book, the perspective just mentioned contains two major pitfalls that divert attention from historical reality precisely because they sound plausible to the casual observer. I will call them "the trap of *wakon yōsai*" and "the trap of the absent populace."

The earliest usage of the phrase *wakon yōsai* cited in Shōgakukan's dictionary *Nihon kokugo daijiten* is from *Nanoriso* (Without Introductions), a play by Mori Ōgai published in 1911: "Talent useful to Japanese state and society today must combine Japanese spirit and Western technique [*wakon yōsai*]." This line is uttered by a pompous "doctor of law" sporting a Western-style suit and whiskers, on his way to an arranged marriage interview with a young lady and her family, so this phrase was likely already in common use at the time, perhaps even a bit of a cliché. Western technology and institutions were being imported, but the traditional foundations of Japanese morality were to be preserved. Huntington's perception that this ideal was widely shared by bureaucrats and intellectuals from the early Meiji period onward seems to provide the basis for his understanding of Japanese modernization.

For example, in the second chapter of *Bunmeiron no gairyaku* (Outline of a Theory of Civilization, 1875), entitled "Western Civilization as Our Goal," Fukuzawa Yukichi questions the argument that Japan can preserve the traditional institutions of "national polity" and government while selectively adopting external forms of Western civilization such as clothing, tools, and housing—an idea similar to *wakon yōsai*.

Yet if we look at the commentary (Fukuzawa's included) in *Meiroku zasshi*, the leading opinion journal of the day, we find that for early Meiji intellectuals, a principal focus of discussion was the extent to which Western culture should be adopted, and what boundaries should be established in this process. Should the Western alphabet be adopted for writing Japanese? Should Christianity, the keystone of Western culture, be encouraged to spread in Japan? Such proposals were vigorously debated. The argument that Japan should learn from Western technology and institutions but strive to preserve its traditional ethos and morality probably began as a counter to such radical proposals and then gradually spread.

The line from Ōgai's *Nanoriso* was a form of self-assertion, essentially saying, "I have succeeded in adopting the Western manner in outward appearances, but in my heart the Japanese spirit lives on!" Subjective unease with the rampant westernization of the era produced such reactions.

But even if early Meiji intellectuals thought they could distinguish between "spirit" and "technique" and selectively adopted the latter, what is more crucial—and

Fukuzawa Yukichi (center, 1835–1901).

left unexplained—is the question of why they were so drawn to "Western techniques." As we shall see in later chapters, from the late Tokugawa period onward, Japanese intellectuals developed an intense interest in the nature of Western politics and society. But this was not because they had vaulted over the cultural differences between Asia and the West to embrace the Western system of values. Nor does the commonly held idea that Japan modeled itself on the West in order to achieve a "rich country and strong army" (*fukoku kyōhei*) provide adequate explanation for why the process of adopting "Western techniques" went so much more smoothly in Japan than in China or Korea. Rather, what we sense here is the realization of Japanese intellectuals, on the basis of values they already embraced, that the Western nations had achieved something much closer to an ideal society.

The trap of the absent populace

The second interpretive pitfall to keep in mind has to do with the relationship between popular consciousness and "civilization and enlightenment." In Huntington's understanding, the leaders of the Meiji state proceeded with a program of assimilating Western civilization while employing the traditional morality of loyalty and filial piety to unite the populace. Thus, efforts to assimilate "civilization" proceeded with no involvement on the part of the general public.

This perspective was stressed by postwar Marxist historiography (frequently referred to as simply "postwar historiography") in discussing the history of the Meiji era. One of its most representative publications, Tōyama Shigeki's *Meiji ishin* (1951), speaks of Meiji government policies supporting the construction of railway and telegraph lines, the installation of gas street lighting, and Western-style brick architecture in the Ginza district of Tokyo: "The victory of civilization and enlightenment was ultimately a victory for the forces of absolutism. The more the transplantation of European and American culture by the rulers was divorced from the reality of the impoverished lives of the masses, the more it was perceived by the masses as a manifestation of ruling power."[10] In other words, "civilization and enlightenment" was forced

upon the common people by the "forces of absolutism" constituted by the officials and bureaucrats
of the Meiji government, and seen by the masses
as nothing more than an additional burden. Huntington's perception of "civilization and enlightenment" seems to share with this interpretation
an emphasis on the elite as the key force driving
Japan's modernization.

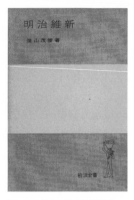

What was the real, lived experience of ordinary
people in Tokyo in the early Meiji years? The Meiji
essayist and journalist Hattori Bushō, who had earlier served the Nihonmatsu domain in what is now

Tōyama Shigeki, *Meiji ishin*
(1951).

Fukushima prefecture as a Confucian scholar, wrote in *Tōkyō shin hanjōki*
(New Tales of Tokyo Prosperity, 1874) of the opening of the new railway line
between Shinbashi in Tokyo and the port of Yokohama, describing the scene
aboard its cars in the following passage. The passengers were a diverse mix of
merchants eager to increase their profits with this new rapid transit, interpret-
ers and others serving as the interface between Japanese businessmen and the
international community of Yokohama, doctors, and casual sightseers.

> All aboard! Mr. A finds it convenient, Mrs. B finds it useful. In other
> words, the railroad is the turnpike to profit, and even blind masseurs
> use it to come up to the capital. People of all classes flock to it; men
> and women mixing together. Young men delight in rubbing elbows
> with slender-armed young ladies, the only hindrance being the purple
> sleeves which come between them and the lovely skin beneath. Teeto-
> talers shrink from contact with the drunken passengers, revolted by the
> fumes of alcohol reaching their delicate nostrils. . . . The long benches
> seat ten, each of whom presents a different mien. This one yawns at the
> ceiling, that one drools into his lap; others read newspapers or smoke
> pipes; some joke and laugh while others engage in serious debate: the
> carriage is truly like a miniature inn.[11]

No one on the packed trains of modern Tokyo is likely to feel sorry for these train-riding "masses" of early Meiji. A few "teetotalers" may have been discomfited by the drunks sitting next to them, but for the most part the napping, joking, debating denizens of these railway carriages come across as a happy lot. The common people were enjoying the modern facilities and conveniences that were springing up so quickly, and by using and profiting from them, engaged actively in the wave of "civilization and enlightenment" engulfing them.

Of course, there were also some unpopular moves to align with Western mores, such as edicts prohibiting public nudity. But for the most part, ordinary people enjoyed "civilization and enlightenment" and hoped that it would bring them greater opportunities for the fulfillment of their desires. Looking at Japan as a whole, it is true that the blessings of *bunmei kaika* did not extend equally to rural farmers and the poorest city-dwellers, but to emphasize this point alone in an overall portrait of the era also seems unfair. Tōyama's approach strikes me as blinkered and fraught with contradiction: historiography claiming to be on the side of "the people" almost never touches on the desire ordinary people had for "civilization and enlightenment" or the delight they took in it.

Seven years before the publication of *Meiji ishin*, at the height of World War II, Tōyama contributed an article entitled "The Character of Mitogaku" to a volume on popular history and thought edited by Nakamura Kōya.[12] At the time, Tōyama, whose interest in history had been stimulated by Hani Gorō's Marxist research on the Meiji Revolution, was working at the Historiographical Institute of Tokyo Imperial University, where he was involved in editing a volume of the great documentary collection *Dai Nihon shiryō* devoted to the diplomatic history of the late Tokugawa period. In 1938, when Tōyama graduated, the department of Japanese history at Tokyo Imperial University was dominated by Hiraizumi Kiyoshi, a historian of medieval Japan who believed the mission of Japanese historiography was to embody the "Japanese spirit." Rebelling against this atmosphere, a group of young historians assembled at the Historiographical Institute under the guidance of Nakamura Kōya as the Kokumin Seikatsu Kenkyūkai (National Life Research Association), which produced a series of collections of articles by its members, of which this work is one.

Tōyama's selection of Mitogaku—a nationalistic Confucian school with its origins in the Mito domain during the Tokugawa period—as the topic of the article he contributed to one of these volumes was likely inspired in part by disagreements with scholars like Nagoya Tokimasa (a year behind him at Tokyo Imperial University) and Arakawa Kusuo (three years behind him) who were working on Mitogaku under the influence of Professor Hiraizumi. Tōyama's article observes that the peasants of the late Tokugawa period, amid the poverty and distress they were experiencing, began to develop a critical consciousness toward the feudal system (*hōkensei*), and that in response to the crisis in foreign affairs there was a growing "awareness among the people of our country of the concepts of national independence and national unity." In this case, the use of the term *hōkensei* is grounded in the concept of feudalism as defined by Marxist historiography—though it is unclear which class Tōyama regarded as the principal feudal landholders, and he could not spell out such matters, as he was writing in wartime Japan.

Tōyama saw the stirrings of this "antifeudal" and "nationwide" movement among the peasantry, spurred by the economic distress experienced as a result of commodity price inflation following the opening of international trade, as manifesting in the rash of peasant uprisings that occurred in 1863. Yet he also concluded that later Mitogaku thinkers (such as Aizawa Seishisai and Fujita Tōko), the daimyo of Mito (Tokugawa Nariaki), and even the lower samurai making up the main force of the *sonnō jōi* ("revere the emperor and expel the barbarians") movement showed virtually no understanding of or sympathy with these developments. The "antifeudal" consciousness of the peasantry was distorted into the *sonnō jōi* ideology of their samurai superiors, and as a result went no further than providing a background to the movement to overthrow the shogunate. This schema for late Tokugawa history would be reproduced in almost all of Tōyama's early postwar work, from his first published article after the war,[13] on the role of the imperial house in late Tokugawa politics, to his influential *Meiji ishin* (1951).

However, in "The Character of Mitogaku," Tōyama points out that there

was one great statesman who directly intuited the consciousness of the peasants and
attempted to connect with concrete political reform: Emperor Kōmei. According
to various documentary sources,[14] the
emperor was concerned about the impact
of inflation on the poor following the opening of the ports, and in the early spring of
1861 sought permission from the shogunate's Kyoto deputy to send "fifty gold
pieces from my personal holdings" to the

Emperor Kōmei (1831–1867).

province of Yamashiro (including Kyoto) for the relief of "distressed people."
The Kyoto deputy, Sakai Tadayoshi, was uncooperative and this donation was
never made, but Tōyama praises this as "one of the most dramatic incidents
in the history of the Meiji Revolution." Had the emperor's plan been realized,
this response to the plight of the people might have worked to begin the dissolution of the feudal system from above, making it an even more important
"incident" than the return of sovereignty to the emperor or the imperial restoration that actually took place. Or so Tōyama seems to have thought.

Tōyama goes on to praise Emperor Kōmei's "boundlessly compassionate wisdom" and writes, "Here the quintessence of our national polity, the
unity of the emperor and his people, was pregnant with the potential for dis-
playing a fresh new vigor, unseen in the *sonnō jōi* movement previously, as
a revolutionary force for the overthrow of the feudal system of the shogunate and domains." In the shadows of the political history of the era there was
at work "the unyieldingly healthy and progressive spirit of the people of the
entire nation, subjects of the emperor's benevolence, a spirit which lay con-
cealed beneath the campaign of the samurai activists," a spirit, the article
concludes, that "all of the people of this nation today, as we struggle for victory in the hundred-year war as the leader of East Asia for independence from
the West" would do well to recall. The various references within this article
to the fact that, unlike the emperor, the court nobles, daimyo, and samurai
did not heed the pleas of the people may have been a veiled allusion to the

military men who, ignoring the people, were leading the national mobilization in wartime Japan. As far as I know, Tōyama did not repeat this assessment of Emperor Kōmei's actions after the war.

Tōyama did not reprint this article in later collections of his papers or in his collected works, but since it is cited in the notes to *Meiji ishin*, it would seem he also made no effort to conceal it. In the unusual circumstances of wartime Japan, he touched on the events of 1861, embracing a fantasy of equality among the people achieved through the compassion of the emperor in a polity based on "unity of the emperor and his people." After the war, bitter recollection of that experience was possibly a factor in his reluctance to write of popular enthusiasm for the "civilization and enlightenment" led by the government bureaucrats and intellectuals of the early Meiji period.

From Tōyama to the present, scholars of modern history taking a stance sympathetic to "the people" have tended, like him, to stress the absence of the people from the narrative of "civilization and enlightenment." A romantic historical vision that longs for an idealized, pastoral Japan prior to "civilization and enlightenment" has also found appreciative audiences, as has an Edo-centric interpretation of history that favors the Tokugawa loyalists and stresses the tyrannical nature of the Satsuma-Chōshū forces that overthrew the shogunate. To the extent that these assessments of the modernization of Japan in the Meiji period also fall into the trap of absenting the people from the process, they seem no more than variations on a theme. But I wonder how many people are aware of the complexities of Tōyama's position, which serves as the point of departure for this view of history.

Differences and similarities

Let's return for a moment to Michael Ignatieff's critique of Huntington, whose book *The Clash of Civilizations and the Remaking of World Order* concludes with an exhortation not to intervene in the internal conflicts of other civilizations under the banner of universalistic concepts of justice. In response to this, Ignatieff proposes the development of a catalogue of "human interests" that should be endorsed by all civilizations. If an immense evil such as genocide is taking place in another civilization, do we not have a responsibility to intervene to prevent it, as it is a threat to all of humanity? At the time, Ignatieff had already posed this fundamental question in *Blood and Belonging: Journeys into the New Nationalism*, a book of reportage based on visits to a number of the ethnic conflicts that broke out after the end of the Cold War.[15] And subsequent to his review of Huntington, he articulates a vigorous argument for recognizing the value of humane interventions in defense of world order in another book, *The Warrior's Honor: Ethnic War and the Modern Conscience*.[16]

Are there indeed values that transcend the differences between civilizations, values that should be universally observed and defended? Indeed, part 5 of Huntington's book, "The Future of Civilizations," takes up this question in a section entitled "The Commonalities of Civilization." In it, he argues that certain values are respected by all the world's civilizations, which he refers to as "Civilization"—capitalized and singular. Here, let us adopt this usage to preserve the distinction with the plurality of civilizations.

Huntington then proposes a third rule for the coexistence of civilizations, following the "abstention rule" and "joint mediation rule" he articulated previously: a "commonalities rule." By working to understand one another and broaden the scope of Civilization, the "political, spiritual, and intellectual leaders" can achieve cooperation among civilizations to secure world peace. In other words, the "core states" should actively support cross-cultural communication in recognition of the values of Civilization and cooperative efforts to preserve and defend them.

The list Huntington provides of what constitutes Civilization is rather vague: "a complex mix of higher levels of morality, religion, learning, art, philosophy, technology, material well-being, and probably other things."[17] Moreover, he mentions Singapore, whose political system is not known for its respect for human rights or the rule of law, as an example of a country that values both its traditional culture and Civilization—a statement that would not escape criticism from Michael Ignatieff.

One of the sources Huntington cites in his discussion of the existence of commonalities is "Moral Minimalism," the first chapter of a work by the political theorist Michael Walzer, *Thick and Thin: Moral Argument at Home and Abroad.*[18] For fourteen years, from 1966 to 1980, Walzer was a colleague of Huntington's in the department of government at Harvard University. He must have taken a political stance opposite Huntington, who was a supporter of the Johnson administration's policies during the Vietnam War.

Michael Walzer (b. 1935).

Walzer begins "Moral Minimalism" with a recollection of seeing a filmed image of a street demonstration in Prague at the height of the Velvet Revolution that toppled the communist regime in Czechoslovakia in 1989:

> It is a picture of people marching in the streets of Prague; they carry signs, some of which say, simply, "Truth" and others "Justice." When I saw the picture, I knew immediately what the signs meant—and so did everyone else who saw the same picture. Not only that: I also recognized and acknowledged the values that the marchers were defending—and so did (almost) everyone else.

What the signs meant by "Justice" was immediately clear: the rule of law and an end to the privileges of the party elite—"common, garden-variety justice," as Walzer calls it. Walzer then develops a vocabulary of different types of moral argument: a "thick" morality, grounded in the particularities of its culture, within which is always embedded a "thin," or minimal morality, which can potentially be shared across different cultures. Thick morality is expressed through the particular customs and conventions of a specific culture and may be difficult for people outside that culture to espouse. But the minimal morality of wishing to escape from brutality and to prohibit murder and tyranny is something that finds expression in various ways in the language of almost any culture. The voices of the people of Prague could be immediately understood by an American political philosopher because they were expressing this type of minimal morality.

Walzer points out that the existence of this type of universalistic morality has been repeatedly confirmed in a variety of times and places through actions of protest and solidarity that transcend cultural differences. Huntington's argument lacks rigor because he fails to do the work of carefully extracting this minimal morality embedded in contemporary realities. In chapter 4 of *Thick and Thin*, Walzer makes the case—in contrast to Huntington—for humanitarian interventions as a practical application of minimal morality in international politics.

If we expand this concept of the relationship between thick and thin morality, it might be applied to a consideration of the crowds of people thronging the newly introduced railways and architecture of the era of "civilization and enlightenment" in Japan. They did not worship these items because they were the products of the more advanced West. They judged the excellence of railways and Western architecture on the basis of a system of values nurtured by the lived experience and customs of the Tokugawa period. Because those values accorded with the values of "Civilization" in the Japanese system of values, these newly arrived artifacts of "civilization and enlightenment" were welcomed and quickly found a place within Japanese society.

The same might be said not only of machinery and tools and clothing, but also of ideas. If we free ourselves from the trap of *wakon yōsai*, then modern Western thought—and by extension, "civilization"—was not something that the Japanese found completely incomprehensible or mysterious. Western ideas gained acceptance because the elements that permitted understanding and sympathy for them were present in Tokugawa Japanese thought and culture.

Now, a quarter century after Huntington's essay and book were published, the world seems, if anything, more opaque and chaotic. The premise that the nations of Europe accept and cooperate with the United States as the "core state" of Western civilization is now in question. The clash of cultures is no longer restricted to conflicts between different countries and regions. As terrorist incidents by Islamic radicals and disputes over immigration and refugees suggest, the advanced nations are also experiencing serious internal problems.

Precisely because of this, people today are confronted with the necessity of asking what "Civilization"—or a minimal morality, in Walzer's terms, which can be shared by a variety of different cultures—might actually look like. Japanese in the late nineteenth century perceived this concept of civilization in the Western culture of their time; many of them longed for Western political institutions and the ideas in which they were grounded, and because of this attempted to integrate them into Japanese culture. The medium for rooting them in Japanese soil clearly existed within the traditional culture. As well, modern Western thought and political institutions, as a result of this process of transplantation into different cultures, matured into a flexible value system open to cultural diversity and coexistence.

In Japan's subsequent history, thought concerning human rights and liberty did not root itself in exactly the same form or manner as it did in Western nations. Japan rhetorically justified its entry into the Sino-Japanese War of 1894–95 as a war for "civilization"; later, a similar hypocrisy attended the International Military Tribunal for the Far East (the Tokyo Trial, 1946–48), which subjected Japan to the "judgment of civilization." Through historical events such as these, the concept of "civilization" acquired certain negative connotations. Even so, Japan's encounter with Western "civilization" is a fascinating model for the advancement of understanding and coexistence among the world's diverse cultures. Exploring the legacy of Japan's quest for "civilization" in the nineteenth century thus serves as a lens for examining our world today.

CHAPTER 1

Meiji Restoration or Meiji Revolution?

Tōshū Shōgetsu, *Samurai of Various Domains Defend the Coast Following the Arrival of the American Ships* (1889).

An introduction to the current terminology

Readers familiar with Japanese history may question the term "Meiji Revolution" in the title of this book, but that is exactly what occurred. In Kyoto, on January 3, 1868, a coalition of samurai centering on the Satsuma domain initiated a coup d'état, overthrowing the Tokugawa shogunate and establishing a new government headed by Emperor Meiji. This change in political regime led to the modernization of virtually all aspects of Japan's political and legal institutions, society, and culture. In light of this massive historical transformation, the title of this book refers to the regime change of 1868 and the various reforms that followed from it as the Meiji Revolution.

The most common Japanese term for the Meiji Revolution is "Meiji Ishin"—*ishin* (Ch. *weixin*) being a term from the Chinese classics that suggests "reform" or "renewal." This was the term generally used by Japanese who lived through the events of 1868 and after to describe the change in political regime. Yet, as we shall see in later chapters, many Meiji intellectuals, such as Fukuzawa Yukichi and Takekoshi Yosaburō, used the word *kakumei* (revolution) to characterize this series of events. Uchimura Kanzō's *Representative Men of Japan* (1908), one of the most famous books in English written by a Japanese author of this era, commences with a chapter entitled "The Japanese Revolution of 1868."

Kakumei (Ch. *geming*) is another term borrowed from the Chinese classics. Strictly speaking, it meant the transfer of the mandate of heaven from one dynasty to another. From the nineteenth century onward in Japan it was used as a translation of the English word "revolution," denoting a major transformation in political institutions, society, and culture. Fukuzawa, Takekoshi, Uchimura, and others used *kakumei*, or revolution, because they felt it described the sweeping changes taking place in their era. In recent years, some of the leading English-language scholarship on Japan has also proposed using the term "Meiji Revolution."[1]

Even so, among English-speaking readers knowledgeable about Japan, "Meiji Restoration" is probably a more familiar term than Meiji Revolution. Japanese-English dictionaries and general histories have tended to use Meiji Restoration to describe the regime change of 1868. The word "restoration," however, suggests a return to imperial rule, such as occurred in England in 1660 with the restoration of the monarchy or in France with the Bourbon Restoration (1814–30), rather than the magnitude of political and social change expressed in the Japanese words *ishin* (reformation) or *kakumei* (revolution).

The edict declaring the "restoration of imperial rule" (*ōsei fukko*)

How is it that the Meiji Revolution came to be called the Meiji Restoration? This English-language usage has its origins in the manner in which the leaders of the new government, which came into being after the collapse of the Tokugawa regime that had ruled Japan for more than 250 years, described the process of creating a new unified nation-state in terms of overthrowing the shogunate and restoring imperial rule.

On the fourteenth day of the tenth month of the third year of the Keiō era (November 9, 1867), the last shogun, Tokugawa Yoshinobu, issued a formal statement in which he expressed the intention of restoring political power to the emperor (*taisei hōkan*), so as to "consolidate authority in the imperial court" (*chōken itto*), but at the same time envisioning a new political system in which this authority would be exercised on behalf of the emperor by a deliberative assembly of powerful daimyo—and the position of the Tokugawa house as "first among equals" would be maintained.

But the Satsuma domain had already set itself on a course to overthrow the shogunate by force. In plotting a coup d'état, Satsuma was joined by a group of court nobles led by Iwakura Tomomi. On January 3, 1868 (Keiō 3.12.9), forces from Satsuma and a handful of other domains seized and held the gates of the Imperial Palace in Kyoto, whereupon Iwakura presented to the emperor a proposal for the restoration of imperial rule. On that day, the edict formally restoring imperial rule (which came to be known as the Ōsei Fukko no Daigōrei) was issued in the emperor's name. Immediately after this, a group of imperial princes, court nobles, and various daimyo and their retainers assembled at the Kogosho (Court Room) within the Imperial Palace. The Kogosho Conference approved a plan for the reorganization of the personnel and institutional structure of the imperial court and the abolition of the shogunate and its associated offices—a decision that was first announced to the imperial family and the court nobility, and then to the daimyo of all of Japan's domains on January 8. The January 3 edict begins as follows:

> The emperor has already accepted the request of Shogun Tokugawa [Yoshinobu] to return governing authority and resign his office as shogun. As everyone knows, from 1853 [the year of Commodore Perry's first mission to Japan] onward, the nation has faced an unprecedented crisis, one that greatly troubled the mind of the previous emperor [Kōmei] for many years. In response to this, the emperor is now determined to firmly establish the basis for a restoration of imperial rule [*ōsei fukko*] and the recovery of our national prestige. To this end, the institutions of the regency [*sesshō*] and shogunate are henceforth abolished, and the three offices of president, senior councillor, and junior councillor are hereby temporarily established to manage all the affairs of state. Based on the example of the founding of our empire by Emperor Jinmu, all matters shall be determined by just and extensive public discussions without distinctions among court nobility, samurai, or commoners, each of whom, in light of the emperor's desire to share the triumphs and travails of his people, should diligently strive to cleanse themselves of the decadent habits of the past and dedicate themselves to public service with complete loyalty and devotion to the nation.[2]

The word "restoration" would eventually become established as the translation for *ōsei fukko* in this document, though it is unclear whether the new government ever recognized it as an official translation. However, on February 8, 1868 (Keiō 4.1.15), the new government presented the envoys of six nations—France, Great Britain, Italy, America, Prussia, and the Netherlands—with letters of state signed by Emperor Meiji establishing diplomatic relations with them. This document, written in classical Chinese, is entitled "Taisei fukko fukoku no kokusho," which might be translated as "Letter of State Proclaiming the Restoration of Imperial Rule," but it appears that there was no official translation at the time into any of the Western languages.

The Kogosho Conference, as portrayed in a mural at the Seitoku Memorial Painting Museum by Shimada Bokusen, entitled *The Restoration of Imperial Rule.*

Francis O. Adams, a diplomat who served as secretary of the British legation in Edo during this period, later published an overview of Japanese history that contains a passage summarizing the content of the edict as proclaiming that "a basis should be formed for a return to the ancient form of government by the Sovereign, and for the restoration of the national dignity."[3] This corresponds to the portion of the Japanese text translated above as "firmly establish the basis for a restoration of imperial rule [ōsei fukko] and the recovery of our national prestige," with the word "restoration" being employed as a translation for the recovery of national dignity or prestige rather than for the revival of imperial rule.

Adams's book was the first overview of Japanese history published by a Westerner in the years immediately following the opening of Japan, and it is possibly the origin of the established practice in English of referring to the events of 1868 as a "restoration." From the standpoint of seventeenth-century English history, which used the term Restoration to refer to the revival of the monarchy, this seemed perfectly appropriate.

The elusive "Meiji Revolution"

The Mikado's Empire, an introduction to Japanese history published in 1876 by the American educator and Congregationalist minister William Elliot

Griffis, who lived and worked in Japan from 1871 to 1874, adopts a different approach. The final chapter of this work, a reprint of an article that originally ran in the *North American Review* in April 1875, is entitled "The Recent Revolutions in Japan" and relates the events leading from the collapse of the Tokugawa shogunate to the establishment of the Meiji government. Griffis begins by speaking of "the restoration of the mikado to supreme power," which has initi-

William Elliot Griffis (1843–1928).

ated "marvelous changes in Japan." He summarizes these changes as comprising "a three-fold political revolution within, a profound alteration in the national policy toward foreigners, and the inauguration of social reforms which lead us to hope that Japan has rejected the Asiatic, and adopted the European ideal of civilization." Phrased in this way, it is clear that Griffis saw the restoration of imperial rule as only one aspect of the "political revolution" in progress in Japan.[4]

In other words, what had taken place was not merely a regime change at the apex of the power structure, replacing the Tokugawa shogun in Edo with the emperor in Kyoto. It was a fundamental reform of the country's political institutions, which had previously given the shogun and his government—the Tokugawa bakufu—ultimate control over the daimyo, the imperial house, and the court nobility. Then, as Griffis also relates, the reforms of the bureaucracy and administrative system, and the end of sanctions against intermarriage among the members of the various classes, effectively put an end to the dominance of hereditary status, and the course of the nation swung decisively toward the assimilation of Western civilization. No word other than "revolution" seems appropriate to express such radical changes in society.

And indeed, the regime change that took place in 1868 was generally described as the "collapse" of the Tokugawa shogunate, and welcomed as *go-isshin*—a "renovation" or "renewal" of the world. In the edict proclaiming the restoration of imperial rule, there is a passage announcing countermeasures for dealing with economic disruption that speaks of "a time for reform in all matters" (*hyakuji go-isshin no orikara*). So the implication of *ishin*, or *go-isshin*, was a movement for the radical restructuring of society. As such, the English equivalent of this idea is probably "revolution." Griffis's use of this term reflects the institutional transformation that took place from Tokugawa to Meiji Japan as experienced by those who lived through it.

In this era, the word *kakumei* was already being used in Japan as a translation of "revolution." The second volume (1868) of Fukuzawa Yukichi's influential three-volume *Seiyō jijō* (Conditions in the West, 1866–70), compiled, translated, and adapted from a variety of English-language source materials, states that "to bring about a sudden change in government through the use of military force is called revolution [*kakumei*]," and goes on to cite three examples: the Glorious Revolution in England, the French Revolution of 1789, and the American Revolution. Fukuzawa's discussion of these events suggests a keen concern for the uncertain situation at the end of the Tokugawa period in Japan; he feared the possibility that "revolutionary warfare" would exacerbate social disorder and invite tyrannical rule by unscrupulous leaders. In any case, the word *kakumei* must have seemed a perfectly appropriate expression of the sequence of events leading from the restoration edict to the Boshin Civil War of 1868–69, which began with the battle of Toba-Fushimi, in which a newly organized Imperial Army defeated forces still loyal to the Tokugawa shogunate.

Although it did not actually do so, if in the early years of Meiji the government had chosen to refer to the reform movement as the "Meiji Revolution," this would probably have been accepted without resistance by society at large and would have become the established historical terminology. As we shall see later, the generation of young intellectuals active from the third decade of the Meiji era, such as Tokutomi Sohō and Takekoshi Yosaburō, liked to use the phrase *ishin kakumei* and called for a second revolution to complete the work of the first.

What was implied by "Jinmu's founding of our empire"?

Let us consider the conflicting aspects of "restoration" (*fukko*) and "revolution" (*kakumei*). Overturning the existing political order in an attempt to restore ancient forms—this "restoration" set the entire nation on a new course that resulted in the dismantling of the hereditary class system, a new centralization of government power, and the wholesale introduction of Western culture. If we focus our attention solely on the word "restoration," this appears to be a complete contradiction.

But there was a logic at work in the revolution of 1868 that enabled the transition to a new political system precisely because it was billed as a restoration, a revival of the past. The restoration edict itself clearly deploys this rhetoric, as in the passage quoted earlier that promises reforms "based on the example of the founding of our empire by Emperor Jinmu." What this implied was an abolition of the regime in which the Tokugawa family wielded ultimate power, to be replaced by an order in which the emperor's ministers—court nobles and daimyo—would directly govern the populace. At least this was the vision that appeared to be shared by the forces urging the overthrow of the shogunate: court nobility such as Iwakura Tomomi and the coalition of samurai led by the Satsuma domain.

But if the idea was to restore things to a state predating the founding of the Tokugawa shogunate, what era in history was to be the goal? The weakened state of the imperial institution during the civil warfare of the Sengoku period (late fifteenth to late sixteenth century) was certainly not a model, and a return to the institutions of Emperor Go-Daigo's failed Kenmu Restoration (1333–36) was also futile.

A confidential position paper believed to have been written in the autumn of 1866 (Keiō 2.10) includes a passage urging that Tokugawa Yoshinobu be induced to surrender his title as *seii tai shōgun* ("barbarian-subduing generalissimo"), arguing that the imperial court should "recover this military post and restore things to the situation before [Minamoto] Yoritomo."[5] While this indicates a period before the Kamakura shogunate, precisely what is envisioned remains unclear.

Iwakura Tomomi (1825–1883).

The second volume of Iwakura's official biography, *Iwakura kō jikki*, relates that Iwakura sought the opinion of the Kokugaku (National Learning) scholar Tamamatsu Misao (1810–72) in the ninth month of Keiō 3 (1867) regarding "the great enterprise of restoring imperial rule." The accuracy of this biography has frequently been questioned, and Tamamatsu's papers suggest that it might have been the summer of 1866, but if we follow the version presented in the biography, Tamamatsu's reply to Iwakura's query is as follows:

> You must work to make the restoration of imperial rule as broad and far-reaching as possible. Thus in reconstructing the system of official ranks and offices, the goal should be a comprehensive renewal [*banki no ishin*] aimed at unifying the realm based on the original foundation established by Emperor Jinmu.[6]

In short, Tamamatsu is saying that in defining the offices and institutions of the government, the precedent set by Emperor Jinmu when he founded the country in antiquity should be followed. Detailed knowledge of the institutions of Jinmu's time was, however, unavailable. In fact, what these words implied was that a complete reform of the system should be undertaken, as at the beginning of a new dynasty. The trope of Emperor Jinmu's founding of the empire would later be extended to legitimize the introduction of new, Western-style institutions. This was a "restoration" that ignited a revolution, in the sense of a sweeping reconstruction of the nation.

"But the mandate is bestowed upon it anew"

We should also note in Tamamatsu's text the use of the expression "comprehensive renewal" (*banki no ishin*), since *ishin* was another key term used to describe the transition from the Tokugawa shogunate to the Meiji government. The locus classicus for the word *ishin* is the "Decade of Wen Wang" in the "Major Court Odes" section of the *Book of Poetry* (*Shijing*). This section of the classic text is a paean to Wen Wang, or King Wen—the name posthumously given to Ji Chang, father of King Wu, founding ruler of the Zhou dynasty (1100–221 BCE)—praising his virtue. In it is a line that reads, "Zhou is an ancient kingdom, but the mandate is bestowed upon it anew." The Ji clan to which King Wen belonged had ruled over an area known as Zhouyuan, to the south of Qishan, since the time of his grandfather Gugong Danfu (known posthumously as King Tai of Zhou), and King Wen himself was given the title of Viscount of the West by the last ruler of the Shang (or Yin) dynasty (1600–1100 BCE), King Zhou. The Ji lineage was said to extend back a millennium or more to its founder, Houji, twelve generations before Gugong Danfu.

According to the Confucian classics, King Zhou of Shang was a tyrant oblivious to the sufferings of his people. He instituted ruinous taxes and used the resulting wealth to fund his own immoderate indulgence in pleasure and entertainment, including banquets featuring "lakes of wine and forests of meat." Any of his ministers who dared to admonish such behavior were brutally executed. In contrast, King Wen was a paragon of exceptional morality, lauded as an ideal character in the later Confucian literature. Hated and feared by King Zhou, he was imprisoned.

After the death of King Wen, his son Ji Fa (later King Wu) raised the banner of revolt and was joined by other members of the nobility. Defeated, King Zhou committed suicide, and the Shang dynasty was destroyed. In its place, King Wu became sovereign (Son of Heaven) of all China, and the Zhou dynasty—the longest in Chinese history—was founded. The phrase "Zhou is an ancient kingdom, but the mandate is bestowed upon it anew" implies that while the Ji family was of ancient lineage, it was from the time of King Wen that it was newly awarded the mandate of heaven to rule as sovereign over all the people and bring them relief. While King Wen chose not to ascend the throne and was awarded the title posthumously, his son King Wu exercised the mandate of heaven to achieve a change of dynasties. This was the new mandate spoken of in the classic text, and the origin of the word *ishin*.

This passage was predicated upon the Confucian concept of the mandate of heaven, which held that the ruler received from heaven an order to rule in its stead. Calling the sovereign of the realm the "Son of Heaven" was an explicit expression of this idea. In the Chinese (and by extension, the East Asian) worldview, the word "heaven" (Ch. *tian*; J. *ten*) was used to refer to the entirety of the natural world in which humans, animals, and plants live. And it was the work of the Son of Heaven to represent the operations of heaven in the eternal process of cultivating and nourishing these living beings.

In other words, insofar as the Son of Heaven had received the heavenly mandate to rule the land, he was obliged to treat his people with benevolence and support them in maintaining peaceful livelihoods. His job was not simply to secure public order and work for the prosperity and welfare of the populace; he was also expected to morally educate the people to live together in harmony. The ruler and the ministers and officials serving him must constantly exert themselves to become moral exemplars—because individuals without high moral character were inherently unsuited to rule.

Thus the idea of the virtuous ruler was conceived; but unique to the Confucian tradition was the attempt to use this concept to explain the transitions from one dynasty to the next. King Zhou of Shang was a tyrant, and so his erstwhile vassal King Wu raised a revolt against him and became the founder of a new dynasty. This was explained as a loss of the mandate of heaven by the old ruler, and its transfer to a new dynasty founded by a ruler of exceptional virtue.

Why was the term *ishin* chosen?

Given these precedents, Tamamatsu Misao's characterization of the restoration of imperial rule (*ōsei fukko*) as a "comprehensive renewal" (*banki no ishin*) could be considered a reasonable choice. At least in terms of who was in de facto control of the country, *ōsei fukko* had brought about a dynastic transfer of sorts, with the "mandate of heaven" shifting from the shogunate in Edo to the imperial court in Kyoto. Moreover, the word *kakumei* used as a translation of "revolution" was also a term rooted in the classics, and literally meant "a change in the mandate." In the sense that they both pointed to a regime change as the result of the transfer of the mandate of heaven, *ishin* and *kakumei* were quite closely related terms.

But the transfer of governmental authority from the shogun to the emperor could not be conceived as a change in dynasties. Instead, it was executed in the form of a surrender of the title and office of shogun and its return to the imperial house, which had granted it, an imperial house that had reigned as Japan's sole royal family since time immemorial. This was certainly not a "revolution" (*kakumei*) in the sense of a dynastic change, and it is not surprising that Tamamatsu Misao chose the expression *ishin* instead of *kakumei*, and that the leaders of the Meiji government followed his lead in describing their activities as a renovation or renewal rather than a revolution.

Tamamatsu was born into a family of the court nobility in Kyoto, and until the age of thirty was a Buddhist monastic at the temple Daigoji. Upon returning to lay life, he studied with the Kokugaku scholar Ōkuni Takamasa (1792–1871), and lectured on Kokugaku himself in Izumi province and in the town of Sakamoto in Ōmi, while at the same time studying Neo-Confucianism. The passage from the *Book of Poetry* that we have been discussing—"Zhou is an ancient kingdom, but the mandate is bestowed upon it anew"—is also quoted in *The Great Learning* (*Daxue*), considered by Neo-Confucian scholars to be one of the Four Books foundational to the Confucian canon, and the first that should be read, since it sets forth an ordered program and method for subsequent study.

Neo-Confucian scholars believed *The Great Learning* to be the work of one of the most important disciples of Confucius, Zengzi (Zeng Shen), and his school. It teaches that those who pursue learning must first cultivate virtue in themselves, then become officials serving the ruler in order to instruct the people and elevate them morally. The section of *The Great Learning* that quotes from the "Decade of King Wen" in the *Book of Poetry* is one that sets forth this effort by those who govern to "renew the people"—Zhu Xi changed the original text from *qinmin* (treating the people with affection; loving the people) to *xinmin* (renewing the people)—as the ultimate goal of scholarship and self-cultivation.

Here, the phrase *ishin* begins to be associated less with dynastic change and more with a process of self-improvement and moral suasion. Considering the fact that King Wen, the subject of this ode, was never monarch, the implications of the

King Wen of Zhou.

phrase *ishin* in Neo-Confucian thought become even further removed from the concept of revolution. Thus minimizing the nuance of dynastic change while simultaneously expressing the idea of fundamental reform, *ishin* is a term that not only Tamamatsu but also many involved in the Meiji government must have found quite convenient.

Moreover, *ishin* would soon acquire additional connotations. After the new government succeeded in crushing the military power of the supporters of the former shogunate in the Boshin Civil War, it decided to locate the seat of government in Edo, which was renamed Tokyo, meaning Eastern Capital. Edo Castle became the Imperial

Emperor Meiji (1852–1912).

Palace, the new residence of Emperor Meiji, who on February 2, 1870 (Meiji 3.1.3), issued an Imperial Rescript on the Propagation of the Great Teaching (Taikyō Senpu no Mikotonori).

The influence on the new government that Tamamatsu and other proponents of Kokugaku and Shinto had, centered in the Jingikan (Office of Shinto Worship), would soon peak and then gradually decline, but at this point their position was still strong. The rescript reflected this, calling for "missionaries" to be sent throughout the country to proclaim the Great Teaching (Shinto) as the official religion of the nation, as in the following passage: "Now that the cycle of heavenly fortune has brought forth renovation in all matters, it is the proper time to clarify the official teachings and proclaim the Way of the Gods [*kannagara no michi*]."[7]

The phrase *kannagara no michi* signifies Shinto, but the two characters used here to write *kannagara* can also be read *ishin*. The great national renovation, or *ishin*, could thus be interpreted, through this reading, as connecting with the Way of the Gods, and a reform of national institutions premised on the continuity of rule by an emperor considered to be a direct descendant of Amaterasu Ōmikami, the sun goddess. This interpretation would place even greater constraints on the nature of this "renovation"—making it even more incompatible, at least linguistically, with the word "revolution."

CHAPTER 2

The Long Revolution

Detail of woodblock print by Hashimoto Chikanobu (Yōshū) celebrating the 1889 proclamation of the Constitution of the Empire of Japan.

The historiography of the Meiji Revolution

It is difficult if not impossible to clearly assess historical events as they unfold; later generations are better positioned for a comprehensive view. Some two decades after the beginning of the Meiji era, the next generation began to articulate the significance of the social transformation that had been set in motion in early 1868—if not before. A leading example of this effort is *Shin Nihon shi* (A History of the New Japan) by Takekoshi Yosaburō, who used the pen name Sansa. *Shin Nihon shi* was published in two volumes a quarter century after the edict announcing the restoration of imperial rule.[1] A third volume had originally been planned but was never completed. Even so, this work is highly regarded as an early attempt to write a general history recording the flow of events from the late Tokugawa period to Takekoshi's time.

Takekoshi belonged to a generation of journalists and intellectuals too young to have played any part in the years immediately surrounding the Revolution. With Tokutomi Sohō and Yamaji Aizan, fellow members of this generation, he was associated with the publishing company Min'yūsha and wrote prolifically on politics and history for its journal *Kokumin no tomo* (The People's Friend) and newspaper *Kokumin shinbun* (The People's Newspaper). The Constitution of the Empire of Japan had just been enacted and the Diet just convened; that is, the institutional framework of the Meiji state was in the process of being established. Standing in opposition to the increasingly conservative power of the *hanbatsu*—the political cliques dominating the government, formed by men from the domains (principally Satsuma and Chōshū) that had overthrown the shogunate—these young journalists used the press and campaigns in support of popular political parties with platforms that included national political reform.

First edition of Takekoshi Yosaburō's *Shin Nihon shi* (History of the New Japan, 1891–92).

The title *Shin Nihon shi* can be read as either "A New History of Japan" or "A History of the New Japan." Clearly the latter was intended, as confirmed by the table of contents for the projected third volume, which appears at the end of volume 2, with chapter titles such as "Critical Biographies of Leaders of the New Japan" and "On the Origins of the New Japan." In other words, as a result of the regime change that had taken place in 1868—traditionally referred to as the Meiji Restoration in English but now known as the Meiji Revolution—the country had undergone a transformation into the New Japan. *Shin Nihon shi* was an experiment in providing a historical overview of that transformation.

The first volume of *Shin Nihon shi* can be characterized as a political history of the period. Beginning with an overview of the institutional structure of the Tokugawa shogunate, it then narrates the major political developments unfolding in the wake of Perry's arrival in Japan in 1853, treating them as "the prehistory of the Revolution." The remainder of the volume then provides a general perspective on developments in politics and foreign policy up to the late 1890s.

Here I would like to draw attention to volume 2, which focuses on social and intellectual developments, and religion. The section dealing with society and thought is quite substantial and is divided into five chapters. The first of these chapters, "The Fundamental Ideology of the Revolution and the Changing Nature of the Monarchy," is followed by "Social Revolution and the Tripartite Division of the World of Thought." If the first volume is concerned with the revolution in the political realm, the second takes up the issue of the revolution of society as a whole. For Takekoshi, it was impossible to describe these historical events as anything other than a revolution in both politics and society. The intensity of the changes could not be adequately expressed with terms such as "transition" or "restoration." An epochal event encompassing the social and cultural realms, it deserved to be called a revolution

Takekoshi Yosaburō (1865–1950).

(*kakumei*)—one that transcended the narrow sense of a change of dynasties (*ekisei kakumei*) implied in the origins of the term *kakumei* in Confucian thought.

Examining the use of the term *kakumei* in *Shin Nihon shi* in greater detail, we find that the Revolution of 1868 is also expressed as a "dynastic revolution" (*daichō kakumei*) in the first chapter of the section of the second volume dealing with developments in society and thought. In this chapter, Takekoshi discusses the concept of *ekisei kakumei* as articulated by Mencius, as well as the violent overthrow and replacement (*hōbatsu*) of tyrannical rulers undertaken by the legendary founders of the Shang and Zhou dynasties, Tang and Wu. Thus it is clear that Takekoshi understood the Meiji Revolution in part as a transfer of dynastic authority and power.

On the other hand, as we shall see, Takekoshi is critical of historians who saw a political movement inspired by imperial loyalism as the fundamental cause of this momentous event. Revolutionary political change was supported, before and after, by a lengthy and continuous process of "social revolution" (*shakaiteki kakumei*). Dynastic revolution had been enabled by "social currents" already manifesting themselves during the Tokugawa period, which was why the government leading the "New Japan" initially undertook reforms that furthered this social revolution. Such is Takekoshi's interpretation of the history of this period.

However, some twenty years after the Meiji Revolution, the government was beginning to show signs of reversing course on the social transformation.

In an opening essay for the second volume of *Shin Nihon shi* that serves as a kind of preface for the entire work, Takekoshi criticizes these tendencies and expresses a determination that this lengthy revolution would not end in betrayal—in this sense prefiguring Leon Trotsky's later characterization of the Soviet regime under Stalin in *The Revolution Betrayed* (1936).

> Now, a mere twenty years or so later, the currents of society have lost track of the great purpose of the Meiji Revolution and are heading down the wrong path. The great ministers of state err in their policies, while activists outside of government err in their opinions; both fall into expedient inactivity. Indignation at this is what has inspired me to take up my pen to attempt an overview of the social transformation that has taken place since the Meiji Revolution.[2]

In other words, Takekoshi is positioning his narrative of recent Japanese history as an effort to remind both government officials and the informed public of the "purpose of the Meiji Revolution" and the nature and significance of "social revolution."

But in what sense were the events of 1868 a revolution? In the previously mentioned chapter "The Fundamental Ideology of the Revolution and the Changing Nature of the Monarchy," Takekoshi begins his discussion with a critique of "conventional notions of the origins of the Meiji Revolution." Of these, he focuses on two: first, the theory of "old-fashioned historians" that an ideology of "imperial loyalism" led to the Revolution; and second, the opinion of "a certain group of historians" that the Meiji Revolution had its origins in "the diplomatic shock" (*gaikō no ikkyo*) of pressure from the Western nations embodied in the appearance of Perry's ships in Japanese waters.

It would be fair to say that even at the beginning of the twenty-first century, these "conventional notions" continued to dominate the image of the Meiji Revolution held by the general public, though there is evidence that this is changing. For example, the 2006 edition of the most widely used ministry-approved high school history textbook, *Shōsetsu Nihonshi* (Comprehensive Japanese History),[3] contains the following passage in the section outlining modern and contemporary history: "In the middle of the nineteenth century, Japan, pressured by Europe and the United States to open itself to the rest of the world, worked to develop into a modern nation-state modeled on the Western powers." Yet in the most recent edition of this textbook (at the time of this writing), published in 2012, this passage regarding pressure from the West has been deleted, suggesting that perhaps it no longer reflects the mainstream opinion in historical and educational circles in Japan.

Even so, as may be seen in the controversy over the Trans-Pacific Partnership, whenever Japan is pressured by other nations seeking free trade agreements, the situation will almost inevitably be compared to the arrival of Perry's "black ships." And in such cases, this comparison implies not merely external pressure, but external pressure demanding internal reform. Considered in these terms, clearly the perspective that sees Western pressure as the principal cause of the Meiji Restoration remains dominant.

On the other hand, the theory that "imperial loyalism" was the driving force behind the Meiji Revolution is no longer included in school textbooks or the work of specialists in the field of Japanese history. The "loyalist" or "imperial" interpretation of Japanese history was widely accepted in academia and the educational system in prewar and wartime Japan, but in postwar historiography, many works adopt criticism of this perspective as their point of departure. Yet in historical novels and television dramas dealing with the late Tokugawa and early Meiji periods, the image of loyalists as the force behind the history of the era remains dominant. In this regard, the loyalist perspective on the Meiji Revolution that Takekoshi criticized lives on to this day.

Yet Takekoshi tells us that both the loyalist perspective and the theory of diplomatic shock overlook the revolutionary nature of political changes of 1868. He follows this with an interesting discussion of revolutionary typology, classifying revolutions into three categories: "revivalist revolutions" like that of England, "idealistic revolutions" like that of France, and "anarchical revolutions" like that of Japan. With the inclusion of England and France in this typology, the term *kakumei* has been divorced from its classical Chinese (or East Asian) sense of "change of dynasties" and transformed into a more universal concept.

The first category of "revivalist revolution" is typified by England, but

Takekoshi's treatment of it extends beyond the English Civil Wars and the Glorious Revolution to include the progressive reform of English political institutions through the establishment of the dominance of the House of Commons, the revision of electoral laws, and so forth.

In short, in England, the principles of liberty and popular rights and of limitations on the power of the monarchy had been established in the Middle Ages, as the example of the Magna Carta would suggest. Thus, in the seventeenth century and after, the English people were able to call for a return to these medieval "precedents" as they sought to free themselves from the constraints of class and establish governmental institutions that asserted their "freedom to bear arms; freedoms of press, speech, and assembly; and local self-government and autonomous municipal police." The English revolution was thus described as the revival of an ancient model.

From this perspective, the "restoration of imperial rule," which proponents of the imperial loyalist interpretation saw as the motive force behind the Meiji Revolution, scarcely deserves to be described as a revolution. This "restoration" simply consisted of a return of sovereignty from the shogun to the emperor—something completely different from the revival of a tradition of liberty and popular rights such as occurred in England. That Takekoshi deliberately describes the English type of revolution as "revivalist" when distinguishing it from the Meiji Revolution can itself be read as an implicit critique of the historical interpretation that saw the Meiji Revolution as a return to the ancient tradition of imperial rule.

Takekoshi's second category is the "idealistic revolution," typified by the American and French revolutions. These took place in societies that lacked an established tradition of "liberty and popular rights" like that of England, and were overshadowed by "the darkness of tyranny and oppression." In the midst of this, "humanistic philosophers with a vision of the future"—Takekoshi was probably thinking of figures such as Jean-Jacques Rousseau and Thomas Paine—advocated for the ideal of "political liberty." Broadly and enthusiastically embracing this concept of liberty, the people of these countries waged "idealistic revolutions" aimed at building "ideal nations."

The Meiji Revolution represented a third type of revolution, distinct from the revivalist or idealistic models. As in France under Louis XVI and in the American colonies, this revolution occurred in a society lacking a tradition of liberty and popular rights—but neither was it guided by a coherent ideology or ideal. The result was something that could only be described as an "anarchical revolution."[4]

> And when, unhappily, history and established institutions are not illuminated by the pleasant light of liberty, and the cruel weight of oppression is like a dark night threatening to extinguish all ideals in the hearts of the people, so they find no hope in the past nor light in the future, then revolution in such a country can be neither idealistic nor revivalist since it occurs merely because the sufferings of the present are impossible to bear. We shall properly call this an undefined anarchical revolution.[5]

Takekoshi's use of the adjective "anarchical" (*ranseiteki*) does not signify ongoing civil strife and upheaval. As we will see in the following section, in the case of the Meiji Revolution, "social currents" had effected gradual change over many years, eventually bringing about a regime change. For him, "anarchical" seems to have implied a movement that was not the product of the intentions or design of specific individuals, but resulted from larger forces impelling society toward revolution.

From the feudal system to the New Japan

In *Shin Nihon shi*, Takekoshi argues that Tokugawa society had been completely enmeshed in the controls of the traditional *hōken* system. He identifies the most prominent characteristic of this system as the "local decentralization of power," in which the shogun delegated regional control to the various daimyo. The Japanese term *hōkensei* is usually translated as "feudal system" but instead describes a structure very different from the centralized system of regional and local government (*gunkensei*) that developed in imperial China.

In China, the imperial court dispatched officials of the central government to rule the provinces; under the feudal system in Japan, the daimyo were granted domains that their families would continue to rule through generations. This dichotomy between a centralized system and a feudal system reflected a traditional typology of government in East Asia, dating back to the Chinese classics. In the Tokugawa period, Japanese scholars and intellectuals understood the ruling institutions of their country as *hōken*. Taking the relationship between the kings of ancient China and their vassal lords as a model, it was possible to conceive of the shogun granting rights to the various daimyo to rule their domains as a similar form of "investiture" or "enfeoffment" (the basic meaning of *hōken*: literally, *divide* land [*hō*] and *establish* [*ken*] lords). And because the shogun, the daimyo, and the samurai serving them as vassals all held their positions through hereditary lineages, this feudal system was also generally regarded as inseparable from the principle of hereditary succession.

Takekoshi interprets the history of the Tokugawa period from the eighteenth century onward as a process in which the social order that had initially been tightly bound by this feudal system gradually unraveled. What sustained the feudal system was the power of intimidation, through a preponderance of military force and political authority. The ruling Tokugawa intimidated the daimyo, higher-ranking samurai intimidated lower-ranking samurai, and the warrior class as a whole intimidated the townspeople and peasants. Such displays of power and dominance were initially effective in maintaining "social cohesion."

But "after the time of the fifth shogun" (mid-eighteenth century onward), the cohesion of this feudal system gradually declined. Successive generations of peace and stability brought by the Tokugawa order resulted in the samurai class becoming corrupted by habituation to a life of luxury and the accumulation of debt. Conversely, the townspeople and peasants were amassing financial power and becoming the creditors of the samurai. On the surface, the feudal caste system was rigidly maintained, but in actuality, the commoners were beginning to reverse the power relationship with the samurai.

This slackening of the power of intimidation that maintained the social order began to influence, and to alter, the thinking of the ruled. In this regard, Takekoshi draws attention to the "headmen and chiefs of townships, villages, and hamlets." Referencing John Hampden, a leader of the rebellion against the crown that initiated the English Civil War, he points to the role of these local notables as representatives of the peasantry in Tokugawa-period protests against increases in the annual taxes on agricultural production:

> Along with this gradual and almost imperceptible alteration in the coercive power that was the sole force maintaining the security of the feudal system, we should not underestimate the early advances toward popular rights. Of course, the concept of popular rights at that time in the Tokugawa period was a far cry from how we conceive of it today, but a reaction against the unbearable depredations of the samurai inspired the appearance of a number of peaceful Hampdens among the headmen and chiefs of townships, villages, and hamlets. Thus even under the feudal system, the passage of more than two hundred years had resulted in the spontaneous emergence of a sort of local self-government. And this is certainly the principal reason the Japanese people have been able to endure terrible oppression to achieve what they have today.[6]

During the Tokugawa period, the collection of taxes and the maintenance of public order were entrusted in large part to the villages and townships under the leadership of local officials such as village headmen. Although they served as the lowest-level units of social control, Takekoshi describes them with terminology borrowed from the Meiji political system as "local representatives, or like the district heads [*gunchō*], being of a semigovernmental nature"; in other words, he saw them not merely as local administrators but as representatives of the local people. Moreover, as their economic position improved, and as publishing and the circulation of manuscripts developed, these village officials were also able to educate themselves. As a result, critiques of the rulers and of the feudal caste

John Hampden (1595–1643).

system from a Confucian perspective began to gradually take hold.

The Confucian tradition, as expressed in the concept of the Mandate of Heaven, demanded that the sovereign and his officials display superior virtue and rule benevolently, with a concern for the peace and welfare of the people. Thus, Takekoshi writes, "the monarch is not a monarch for his own sake; he exists only because of the people." The chapter on the house of Chen in Sima Qian's classic of Chinese history, *Records of the Grand Historian*, contains a passage in which Chen Sheng justifies his rebellion by declaring, "It is not blood that makes a man king or minister or general"; this questioning of the validity of hereditary rule had begun to spread through society. Takekoshi's commentary on this subject no doubt reflects his personal experience of having grown up in the family of a local notable and proprietor of a sake brewery in the provincial town of Kakizaki in Echigo (now Niigata prefecture).

During the late Tokugawa period, "a great transformation of society itself" was steadily underway in the realms of scholarship and thought. Thus, Takekoshi argues, rather than an ideology of imperial loyalism seeking the emperor's return to power, the "major factor" sustaining the political movement toward the Meiji Revolution was based in the philosophies of Mencius and Wang Yangming, which gave theoretical articulation to dynastic change and the forcible overthrow of rulers who had deviated from the Way. The crisis in foreign relations and imperial loyalism had merely been catalysts for the emergence of this political movement. And the fact that the new Meiji government had not stopped at the seizure of political power but had plunged ahead to dismantle the entire system of feudal caste and status was seen as evidence of this. If the Meiji Revolution had been motivated solely by the goal of "dynastic change," then the Meiji government would not have found it necessary to push forward with the social changes that dismantled the samurai class, such as the return of domainal sovereignty to the central government (*hanseki hōkan*) and the creation of a national army based on a system of universal military conscription.

So Takekoshi interprets the fundamental nature of Meiji Revolution as a "social revolution" that had proceeded steadily at the deepest levels of Japanese society. If we might borrow the title of a famous work by Raymond

Williams,[7] the twentieth-century British critic regarded as one of the founders of the field of cultural studies, the Meiji Revolution was a "long revolution" with a far greater temporal span than that of the comparatively superficial political events of the years surrounding 1868.

The Meiji Revolution as a long revolution

Some readers may feel they have heard this argument somewhere before—that at the root of the political transformation wrought by the Meiji Revolution was a gradual disintegration of the existing social order. And in fact, this was the Marxist interpretation of the Meiji Revolution. One of the earliest works of this type of historical research is Noro Eitarō's monograph "Nihon shihon shugi hattatsu shi" (A History of the Development of Japanese Capitalism),[8] which defines the Meiji Revolution as "a forcible social transformation aimed at establishing the dominant position of capitalists and capitalistic landowners," a bourgeois revolution that Noro was moved to call the "Meiji Revolution."

This characterization of the Meiji Revolution as a bourgeois revolution was one that Noro would soon have to abandon in light of the Comintern's 1927 "Theses on the Japan Problem," but what is noteworthy here is the historical image of the progressive disintegration of the established social order of Tokugawa Japan in the areas of agriculture, trade, and industry.

Of course, Noro's description of the feudal system of the Tokugawa period has in mind a concept of feudalism derived from the Marxist theory of the West (a system of landownership and relations of production in which the feudal lords dominated village communities comprised of serfs)—something quite different from Takekoshi's *hōkensei* as discussed earlier. Yet at least in terms of his perception of the phenomenon of the "long revolution," it may be possible to see Takekoshi's analysis as flowing—some forty years after it was written—into the Marxist historiography of the 1920s and later.

Noro Eitarō (1900–1934).

But compared to Noro's tight focus on relations of dominance and subordination in the economic sphere in describing this long revolution, Takekoshi's perspective is much broader, depicting a comprehensive process of social transformation considered in a diversity of aspects, from the social relations of the class system to the development of communications and the diffusion of ideas.

The Kōza-ha ("Lecture Faction") school of Marxist historical interpretation with which Noro was associated also went beyond a simple analysis of the economic structures of capitalism and imperialism, expanding its scope to address the issue of "feudal remnants" in social consciousness and analyze the political system that had situated the emperor at its apex. In this sense, it might be said that in their analysis of the "feudal system," these historians were also aiming at a total history that did not confine itself merely to a depiction of economic structures.

But the perspective that Takekoshi brought to his depiction of history had even stronger tendencies toward total history than that of Kōza-ha Marxism. The attempt to narrate the history of a nation not merely in terms of political and economic developments, but to embrace the broader movements of culture and society, was characteristic of the histories of civilization written in nineteenth-century Europe, and the intellectuals of Meiji Japan received these as a contemporary influence.

This type of comprehensive attention to historical change, from a perspective grasping the Meiji Revolution as a phase in a longer revolution, was already apparent in the work of another writer referenced by Takekoshi in *Shin Nihon shi* Fukuzawa Yukichi, and especially in Fukuzawa's *Bunmeiron no gairyaku* (Outline of a Theory of Civilization), published in 1875. Takekoshi was a student of Fukuzawa at his private academy, Keiō Gijuku, an experience that seems to have

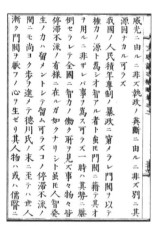

A page from chapter 5 of Fukuzawa Yukichi's *Bunmeiron no gairyaku* (1875).

strongly influenced Takekoshi's understanding of the Meiji Revolution.

Fukuzawa directly engages the nature of civilization in *Bunmeiron no gairyaku*. We will touch on this in greater detail in chapter 3 of this book, but according to Fukuzawa, civilization is a universal ideal of humankind, and the highest human aspiration is to effect the progress of one's nation from "barbarism" to a civilized state.

The fifth chapter of *Bunmeiron no gairyaku* continues an argument begun in the preceding chapter regarding "the intellect and virtue of the people of a country." In it, Fukuzawa asserts that the index of progress toward civilization achieved by a nation as a whole is the level of development that its people have reached in intellect and virtue. As concrete examples of this he cites two events that occurred, respectively, a mere eight years earlier, or four years prior to the publication of his book: the "restoration of imperial rule" (*ōsei isshin*), and the abolition of the feudal domains and establishment of prefectures (*haihan chiken*). It is worth noting that here Fukuzawa treats these two events separately, not seeing them in terms of a single historical event called the Meiji Revolution.

With regard to these two great events, the intellectuals of the day, and especially the imperial loyalists, saw the overthrow of the shogunate as a result of the appeal to the people of "the glory of the imperial house," and the decision to replace the domains with prefectures as "heroic decisions by those in power." But Fukuzawa sternly rejected such popular opinions. He believed that the real force driving this series of great reforms that reshaped Japan as a nation was in fact the increase in the "intellect and virtue" of society as a whole.

> The people of our country suffered for many years under the yoke of tyranny. Heredity was the source of power, and even men of talent could find an outlet for its expression only through heredity. The whole age was oppressed by hereditary power, and throughout the land there was no room for the workings of the intellect; everything was in a state of stagnation. But the creative powers of the intellect are irrepressible. Even amidst stagnation, there was progress, and by the end of the Tokugawa period, antipathy to hereditary power had arisen in the minds of the people.[9]

Even in the society of the Tokugawa period, which appeared to be shackled by a system of hereditary power, currents of discontent roiled members of the broader populace who, because their birth and station were too low, could find no place to demonstrate their talents and abilities. As long as the shogunate continued to exercise its repressive power over the people, overt manifestations of this discontent were impossible, and instead found expression in scholarship and literature. Fukuzawa notes that such dissidence could be found by reading between the lines of treatises by Confucian scholars and the popular satirical writers known as the *gesakusha*.

Yet just at the point that this "antipathy to hereditary power" had built up to the verge of explosion, Perry's squadron arrived in Japan and exposed the weakness of the authority of the shogunate. The populist cry to "expel the barbarians" born of this encounter served as the catalyst for the "antipathy to hereditary power" to explode into a political movement culminating in a revolutionary overthrow of the shogunate, which was further impelled to proceed with the dismantling of the caste system represented by the abolition of the domains and the creation of prefectures.

Thus, in Fukuzawa's understanding, the arrival of Perry did no more than light the fuse for the explosion of the "antipathy to hereditary power" he describes. Antiforeign agitation and imperial loyalism simply rode the crest of this outburst. On the surface it appeared that the rhetoric of "revere the emperor and expel the barbarians" (*sonnō jōi*) was the force that toppled the shogunate, but what really sustained this movement was the critique of the hereditary caste system that had accumulated and deepened through the course of the Tokugawa period.

For Fukuzawa, the "antipathy to hereditary power" was the result of the ways in which the development of the "intellect and virtue" of the people had been distorted by the constraints of the class system. And he notes that this began to find social expression in scholarship and literature "from the Tenmei to the Bunka era" (c. 1780–1820). This differs somewhat from "after the time of the fifth shogun" (Tsunayoshi, who ruled from 1680 to 1709) alluded to by Takekoshi, but both of these writers envisioned a long process of social change stretching back to the mid-eighteenth century or the beginning of the nineteenth, in which they discerned a power at work that shaped the undercurrents of the transformation known as the Meiji Revolution.

So there was intellectual and social transformation that spanned the long years of the nineteenth century, centering on the Meiji Revolution. What exactly was this, and what significance did it have for the history that followed? With Takekoshi's and Fukuzawa's insights in mind, would it not be intriguing to rethink such questions?

CHAPTER 3

History in Reverse

Expo '70 in Osaka.

The impact of the history of civilization

According to the Western perspective, the ideal civilization lies in the future. This stands in stark contrast to the Confucian view of history, in which the ideal civilization is found in the Way of the Ancient Kings of remote antiquity. How have the contradictions between these two perspectives on history played out in modern Japan?

The theme of Expo '70, the world's fair held in Osaka in 1970, was "Progress and Harmony for Mankind." This can be read as a full-throated paean to historical progress, in which the history of the human race follows a path of consistent improvement. At the time, Japanese society was in the midst of dizzying economic growth, living conditions were steadily improving, and the word "progress" resonated with people's experience. In contrast, the theme of Expo 2005 in Aichi prefecture was "Nature's Wisdom." While this did not necessarily contradict the idea of history as steady progress, it did point to the timeless truths of the natural world. For the people of the twenty-first century, unqualified praise for "progress" seems to have become somewhat problematic.

As the sociologist Yoshimi Shun'ya has shown, such doubts concerning progress had already been articulated during the initial deliberations for the theme of Osaka Expo '70.[1] According to his research, "The Wisdom of Mankind" had been under serious consideration by the committee charged with drafting the theme. Members of the committee who promoted this theme believed that wisdom was crucial in tackling the problems associated with scientific and technological development and contemporary conflicts such as the Cold War and the Vietnam War. Clearly, skepticism regarding progress was already stirring behind the colorful and festive facade of Expo '70. Such doubts were alien to Meiji intellectuals like Fukuzawa Yukichi. They lived through the transfer of power from the Tokugawa shogunate to the Meiji government and the massive social and political changes that ensued, which they saw as having been brought about by the progressive movement of society toward "civilization." They believed, without question, that history would continue along the path of progress.

Let's consider Fukuzawa's masterwork, *Bunmeiron no gairyaku* (Outline of a Theory of Civilization, 1875). Beginning in the waning years of the Tokugawa shogunate, Fukuzawa had worked to disseminate the thought and institutions of the Western nations—seen

The beginning of chapter 3 of Fukuzawa Yukichi's *Bunmeiron no gairyaku* (1875).

as the vanguard of "civilization"—in a series of works that include *Seiyō jijō* (Conditions in the West, 1866–70) and *Gakumon no susume* (An Encouragement of Learning, 1872–76). Seven or eight years after the collapse of the Tokugawa regime, Fukuzawa felt that social conditions had gradually stabilized, and he resolved to renew his study of Western works dealing with the topic of civilization with the intention of writing a comprehensive introduction to the theory of civilization for Japanese readers. The result was *Bunmeiron no gairyaku,* published in August 1875 in a six-volume edition.

In chapter 3 of this work, "The Essence of Civilization," Fukuzawa argues that "civilization" signifies not only the provision of comfort and convenience in the material aspects of daily life, but also the process of refinement and enhancement of the intellect (*chie*, a term that reappears as the focus of chapter 6 of the work) and virtue. Thus the gradual ascent from barbarism to civilization becomes the consistent principle underlying the history of humankind.

What, then, does civilization mean? I say that it refers to the attainment of *both* material well-being *and* the elevation of the human spirit. It means both abundance of daily necessities and refinement of human character. Is it civilization if only the former is fulfilled? The goal of life does not lie in food and clothes alone. If that were man's goal, he would be no different from an ant or a bee. This cannot be what Heaven intended for man.

On the other hand, is mere spiritual elevation to be termed civilization? In that case, everyone should be like Yan Hui, who lived in a humble hut and survived only on water. This cannot be called Heaven's will either. Therefore, there must be both material and spiritual aspects before one can call it civilization.[2]

One might also ask whether material abundance has led to a decay of the human spirit. This is an analysis of present conditions that we often hear in the words of ecological activists, but as a critique of "civilization" it had already been developed in the eighteenth century by Jean-Jacques Rousseau in works such as *Discourse on the Arts and Sciences* (1750) and *Discourse on the Origin and Basis of Inequality Among Men* (1753).

François Guizot (1787–1874).

Fukuzawa was deeply influenced by nineteenth-century European writing on the history of civilization, from the French thinker François Guizot's *History of Civilization in Europe* (1828; Fukuzawa read an American edition of William Hazlitt's English translation) to Henry Thomas Buckle's *History of Civilization in England* (1857–61). These works are cognizant of critiques such as Rousseau's, while continuing to point to the refinement of human spirituality, rather than simply material development, as a central element of civilization. Fukuzawa's argument, which advocates a balanced development of body and mind, and the refinement of the intellect and virtue, draws upon these contemporary developments in Western intellectual history. Following upon the passage quoted above, Fukuzawa continues:

Moreover, there is no limit to the material well-being or spiritual refinement of humanity. By material well-being and spiritual refinement is meant a state in which these two aspects are really making progress, and by civilization is meant the progress of both man's well-being and his refinement. Since what produces man's well-being and refinement is intellect and virtue, civilization ultimately means the progress of man's intellect and virtue.[3]

The essence of civilization lies less in material, physical well-being than it does in the development of the intellect and virtue—which generates such well-being—and spiritual refinement. And there are no limits to such progress. Fukuzawa argues that human history is a limitless process of the enhancement of the intellect and virtue. His position is frequently interpreted as an exhortation to Japan to exert itself to catch up with the advanced civilization of the West. But if we accept this rather simplistic conclusion, we run the risk of overlooking some of the more important aspects of Fukuzawa's perspective on civilization.

The second chapter of *Bunmeiron* is entitled "Western Civilization as Our Guide"; here, Fukuzawa articulates a vision of the contemporary nineteenth-century world in which the European nations and the United States are "the most civilized nations," the Asian nations such as Turkey, China, and Japan are "semi-civilized" (*hankai*), and Africa and Australia are described as "barbarous" (*yaban*).

In the twenty-first-century world, this view of civilization has fallen into disrepute; it is regarded as a flawed ideology that once served to legitimize the colonization of Asia and Africa by Western powers. It is also clear that Fukuzawa thought of Western nations as the most advanced along an index premised on the opposing values of "barbarous" and "civilized." Moreover, in *Bunmeiron no gairyaku*, he declares that to become a truly civilized nation, Japan must learn from the "spirit of civilization" that lives in the West.

Today, when cultural relativism has become something of a norm, Fukuzawa's argument, which at least superficially appears to praise the West and denigrate traditional Asian culture, is akin to an endangered species. Yet at the heart of his discussion of civilization in chapter 2 of *Bunmeiron,* he asserts that the designations civilized, semi-civilized, and barbarous are all "relative."

"Civilization is a living thing; it moves and progresses. And things that move and progress must go through sequential stages." Viewed from the perspective of the totality of human history, every nation is always progressing somewhere along the road from barbarous to semi-civilized to civilized, and the difference between the West and Asia may be ascribed simply to the

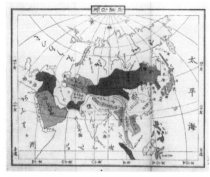

Map of Asia from *Sekai kunizukushi* (1869), a world atlas compiled and translated by Fukuzawa Yukichi.

speed of that progression to date. Thus the contemporary West is still in the process of development, and has not attained the pinnacle of civilization.

Moreover, although we call the nations of the West civilized, they can correctly be honored with this designation only in the modern world. And many of them, if we were to be more precise, would fall well short of this designation.

For example, there is no greater calamity in the world than war, and yet the nations of the West are always at war. Robbery and murder are the worst of human crimes, but in the West there are robbers and murderers. There are those who form cliques to vie for the reins of power and who, when deprived of that power, decry the injustice of it all. Even worse, international diplomacy is really based on the art of deception.[4]

It is important that Fukuzawa devotes such critical attention here to the fact of warfare among the Western nations and their efforts to extend their power over other parts of the world, as well as the "art of deception" they employ to advance their interests in the arena of international affairs. What this meant was that the West, too, was still on the path of progress; it was still far from having attained "the ultimate good." As the intellect and virtue of the peoples of the earth progress over the passage of several centuries, or several millennia, they might eventually arrive at a "perfection of peace and well-being" from which, Fukuzawa predicts, these denizens of the future might look back with pity upon the primitive conditions represented by "the state of the Western nations today."

Reflecting in later life on his motives for writing *Bunmeiron no gairyaku,* Fukuzawa said he "thought it would be most wondrous if I brought my argument to the attention of the old Confucian scholars and might win their approval."[5] In fact, the Confucianism these scholars believed in was a philosophy dating back to remote antiquity, when China existed in a much more barbarous state than now, and Fukuzawa was harshly critical of it as unsuited to a civilized era.

In chapter 7 of *Bunmeiron no gairyaku,* "The Proper Times and Places for the Intellect and Virtue," Fukuzawa tells us that because remote antiquity was "barbarous," "a world blind to reason" in which human intelligence was completely uncultivated, tyrants ruled by "brute force," maintaining order by instilling fear or reverence in the populace. Confucian teachings frequently allude to the ruler as "father and mother of the people" and speak of him as compassionately ensuring the welfare of the people through his benevolence—but he also used intimidation to control their behavior.

> The country was like a single family or a classroom, with the ruler as the parent or teacher. To the extent that his authority was inscrutable, he was like a god. He was simultaneously parent, teacher, and god. In such a situation, if the ruler of the country checked his selfish desires and cultivated virtue, even if he were not too intelligent, he was praised as a benevolent ruler and enlightened emperor. This is what was called "the tranquility of the barbarians." Of course, in such an age, this was unavoidable, it might even be called admirable.[6]

An outstanding ruler was one who exercised the kingly virtues—exemplified by benevolence—in governing the land, and who also exerted himself to educate the people and elevate them morally and ethically. This was the ideal order envisioned by Confucianism. But Fukuzawa saw this as an approach that was viable only in a "barbarous" world in which the human intellect was not far advanced and the patterns for life and behavior were limited. With progress toward civilization, the world grows increasingly diverse and complex, and virtue alone, backed by love and compassion shown toward individuals, no longer suffices to maintain order: the development of the human intellect is also required.

Here it should be noted that the question of the nature of historical progress is inextricably bound with issues of morality. The progress of civilization lies not merely in the development of science and technology and a more comfortable and convenient material existence. Only when it is accompanied by enhancement of the intelligence and virtue of ordinary people can we expect it to reach the ultimate goal of progress, "the perfection of peace and well-being." In contrast, the moral and ethical vision of the traditional Confucian teachings saw the first step toward moral progress in society strictly in terms of the exercise of "benevolent authority" by a virtuous ruler. But for Fukuzawa, this was a barbarous concept of social order that was no longer valid in a civilized world.

Overturning the idealization of the past

To speak of the progress of civilization, and to believe in the unlimited capacity for improvement of the human race, was a new vision of history that Fukuzawa and other Western-influenced intellectuals had come to embrace as a result of their exposure to the Western narratives of the history of civilization. The explosive power of this perspective led to a revision of traditional concepts of human nature, morality, and politics such as those of Confucianism, and to the establishment of new modes of thought that took Western modernity as their model.

But here let us pause for a moment to reconsider the Confucian view of history that was being rejected. The idea that the Tokugawa shogunate, from its founding, deliberately disseminated Confucian thought (and especially that of the Neo-Confucian Zhu Xi school) as an ideology legitimating its rule has been largely rejected by recent historical scholarship, such as Watanabe Hiroshi's *Kinsei Nihon shakai to Sōgaku* (Early Modern Japanese Society and the Zhu Xi School).[7] Instead, amid the stability and peace brought by the

Tokugawa regime, Neo-Confucianism was championed by independent scholars working outside official circles, while the unique perspective on Confucianism developed by critics of Neo-Confucianism such as Itō Jinsai and Ogyū Sorai also had a major impact on the world of thought.

As a result, beginning in the late eighteenth century, daimyo in every part of Japan began to found domain academies, and the shogunate created its own official academy, the Shōheikō. In these academies, the Zhu Xi school of Neo-Confucianism and other Confucian schools grew into an official orthodoxy that became the shared premise of discourse among the intelligentsia of Tokugawa Japan.

Ogyū Sorai (1666–1728), from Hara Tokusai, *Sentetsu zōden* (Illustrated Biographies of Great Scholars, 1845).

The scholar of Chinese history Masubuchi Tatsuo once described the Confucian perspective on history as characterized by "idealization of the past" (*shōko shugi*).[8] Here, as a concrete example of this, I would like to consider *Gakusoku* (Instructions for Students, 1727), a work by the great Confucian thinker Ogyū Sorai (1666–1728).[9]

Sorai began as a Neo-Confucian scholar but eventually turned his attention to the early canon of Confucianism, the ancient texts comprising the Six Classics[10] (*Book of Poetry*, *Book of Documents*, *Book of Rites*, *Book of Music*, *Book of Changes*, and *Spring and Autumn Annals*). In order for them to be properly read, he conceived a methodology that was grounded in meticulous mastery of the language of ancient China, in an effort to enable the reader to experience the thought processes and sensibility of the people who created these texts. His work was an attempt to understand the Way of the Ancient Kings (*sen'ō no michi*) contained in the Six Classics through study of such ancient writings, and thus to clarify the true nature of Confucian thought.

Gakusoku is a brief work outlining Sorai's scholarly method. His fourth instruction begins:

In ancient days there were sages. Now there are no sages. Hence, to study necessarily means to study the past. Yet if there were no antiquity, there could be no present; and if there were no present, there could be no antiquity. How could we do away with the present? The many ages appear in turn: which is not past? and which is not present? One is conversant with the past and thereby sets himself facing the proper standard. One knows the present and thereby makes this standard his own. He distinguishes among the ages and thereby observes their histories. If he does all those things, then their customs and human feelings will become as clear to him as if he were seeing them in the palm of his hand.[11]

In Sorai's view, the Confucian teachings were in their essence a science of government. And the great rulers who had embodied and actualized this ideal of governance were the "sages" and "ancient kings" of China: Yao, Shun, and the monarchs of the Three Dynasties—Xia, Shang, and Zhou. The "Way" that Confucians must study and practice consisted in the totality of the institutions that these sage kings had created over the course of many years, centering on "rites, music, punishment, and rules" (*rei-gaku-kei-sei*). "Rites" in this sense was a comprehensive term for a broad range of institutions, from the elaborate ceremonials of the royal court to the customs and etiquette of everyday life. "Music" signified both the music and dance performed in the rituals of the court. "Punishment and rules" meant the legal framework provided by penal and civil law, as well as its administration.

This view of history was premised upon the belief that the ideal social order that humanity should universally adopt as its model had actually existed in ancient China. The great institutions established by the early kings had realized a gently ordered world in which the customs and behavior of the people inclined toward goodness. Yet gradually this world fell into disorder, and Confucius, deeply troubled by the sense that the concrete institutional expressions of the Way of the Ancient Kings were being forgotten, labored to compile them into the Six Classics and other texts as a standard for later generations to study and emulate.

Thus human history was conceived as a gradual falling away from the ideal world of Yao, Shun, and the Three Dynasties of ancient China. But as the citation above suggests, Sorai neither argues that the present age was so decadent that nothing could be done to correct it, nor asserts that the institutions of antiquity could or should be revived without modification.

He believed that each "present" had institutions appropriate to it, as revealed through historical research and an assessment of the strengths and weaknesses of each period ("distinguishing among the ages and observing their histories"). Then, while of course taking the institutions of the early kings as the model ("facing the proper standard"), they should be reconfigured in a contemporary manner to create an institutional framework appropriate to governance in the present time. Sorai thought that in this way, even in a present far removed from the era of the sage kings, stable government could be achieved.

Sorai, it seems, believed that the practice of an ideal Way had occurred not only in China under the rule of the sage kings but also in Japan. In his *Taiheisaku* (Policies for Great Peace), said to have been submitted to the shogun Yoshimune as a policy proposal in 1721,[12] he touches briefly on the subject of the Way of the Gods (*shintō*). According to Sorai, the Way of the Sages (*seijin no michi*) described in the Six Classics was the universal Way for all humanity, and it was impossible for a distinctive "Way" for a particular country to coexist in parallel with it. Yet Sorai notes that in Japan, before the introduction of written language, the imperial court (*chōtei*) practiced rituals similar to those by which Yao, Shun, and the rulers of the Three Dynasties venerated heaven and their own ancestors. Sorai's commentary on the rituals associated with the gods of Japan are fragmentary, and it is difficult to interpret them with certainty, but it would appear that the mentality that sought utopia in ancient China was, at the same time, connected with a desire to discover a similar ideal embodied in ancient Japan. Sorai thought that in remote antiquity, long before any written records, the Way had been transmitted to Japan from China—fragments of which survived as the rituals conducted by the Japanese emperors in veneration of the gods and recorded in later Japanese texts. To this extent, the idealization of the past transcended the distinction between China and Japan to become a universal standard of historical judgment.

In 1862, more than 130 years after Sorai's death, a young Japanese scholar who had studied his works attentively set out on a journey to study in the Netherlands. Nishi Amane (1829–97) had grown up in the domain of Tsuwano, in present-day Shimane prefecture. Recognized for his talents in Western learning, he was hired as an assistant lecturer at the shogunal institute for foreign studies, the Bansho Shirabesho. In his youth he had studied Neo-Confucianism at the domainal academy Yōrōkan in Tsuwano; he had also come into contact with the works of Sorai and found them compelling.

Later, sent by the Tsuwano domain to Edo to report on the situation following the arrival of Perry's warships in Japan, he felt keenly that traditional scholarship based in the Chinese classics would prove completely inadequate for dealing with developments in the contemporary world, and he decided to devote himself to Western studies. After the Meiji Revolution, Nishi would become a member of the influential intellectual journal *Meiroku zasshi* and a government bureaucrat in the fields of military affairs and education, but even after his shift to Western studies, the influence of the Sorai school on his thought remained strong.[13]

But here I would like to focus on an essay entitled "Suehiro no kotobuki" (A Celebration of Continual Progress), believed to have been written by Nishi sometime in the first three years after the Meiji Revolution, between 1868 and 1870, after he had returned from study in Europe and had moved to Numazu in Shizuoka, accompanying the former shogun Tokugawa Yoshinobu. In this essay, Nishi employs the traditional metaphor of the spreading fan as a symbol of good fortune and longevity to express a progressive vision of history and the development of the human race.

Nishi affirms that through the ages "the Way of the human world" has become more "fully endowed" and more "enlightened," and the "truth of things" revealed by the human intellect has grown increasingly more detailed and precise. "Indeed, there can be no doubt

Nishi Amane (1829–1897).

that prosperity begets prosperity, and enlightenment further enlightenment."[14] "Suehiro no kotobuki" was an unfinished and unpublished manuscript, but one that proudly proclaims a progressive historical perspective similar to that advanced by Fukuzawa in *Bunmeiron no gairyaku*.

Moreover, in this essay Nishi specifically cites "the *Gakusoku* of Master Sorai" as a prime example of a mode of thought that seeks an ideal world in antiquity and looks upon the present as a decline from former glory. In Nishi's judgment, this was a consequence of the failure of the Sorai school to give sufficient attention to the laws and principles of the universe, and its conception of the Way as consisting only in "rites, music, punishment, and rules." Sorai and his followers made the mistake of idealizing antiquity because they believed these institutions and practices to be the invention of the ancient sages. Nishi goes on to criticize Daoism, Buddhism, and Kokugaku (National Learning, the study of Japanese classics) for having similarly erroneous antiquarian perspectives on history.

In contrast to this, Nishi speaks of a historical truth to be learned from Western studies, based on "the truths of the universe" or "the mind of God, expressed without being uttered by Heaven."

> To conceive of the Way of mankind as the truth of the universe... means that without question the human world will grow increasingly more enlightened and abundant, until at last we shall ascend to the realm described by Kant as *pacem aeternam* or *harmonia aeternam*.[15]

According to Nishi, human beings are different from other living things by virtue of being equipped with an innate capacity to develop new knowledge and to make things, cultivating for themselves a "way of utility and well-being." Eventually, as this material "civilization" (*kaika*) was accompanied by the perfection of human "ethical nature" (*jingi no sei*), the progress of the human race as a whole would lead to the advent of the harmonious world described in Immanuel Kant's *Perpetual Peace: A Philosophical Sketch* (1795).

Thus both Nishi and Fukuzawa reversed the idealization of the past represented by Confucian thought, replacing it with a progressive view of history that sought the ideal world in a distant future, successfully positing that society was headed toward civilization and enlightenment. Despite the boldness of this shift in perspective, it is difficult to see in their prose—especially Nishi's—a complete parting of the ways with traditional thought. Stylistically, in contrast to the content, his writing displays considerable continuity with the texts of Neo-Confucianism, the Sorai school, and the Kokugaku that he encountered in his youth.

Immanuel Kant (1724–1804).

It might be natural to assume that as an eyewitness to the epochal transition from the Tokugawa shogunate to the Meiji government, and as a result of his own experience of study in the West, Nishi's thought underwent an abrupt and complete transformation. But the vocabulary with which Nishi voices his new conception of history is not based solely upon Kant's discourse on perpetual peace and human progress.

Instead, Nishi's "Suehiro no kotobuki" is studded with phrases that at least superficially resemble those commonly employed by the Neo-Confucian scholars: "the principles pervading the universe," "human nature," "the nature of humanity and justice," "the Way of mankind." In other words, Nishi himself sensed no contradiction in proposing his new vision of history in the language of traditional learning, which had supported the idealization of the past.

We should not be too quick to assess this as evidence of the limitations of Nishi's—or Fukuzawa's—understanding of Western thought. During the Tokugawa period, well before either made their appearance as intellectuals, ways of thinking about history were already beginning to change. Perhaps because it had already become somewhat conventional to employ the existing vocabulary of Confucianism and Kokugaku to express this sense of a transformation at the deepest levels of thought, they felt no hesitation at using the same vocabulary to introduce the progressive concept of history originating in the West.

A new historical vision was introduced through Japan's encounter with the civilization of the West. But did this vision not overlap, in part, with the consciousness of a changing world that was already being intuited by the people of Tokugawa Japan? Such questions arise out of the works of Fukuzawa Yukichi and Nishi Amane.

CHAPTER 4

The Voltaire of Osaka

Hanegawa Tōei, *The Korean Embassy Visits the Capital*, c. 1748.

The Korean embassy to Japan

Let us begin with the 475-member embassy sent by the Korean royal court, which arrived in Osaka on October 16, 1719. Three years before, the seventh Tokugawa shogun, Ietsugu, had passed away at the tender age of eight, and the Tokugawa council of elders selected Yoshimune, from the Kii branch of the family, as the eighth shogun. The Korean embassy—the first in eight years—traveled to Japan in 1719 to present a letter of congratulations on Yoshimune's accession to the office of shogun. Shin Yu-han, who was attached to the embassy as a secretary and official recorder, left a detailed diary of the mission, *Haeyurok* (Record of a Journey across the Sea).[1] In his role as secretary, Shin also performed the function of communicating in poetry and prose with the Japanese Confucian scholars who came to visit the members of the embassy. As Confucianism was beginning to permeate Japanese society during this period, these Japanese scholars were eager to learn authentic classical Chinese literary style from the Korean officials of the embassy, all products of the rigorous civil service examination system of the Korean royal court.

The Korean embassy was also the object of intense curiosity and interest on the part of the general populace, who were excited by the rare opportunity to encounter foreigners and their customs that was afforded by the stately procession of the embassy along the highways from Osaka to Edo. In this era of strictly limited contact with the outside world—later known as *sakoku*, or the closing of the country—the visit of the Korean embassy to Japan was a remarkable international event.

Shin Yu-han and the other members of the embassy embarked on a ship at Busan, and after stopping at the island of Tsushima, the established transit point between Korea and Japan, passed through the straits of Shimonseki, crossed the Inland Sea, and then sailed up the lower reaches of the Yodogawa river to disembark in Osaka. There, the members of the embassy formed a procession that set out through the streets of the city to the official guesthouse that had been established for them at the great Nishi Honganji temple. Shin Yu-han writes with wonder of the scene that greeted their eyes:

Then, bearing the letters of state and accompanied by the music of the drums, we reached the guesthouse after six or seven *li* [24–28 km]. Long buildings lined the streets along the way, none of them less than two stories, and all of them shops trading in a wide variety of goods. Waves of onlookers thronged the sides of the street, almost dazzling in the finery of their dress. Their numbers had increased several-fold since our landing at the riverbank, and by now made one feel almost faint. I don't know how many streets we passed, nor how many neighborhoods, but the avenue we were on was straight as a die and without a spot of dirt or dust. Lining it were shops selling bead screens, albums of art, and embroidered cloth. Both street level and the upper stories were occupied by a wall of humanity, male and female, old and young, all dressed in clothing patterned in blue, crimson, indigo, purple, green, and yellow.[2]

Contemporary Japanese accounts of the embassy's visit tell us that the shogunate, which had direct control of the city of Osaka, had commanded residents of the streets and neighborhoods visible along the route of the embassy's procession to take special care to make them clean and presentable. So the splendid appearance remarked upon by Shin may have had an element of exaggeration underlying it, compared with everyday life. Even so, it is clear that the liveliness and prosperity of the city of Osaka surprised the foreign visitors and left a vivid impression.

In the previous chapter we touched on the way in which the idealization of the past embraced by Tokugawa-period intellectuals, which sought models for morality and social order in distant antiquity, was reversed by the discourse on "civilization" in the early Meiji period, which articulated a historical vision oriented toward a future of limitless progress. This shift in thought did not occur solely as a result of exposure to the progressivism upon which much of eighteenth- and nineteenth-century Western thought was premised. People sensed, on a completely different plane from the arguments of the Confucian thinkers, that the world was actually, if gradually, changing for the better—and precisely because of this, they were able to appreciate the progressive view of history and make a place for it in Japanese society. So let's return briefly to the eighteenth century, when this intuitive sense began to make itself felt, and examine some of the thinkers who were the first to clearly apprehend it and incorporate it into their own discourse.

In the early twenty-first century, against a background of global recession and rising energy costs, there has been considerable support in Japan for the idea of abandoning the goal of economic growth and replacing it with the aim of a zero-growth reduce-reuse-recycle economy. The Tokugawa society might serve as a model for the zero-growth society of the future: this period saw little demographic expansion and had a low rate of economic growth, and for more than two centuries Japan remained stable and peaceful. Indeed the image of Tokugawa Japan as an economically stagnant society has become so widely accepted that assertions of this sort are being advanced by economists who once preached strategies for economic growth.

Current research in economic history is completely at odds with this image, however. In their 1988 overview of Japanese economic history in the seventeenth and eighteenth centuries,[3] Hayami Akira and Miyamoto Matao describe the Tokugawa period as one in which Japan was advancing broadly toward becoming an "economic society." Along with expanding rice production in rural villages, there were considerable advances in the commodification of other types of agricultural produce during this period.

The seventeenth century saw the formation of a nationwide commodity distribution network centered on Osaka, and as this grew, it encouraged the development and production of a greater variety of commodities. Japan was thus transformed into an economic society: one in which the economic value of trying to secure the greatest gain for the least expenditure would shape the behavior of many people. This mentality would eventually pave the way for the relatively smooth acceptance of the introduction of modern industrial technology from the West.

Hayami and Miyamoto point out that as the unified authority of the Tokugawa shogunate brought peace and stability after the disorder of the Sengoku period, the seventeenth century became an era of economic growth, enabled by "a major opening of new land to agriculture and a population explosion." From the seventeenth into the early eighteenth century the annual rate of population growth ranged from 0.61 to 0.96 percent. These are remarkable figures for a premodern society—comparable to the population growth rates recorded after the Meiji Revolution. The opening of new land to cultivation was accompanied by an intensification of agricultural labor and technological innovations that significantly increased per capita productivity. Demographic expansion stagnated for a time during the eighteenth century, but the development of better fertilizers and new crops led by the early nineteenth century to a resumption of population growth. In addition, the spread of handicraft production as a supplement to agriculture contributed to economic growth that paved the way for modernization.

Thus, what Shin Yu-han witnessed in 1719 was a time of unprecedented prosperity in Osaka, which was then the epicenter of Japan's economic development. Osaka had come under the direct control and administration of the Tokugawa shogunate after the summer siege of Osaka Castle in 1615 had eliminated Toyotomi Hideyoshi's heir, Hideyori, and with him the last major threat to Tokugawa rule. Under this new regime the city saw development of its port and harbor facilities, digging of new canals, and other significant urban development. Many of the daimyo built warehouses in the city and began selling their tax rice on the Osaka market.

The Dōjima Rice Market in Osaka (from *Settsu meisho zue*, 1796–98).

Creation of coastal shipping routes connecting the Sea of Japan ports with Edo (the *higashi mawari*, or eastern circuit) and with Osaka, en route to Edo (the *nishi mawari*, or western circuit), placed Osaka at the hub of a nationwide network of commodity distribution, and eventually established a mechanism by which the price of rice on the Dōjima rice market in Osaka determined the market price for the entire country. By the beginning of the eighteenth century, the population of Osaka was nearing 350,000 people.[4] This was not as large as Beijing, Edo, Istanbul, London, or Paris, but still placed it amid the ranks of the largest cities in the world at that time.

Kaitokudō: An academy for townsmen

The economic prosperity of Osaka gave birth to a prosperous merchant class—like the characters in the works of Ihara Saikaku, who turn their talents to trade and, with a keen eye for the main chance, transform themselves into men of wealth and influence. They were the ones who handled the sale of rice from the daimyo warehouses, who loaned money to the daimyo in times of financial distress, and who developed a variety of other financial institutions and instruments, including a commodity futures market, that created enormous profits for themselves.

These Osaka merchants enjoyed a sumptuous consumer culture and a lively network of social contacts. Among their various pursuits and entertainments, scholarship was something many inclined toward. In 1724, five years after the Korean embassy visited Osaka, five wealthy Osaka merchants (Nakamura Ryōsai, Tominaga Hōshun, Nagasaki Katsuyuki, Yoshida Kakyū, and Yamanaka Sōko) established a private academy called the Kaitokudō in the Amagasaki district of central Osaka (now Imahashi Sanchōme). The curriculum was largely grounded in Neo-Confucianism.

From a present-day perspective, it might seem strange that the interests of a group of affluent merchants would run in the direction of seeking further schooling, but in the Tokugawa period there was nothing comparable to today's system of public education. Domain academies and the shogunate's Shōheikō—schools officially established by ruling authorities to teach

Confucianism—generally appeared from the eighteenth century onward, and even the majority of samurai never studied in such institutions. Schooling was left to the *tenaraijo* or *terakoya*, small local schools that taught commoners the rudiments of reading, writing, and arithmetic, or to private schools and academies established by individual scholars.

Given these circumstances, it seems only natural that the interests of prosperous merchants, and the broader strata of townspeople in general, would turn to education in addition to more conventional sources of amusement and entertainment. In Japan today, we are all too familiar with the type of education forced on us by the school system and may find it difficult to imagine a situation in which innate curiosity would motivate an interest in scholarship. But in Tokugawa Japan, study at a private Confucian academy—like practicing the tea ceremony, ikebana flower arrangement, haiku, or Noh drama—was an expression of intellectual curiosity. In *Haeyurok*, Shin Yu-han notes the considerable number of Japanese reprint editions of Chinese and Korean books in classical Chinese arrayed on the shelves of bookstores in Kyoto. Kaitokudō would have a 145-year history, from its founding in 1724 to its closure in 1869, testimony to the strength and sustainability of this passion for learning.

The founding of Kaitokudō was occasioned by the loss to fire of a private academy operated by Miyake Sekian, a scholar whose lectures combined interest in both the Zhu Xi and Wang Yangming schools of Confucianism. The five founders of Kaitokudō had studied with Sekian and now donated funds to establish this new academy, with Sekian as its first director. Eventually, a Confucian scholar named Nakai Shūan, who had trained under Sekian, traveled to Edo to make an appeal to the advisors of shogun Tokugawa Yoshimune to extend recognition to Kaitokudō as an academic institution, and in 1726 this request was granted.

At the time, Yoshimune was in the midst of implementing the Kyōhō Reforms. He employed Ogyū Sorai as a policy advisor, published a Japanese translation of a Chinese Neo-Confucian primer for commoners (*Rikuyu engi taii*), and was enthusiastic in his support for Confucian scholars and the dissemination of Confucian teachings. Whether official recognition of Kaitokudō was accompanied by any financial assistance from the shogunate is not known, but the authority conveyed by such recognition appears to have been part of a policy of support for private Confucian academies for the common people.

In Japan, unlike China and Korea, there was no official examination system used for staffing the government bureaucracy with Confucian

Entrance to Kaitokudō (computer graphic recreation, courtesy of the Kaitokudō Archive, Osaka University).

scholars. Government was administered by samurai, in their capacity as military men, and their ranks and positions were determined to a considerable extent by heredity. Since there was no real need for the rulers to establish schools or academies to train these men in the Confucian canon, the dissemination of Neo-Confucianism in Japan initially centered on unofficial private academies. However, in the latter half of the Tokugawa period, the activities and presence of the growing number of private-sector Confucian scholars eventually led, as noted above, to the establishment of official academies by the shogunate and the domains. The recognition extended to Kaitokudō, seen in terms of long-term historical change, might be regarded as a milestone in the elevation of Zhu Xi's Neo-Confucianism, and Confucianism in general, to an officially approved philosophy.

Official recognition did not necessarily mean the transformation of Confucian academies into institutions whose role was limited to training samurai for official duties. In fact, Kaitokudō took the opposite tack. Eventually Miyake Sekian's son Miyake Shunrō became the third headmaster, while the practical affairs of the academy were handled by Nakai Chikuzan, Nakai Shūan's son, who served as its chief administrator. A dormitory was established for students coming to the academy from outside the Osaka area, and in 1758, a set of "regulations" (*sadame*) was posted there. The first read: "Relations among the students will be conducted without reference to hereditary or economic status; all shall treat one another as equals." In this academic realm, all students were expected to set aside birth and social rank to debate and instruct one another as classmates.

The historian Miyagawa Yasuko has also drawn attention to the importance of the Kaitokudō regulations, persuasively arguing that in contrast to the mentality of the samurai, who emphasized hierarchical status relations, Kaitokudō created "an environment for free and open discussion," permitting the questioning of established academic and political authority.[5]

Neo-Confucianism had always valued free debate among equals as a method for seeking *ri* (Ch. *li*), the principle or reason pervading heaven and earth and the world of humankind. Neo-Confucianism conceived the universal principle of *ri* as inherently manifesting in the hearts and minds of all human beings as a commonly shared human nature, or *sei* (Ch. *xing*). Thus, regardless of the circumstances of their birth or position in society, anyone who followed the proper procedures could gain complete awareness of their inherent human nature and, by extension, a clear understanding of the principle animating the entire universe. One of the most important methods for achieving such insight was thought to be free intellectual discussion.

Moreover, Neo-Confucian education prized free and equal discussion among teachers and students concerning the interpretation of classic texts. Although he was himself critical of Neo-Confucianism, Itō Jinsai's private academy Kogidō in Kyoto was famous for its classes in which line-by-line interpretation of texts such as the *Analects* and *Mencius* was carried out through free discussion among participants. The Kaitokudō regulations seem to have envisioned a similar environment for unrestricted discourse. From the midst of this intellectual freedom, new thinking would emerge that would challenge the Confucian and Neo-Confucian traditions.

Tominaga Nakamoto: "The Voltaire of Japan"

Tominaga Nakamoto (1715–46) is a rather isolated and mysterious presence in the landscape of Tokugawa intellectual history. He was a son of Tominaga Hōshun, one of the five original merchant benefactors of Kaitokudō. Ten years old when Kaitokudō was established, he probably studied there under his father's teacher, Miyake Sekian. But at the age of fifteen or sixteen, he is said to have angered his teacher by writing a treatise entitled *Setsuhei* that presented an overall critique of the Confucian teachings, whereupon he was expelled from the academy. There is almost no subsequent biographical information on him, but he eventually left his merchant

Amemiya Shōteki, c. 1760, Ogyū Sorai (seated at center, top) and his disciples.

family to establish himself as an independent scholar, taking on a small number of students and leaving a handful of scholarly works as his legacy before dying an untimely death at the age of thirty-two.

The manuscript of *Setsuhei* has been lost, but its contents can be surmised from the brief text *Okina no fumi* (Notes of an Old Man) published in 1746, the year of Tominaga Nakamoto's death. This work offers a thoroughgoing critique of the three great traditions of Shintoism, Confucianism, and Buddhism, accompanied by an outline of a "Way of Truth" (*makoto no michi*)—"a Way that can be called the Way of all Ways" (*michi no michi to iu beki michi*).

The criticism of Confucianism that was probably the focus of Miyake Sekian's ire is found in section 11 of *Okina no fumi*. It begins with a scathing attack on the character of Confucius himself. "Also, Confucius considered as his predecessors Yao and Shun, idealized Kings Wen and Wu and preached the Kingly Way, thus going beyond the customary belief of his time when the Way of the Five Nobles, such as Duke Huan of Ch'i [Qi] and Duke Wen of Chin [Jin], was highly esteemed."[6]

Here, "of his time" draws attention to the context in which Confucius began compiling the Five (Six) Classics and establishing what would become the Confucian canon, and it is significant that Tominaga interpreted the nature of Confucian thought in terms of its relationship to this context. Confucius lived during the Spring and Autumn period of the declining Zhou dynasty, when China was divided into a number of smaller states ruled by various noblemen. Among them, the Five Nobles (also known as the Five Hegemons),

A spread from the printed edition of Tominaga Nakamoto's *Okina no fumi* (Writings of an Old Man), 1746.

including Duke Huan of Qi and Duke Wen of Jin, were praised for the way in which they managed their states. But Confucius turned his attention to far more ancient models—Yao, Shun, and King Wen and King Wu of the early Zhou dynasty—idealizing their rule and using it as the basis for the dissemination of a "Kingly Way" of government by virtuous rulers personified by these figures.

The tactic of brandishing the thought of an earlier era as an authority to destroy the arguments of rivals and legitimate one's own views was given a name that Tominaga himself coined: *kajō*, meaning to go beyond or supplant. In Tominaga's understanding, the entire history of Confucian thought was founded upon a process in which the various thinkers of a particular period strove to supplant their rivals in this manner. Tominaga was critical of both Itō Jinsai and Ogyū Sorai for failing to escape this tendency in their own critiques of Neo-Confucianism.

As previous research such as that of Miyagawa Yasuko has shown, the method of analyzing the thought of the past by placing it in its historical context and using this to point out its limitations and deficiencies was actually something that Tominaga learned from the writings of Ogyū Sorai. We may surmise that initially, in his early years, Tominaga was an assiduous student of Sorai in addition to the Neo-Confucianism he was taught at Kaitokudō, and only later shifted to a more critical stance.

In his treatise *Bendō* (Distinguishing the Way), written in 1717, Sorai deploys the following critique of his Confucian predecessors. After Confucius himself had compiled the Way of the Ancient Kings into the classic texts he left for posterity, his disciples Zisi and Mencius, in an effort to contend with other contemporary streams of thought such as Daoism, Legalism, and the followers of Mozi, and to win people over to their side, emphasized certain aspects of the Way of the Ancient Kings and incorporated elements of other schools of thought into their teachings, in the process losing sight of the totality of the Way. This method of inferring the context of the philosophical debates of the past and interpreting various aspects of the thought of a particular era as selfishly motivated ideology was adopted by Tominaga, who deployed it as a tool for critiquing all Three Ways (Shintoism, Confucianism, and Buddhism), including the thought of Sorai himself. The critic and writer Katō Shūichi describes Tominaga's thoroughgoing critique as "recalling the relentless critical spirit with which Voltaire unflinchingly opposed the clerics."[7]

For his own part, what Tominaga proposes is a "Way of Truth" in contradistinction to the Three Ways he had exposed as mere ideologies. But what was this Way of his?

To write with present-day script, to speak with present-day language, to eat present-day foods, to wear present-day clothes, to use present-day utensils, to live in present-day houses, to follow present-day customs, to respect present-day rules, to mingle with present-day people, not to do bad things, but to do what is good—that is the Way of Truth, the Way which is practicable in present-day Japan.[8]

If this is the sum total of Tominaga's explanation of the Way of Truth transcending Shintoism, Confucianism, and Buddhism, it is a bit disappointing. But no doubt he would reply that living according to the ways of the present is sufficient; belief in superfluous creeds and dogmas suffused with the authority of previous eras or foreign lands only alienates us from the living, breathing morality and ethics of the present day.

Tominaga's critiques of Confucianism and Buddhism pointed out differences with the "national ethos" (*kokuzoku*) of China and India and argued that the teachings derived from these countries did not suit the customs of Japan—a view that had elements in common with the nationalism of later generations. But here I would like to focus on Tominaga's historical consciousness, and specifically his insistence on careful scrutiny of the discontinuity between past and present.

Some sixty years after Tominaga's death, another merchant-intellectual trained at Kaitokudō, Yamagata Bantō (1748–1821), would publish a work entitled *Yume no shiro* (In Place of Dreams) that also comprises a radical critique of all previous modes of thought. In its eighth volume, "Miscellaneous Writings," Bantō argues that the "Kingly Way" of "the Three Dynasties of

Statue of Yamagata Bantō in Takasago, Hyōgo prefecture.

China" stressed by generations of Confucian thinkers was inappropriate to the task of political reform in "today's Japan," and points out that Ogyū Sorai's *Seidan* (Discourse on Government), published circa 1726, was not, in fact, an articulation of the Way of the Ancient Kings but a reform proposal addressing "the politics of his day." Analogously, we might assume that Tominaga also perceived that Sorai's discourse was based upon an acute awareness of discontinuity between the thought of antiquity and the present day.

The clearest expression in *Okina no fumi* of Tominaga's understanding of the difference between past and present is contained in the section dealing with Shintoism. According to him, Shintoism is yet another example of a dogma based on the rhetoric of supplanting or delegitimizing earlier scholars, as described above. "As for Shintoism, it was also invented during the medieval age by some people who pretended to trace it back to the age of Gods, and called it the Way of Japan in an attempt to outdo Buddhism and Confucianism."[9]

As a doctrine, Shintoism first emerged out of the Ryōbu Shinto developed within the Shingon sect of esoteric Buddhism, which Tominaga understood as "a mixture in convenient proportions of Buddhism and Confucianism." Later, a variety of Shinto schools would emerge: *honjaku engi*, which taught that the Shinto gods were local incarnations of the buddhas; *yuiitsu sōgen*, which attempted to unify Shinto beliefs into a systematic, unified teaching;

and Hayashi Razan's ōdō shintō, which taught that the emperors were descendants of the gods and thus the Kingly Way (ōdō) was indistinguishable from the Way of the Gods (shintō). All of these claimed to date back to ancient Japan, despite admixtures of Buddhist and Confucian thought, which of course had not been present in Japan during the "Age of the Gods."

Moreover, Tominaga Nakamoto argues, even if these teachings were actually based on the customs that had existed in the Age of the Gods, it would be a mistake to try to apply them in the present day.

> In old Japan it was good manners for people to salute each other four times, turning to each other and clapping hands. Food was served on an oak leaf as a dish. At times of mourning, songs were sung, people wailed over their loss, and when the mourning was over they went to the river to perform the purification rites. People who learn Shintoism must practice these things, every one of them, exactly in the manner of ancient times. Since the gold or silver money we use today did not originally exist in the Age of the Gods, those who learn Shintoism would do well to throw it away and make no use of it.[10]

This is a biting satire of adherents of Shinto who attempted to lend authority to their ideas by claiming to base them in Japanese antiquity. Tominaga continues in this vein, citing other examples of dress and language in which antiquity and the present differ considerably, making the point that it is a fundamentally mistaken idea to try to live in the present day according to the models offered by the Age of the Gods. Especially since, as he says, "there are very few people today who remember recent events of only five or ten years ago."[11]

It is noteworthy that Tominaga immediately refers to gold and silver currency as emblematic of things in use in the present day, and it is also intriguing that he mentions how people forget the events of only five or ten years previous. In the writings left to us by Tominaga, there are no detailed depictions of contemporary society or concrete discussions of policy. Yet here we glimpse a consciousness of his present as an era of intense societal change spurred by rapid economic growth. And as it was an age of peace and plenty,

this may have led him to see living according to
the common sense of the present day as leading
to the Way of Truth.

Around the time that Tominaga died, in the latter
half of the eighteenth century, a school of thought
emerged that proposed taking the narrative of the
chronicle *Kojiki* (Record of Ancient Matters, 712)
literally as the Way, with no reliance on Buddhist or
Confucian thought. This was Kokugaku (National
Learning), given its most complete articulation by
Motoori Norinaga (1730–1801).

Kamogawa Seitoku, *Portrait
of Motoori Norinaga in His
Seventy-Second Year*, 1801.

Norinaga was raised as the second son of a
wealthy merchant family in Matsusaka (in present-day Mie prefecture). Perhaps because of this, the eighth volume of his fourteen-volume essay collection *Tamakatsuma* (The Precious Basket, 1795–1812) contains a brief review
of Tominaga Nakamoto's *Shutsujō gogo* (Words after Enlightenment, 1745),
a work that employs Tominaga's rhetorical analysis to provide a historical
overview of Buddhist theory. Norinaga praises its critique of Buddhism as
"eye-opening."

In the fourteenth volume of *Tamakatsuma*, in an essay entitled "Inishie
yori mo nochi-no-yo no masareru koto" (Why the Present Is Superior to
the Past), Norinaga takes the example of citrus fruit, and says that while
in the past only the *tachibana* orange was available, in recent times many
other, more delicious citrus varieties have emerged: the *mikan, kōji, daidai,*
and so on. The present is materially superior to the past because so many
things that did not exist in the past have come into being. "And if one thinks
of this, imagine what things might be like in the times to come."[12]

It is interesting to see Norinaga—who preached an Ancient Way (*inishie
no michi*) grounded in the Age of the Gods—expressing such a naively progressive view of history. It would seem that, whether conscious of it or not,
both Norinaga and Tominaga intuitively sensed that economic progress was
gradually producing a more affluent world.

CHAPTER 5

Is Commerce Evil?

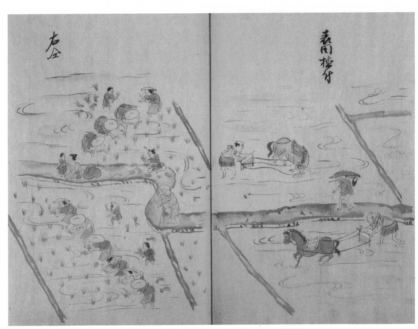

From a late Tokugawa copy of *Kōka shunjū* (Farmer's Almanac, 1707).

Economic development and Confucian thought

As we have seen in the preceding chapter, the Tokugawa period was one of startling economic growth. During the seventeenth century, a nationwide commodities market centered on Osaka had already come into being, agricultural productivity was expanding, and Japan had suddenly entered an unprecedented era of prosperity.

This image of rural prosperity is but one side of the story, as historical records demonstrate in numerous accounts of suffering caused by famine and natural disasters. Still, research in the history of agriculture has unequivocally shown that during this period the Japanese economy benefited from an ongoing rise in standards of productivity due to improved crop varieties and progress in agricultural technology. In his highly regarded work on this subject, Takei Kōichi reports that because of the widespread development of paddy cultivation and the use of fertilizer, there were cases in which peasants overworked and exhausted the soil and abandoned their fields.

Rising agricultural productivity is also reflected in demographic data: mortality rates and average life expectancy steadily improved during the Tokugawa period. In recent times, population increases in poorer countries are often tied to dramatic declines in infant mortality, thanks to improved medical care. But in the absence of such improvements, these increases in average life expectancy could not possibly have occurred if premodern rural villages were continually suffering under extreme poverty. Generally speaking, the stereotypical image of a starving peasantry is not supported by the evidence.

If this is the case, why is it that the historical perception of impoverished villages and a desperate peasantry struggling under the crushing burden of annual land taxes continues to be so widely accepted? Mizutani Mitsuhiro offers an intriguing answer to this question.[1] Under the rule of the Tokugawa shogunate, the daimyo were required to bear the cost and responsibility for carrying out a variety of public works projects, including irrigation and flood control. Mizutani argues that in order to avoid or limit as much of this burden as possible, the domain officials stationed in Edo plied the shogunate officials with pleas concerning the economic hardship experienced by their domains—including exaggerated accounts of the suffering caused by famines and natural disasters.

In one example, a domain reported to the shogunate that its population had declined by 60,000 as the result of a famine, when its internal documents showed a population increase for the same period of 250 people. It seems likely that such exaggerations of population loss were widespread to reduce the public works burden imposed by the shogunate on the domains. Moreover, in the relationship between the domains and the rural communities under their control, grassroots administration was customarily left to village elders, who handled the collection and delivery of the annual tax on agricultural production. It is not difficult to imagine that here as well, there was a certain amount of false accounting. If we take at face value the documents making pleas of hardship at every level—from the villages to the domain governments, and from the domains to the shogunate—then the image created, as Mizutani observes, is one of a starving and suffering peasantry.

Yet another factor that likely contributed to the pervasive image of a suffering peasantry was the belief system of contemporary commentators concerned with the economy of their time and seeking to analyze and resolve its problems. Simply put, writers grounded in an anti-commercial perspective were predisposed to be critical of the merchants profiting from periods of economic growth and sympathetic to the poverty and plight of the primary producers, the peasants.

As noted above, the dynasties of imperial China and the Korean royal court used a system of civil service examinations based on Confucian teachings to select individuals of erudition and good judgment to serve in official posts—a system that was never introduced in Japan. However, as we see in the example of Kaitokudō in Osaka, the idea of Confucianism as an essential element in the training of an educated man was gradually spreading throughout the country, and by the latter half of the eighteenth century, many daimyo houses had established Confucian academies for their retainers. However, no system had been adopted—including at the official shogunal academy, Shōheikō, founded at the end of the eighteenth century—directly linking academic performance with advancement along a career track as a government official.

Even so, when Japanese intellectuals attempted to look at their world, define its problems, and propose solutions, they often turned to Confucianism to provide a conceptual framework. Confucianism (or Neo-Confucianism), rather than military science or Legalism, flourished under the Pax Tokugawa probably because it was unique in possessing a capacity for addressing the issues of how to rule the realm from a comprehensive perspective, backed by a systematic philosophy of human nature and of history.

Kumazawa Banzan (1619–91) was an exception among the Confucian scholars of the early Tokugawa period in that he was directly involved in presenting policy proposals to the rulers. As a samurai in the service of the Okayama domain, he was highly regarded by the daimyo, Ikeda Mitsumasa, and was involved in reforming government administration. In the seventh volume of his major work, *Shūgi washo* (Japanese Writings on the Accumulation of Righteousness, published in 1672), Banzan gives us a clear expression of how he viewed the economic prosperity of his times.[2]

Banzan believed that the "customs and manners of remote antiquity," regarded as the Confucian ideal, "freed people from greed and led them to appreciate what was sufficient." Because selfish desires were appropriately constrained, rulers exercised frugality, aided the poor, and governed in a way that "took from those above to benefit those below." But how did Banzan see his own times? "In later generations, the progress of civilization [*bunmei*] gave rise to ostentation." Here, *bunmei* seems to signify a glittering achievement of affluence and material well-being, characterized by an abundance of luxury goods.

According to Banzan, "Times of excessive luxury incite desire, which produces greed." When surrounded by desirable things, human desires

Kumazawa Banzan (1619–1691).

proliferate endlessly. In response, rulers must prescribe "rules of behavior" (*reigi no nori*) to channel these desires and transform them into "habits of simplicity and restraint." In this regard, Banzan proposes that rulers should minimize the circulation of money, and that the daimyo should directly control "commodities essential to the daily life of the people" and establish a system for allocating them. By forcefully breaking the power of "the artisans and merchants who have based their livelihoods on decades of greed and ostentation," a government that "takes from those above to benefit those below" can be achieved. This is the solution that Banzan advocates. The majority of the population would then continue to lead simple and modest lives as farmers. In the sense that this was his ideal image of society, it is a thoroughly anti-commercial stance. In one of his late writings, *Daigaku wakumon* (*Questions on The Great Learning*), Banzan argues that the samurai should reside in rural villages, cutting off their connections to the urban lifestyle that was drawing them into a consumer culture. This in turn would help suppress the bloated power of commerce and revive an economy based on local self-sufficiency.

This anti-commercialism—or, from a different perspective, agrarianism—was not unique to Banzan, but was instead a common premise of Confucian thought. The standard for "benevolent government" (*jinsei*) was one in which food and the necessities of everyday life reached all the people, permitting them to live without deprivation; though even this acknowledged the need for sufficient trade to allow the exchange of essential goods. The foundation of Confucian ethics was stern condemnation of any pursuit of profit that would threaten the overall social harmony brought about by benevolent government. Confucius tells us in the *Analects* that "the mind of the superior man is conversant with righteousness; the mind of the mean man is conversant with gain."[3] The proper practice of morality takes no heed of a result; it does what is right because it is right; this is the attitude of the superior individual. On the other hand, those who act only with some specific result in mind are chastised for being controlled by their desires, losing sight of morality in pursuit of profit. Thus, "distinguishing between righteousness and profit" (*giri no ben*) was taken seriously by Confucianism.

Obviously, as seen from the previous example of making allowances for limited trade in essential commodities, it would be difficult to completely reject commerce or forms of behavior in pursuit of some type of gain. But as passages from the classics inform us—"In a State, gain is not to be considered prosperity, but its prosperity will be found in righteousness,"[4] or "Genuine profit is the harmony of righteousness"[5]— true profit and gain are to be found in pursuing the correct path and achieving social harmony. Conversely, profit-making activities that do not give due consideration to the achievement of social harmony are not profitable in a genuine sense, for they misconstrue the very nature of profit.

For intellectuals trained in Confucian theories of government, grounded as they were in this mode of thought, it was difficult to morally and ethically accept the development of commerce and industry, the urban growth that made it possible, or the lively consumer lifestyle being enjoyed there. To the very end of the Tokugawa period, discourse on government maintained at least a facade of this anti-commercialism. The prevailing image of Tokugawa-period peasantry as impoverished probably inherits something of this moral opprobrium with regard to commercial activity.

The pursuit of wealth

Although no civil service examinations were conducted, and in the early Tokugawa period neither the shogunate nor the daimyo had established academies to instruct their retainers in the Confucian teachings, Confucianism had a fairly deep hold in Japan. Even if the worldview and theoretical framework of Confucianism (or Neo-Confucianism) were not completely understood, Confucian virtues such as filial piety were widely promulgated in instructional tracts for peasants and townspeople, and dramas extolling the beauty of loyalty to one's feudal lord were greeted with the applause of the common people. Even if the content of these concepts was somewhat different from that expounded by the Confucian scholars, the vocabulary of Confucian virtue was something that had become familiar to ordinary people.

But did the Confucian conception of the pursuit of profit as immoral, and its low estimation of the significance of commerce, achieve a similar degree of social diffusion? Amid the unprecedented economic development of the Tokugawa period, did the townsmen devoting themselves to business pursuits in the great cities of Osaka and Edo really agree with Confucian moral teachings of such an anti-commercial bent?

From one perspective, the answer to this query is yes. For example, Shingaku, the teachings of Ishida Baigan (1685–1744), urges farmers and townsmen to be diligent in pursuing their trades, and has been interpreted as providing an ethical foundation for the development of commerce. The accumulation of wealth is praised, but only for the purpose of ensuring the sustainability of the "family business" (*kagyō*). The family business or trade is something to be inherited from the ancestors and passed on to later generations; this is seen as a type of filial piety. But like the ascetic tendencies of the Protestant sects of modern Western Europe that Max Weber famously points to in *The Protestant Ethic and the Spirit of Capitalism* (1921), the accumulation of wealth for its own sake was not accorded a positive moral significance.

Yet it is difficult to believe that the merchants who amassed great wealth in the midst of the development of the market economy exercised self-restraint in the pursuit of profit beyond what was necessary to practice filial piety and maintain the family business. In a time of great economic expansion, the essential motive for their behavior must have been competition to seize business opportunities and make as much profit as possible. Merchants naturally sought a language capable of legitimizing their commercial activities. *Chōnin bukuro* (Bagful of Knowledge for Merchants, 1692, published 1719) by Nishikawa Joken (1648–1724) is an early example. Joken was a major intellectual figure, the scion of a merchant family in the commercial entrepôt and trading port of Nagasaki who studied Neo-Confucian thought and astronomy and who, through contacts with visiting Dutch traders, became well versed in world geography. His volume of teachings for merchants and townspeople was widely read, as we know from the number of times it was reprinted throughout the Tokugawa period.

Chōnin bukuro contains a sharp critique of commonplace ideas emphasizing the importance of the hereditary class system, which held that since Japan was a country that honored and respected lineage, superior talent could come

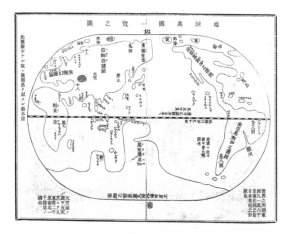

Map of the world by Nishikawa Joken, from *Zōho ka'i tsūshō kō* (An Inquiry into Commerce among the Civilized and Barbarian).

only from the high-ranking noble or samurai houses. According to Joken, no matter how humble one's birth, it was possible with appropriate education to develop into "a virtuous and broadly talented individual."

> No matter how vulgar one's bloodline, if proper prenatal training is observed, so that the infant is set on the correct path while still in the womb; and if after being born the child receives instruction in the virtues appropriate to childhood at the side of a gentleman and scholar; and if he is endowed with talents and ability, then the quality of these natural endowments, with some variations in beauty of appearance or quickness of wit, will give him a character in no way different from that of a high official. Ultimately there is no fundamental reason for regarding people as noble or base. We should know that it is all a matter of upbringing. The majority of courtesans are born into the lowest of families, yet they are trained in elegant accomplishments from an early age and acquire an appearance and manners that could deceive anyone. How then can we think that in the very heart of human nature there can be any distinction between noble and base?[6]

Despite this denial of "any distinction between noble and base," Joken is not criticizing the hierarchical relationships among samurai, townspeople, and peasants characteristic of the Tokugawa period, nor was he preaching egalitarianism. His argument was grounded in the Neo-Confucian idea that the minds of all human beings, regardless of birth, are endowed with an innate human nature, and that by study and learning they can bring this natural endowment to fruition. Joken's encouragement of learning, beginning with prenatal training (*taikyō*, literally "instruction in the womb") suggests a mania for education similar to that in present-day Japan. But what is fascinating here is his use of the courtesans of the pleasure quarters—those paragons of contemporary urban fashion and manners—as exemplars of the latent capacities and abilities common to all humankind.

For Joken, eyewitness to urban prosperity and the activities of wealthy merchants and artisans, it probably seemed a perfectly obvious phenomenon that talented individuals could arise among the townsmen regarded as inferior in status to the samurai, and that many such individuals might emerge to lead successful and even splendid lives.

Toward the end of his life, in the same year (1719) that *Chōnin bukuro* was published, Joken was summoned to Edo in recognition of his erudition in the field of astronomy, and honored by a personal audience with shogun Yoshimune. No doubt this experience confirmed his faith in the validity of his own opinions and perceptions.

In *Chōnin bukuro* we also find an affirmation of the positive value of competition among merchants:

> Decrease in the fortunes of the wealthy increases the wealth of poorer families. Poorer families, hoping to increase their wealth, do not neglect their daily labors. If you want to hold on to what you have, do not neglect to be diligent in your family business. Society [*seken*] is built upon the challenge of this hopeful mutual striving among people.[7]

The competition (*hariai*, "mutual striving") among families to amass wealth, and the schadenfreude experienced when a wealthy neighbor lost his fortune, would no doubt be sternly condemned by strict Confucians as manifestations of humanity's baser desires. But according to Joken, the competition among

Chōnin bukuro (Bagful of Knowledge for Merchants) by Nishikawa Joken.

merchants seeking to increase their fortunes was what fueled the circulation of money throughout the realm, preserving a balanced flow "of yin and yang, the two great forces of the cosmos."[8]

Here, market competition and the circulation of money are seen as contributing to the smooth operation of the universal forces (*ki*) of nature, of which the human world is a part, and thus serving to help sustain human existence. Nomura Maki, a historian of political thought, has written in detail of the unique vocabulary developed by Osaka merchants who made their fortunes in the rice exchange to understand and describe the self-regulating behavior of the market.[9]

For example, the merchant-scholar Kusama Naokata, educated at Kaitokudō, wrote of the phenomenon in which a precipitous drop in the price of rice would create an impulse to buy up the commodity in anticipation of a future increase in value—thus fueling demand and creating "a natural rise in price." The collective impulses of many people create a type of energy that moves society as a whole. A vocabulary and mode of expression capable of grasping the behavior of the market in this way, and describing this insight using the energetic concepts (J. *ki*; Ch. *qi*) of traditional East Asian thought, had become widely accepted among the townspeople. This was a mentality that welcomed the ongoing economic growth of that era and saw commercial activity in the context of a self-regulating market and the acquisition of wealth through such activity in a positive light. Such a worldview and sensibility, though still in a somewhat naive and unsophisticated form, spread throughout eighteenth-century Japan.

The twilight of anti-commercialism: Ogyū Sorai and Dazai Shundai

If Confucian thought was fundamentally anti-commercial, the policies of the shogunate and the daimyo, at least in the first half of the Tokugawa period, also adopted a position of controlling commercial development. In what has been called a "rice-based economy," the fundamental revenues of the shogunate and the domains were collected in the form of an annual tax in kind on rice production. The rice collected from the peasants was then sold on the rice market, converting it to currency to support government expenditures. The goal was to ensure a stable livelihood for the peasantry in order to provide a reliable source of revenue, while at the same time exercising fiscal restraint in terms of expenditures.

In contrast to this, the development of commerce and the growth of cities were looked on with severe apprehension, as it was feared they would accelerate the shift of population to urban areas, leading to the desolation of rural villages, while commodity price inflation and a taste for luxury seemed to invite the impoverishment and moral degeneration of the samurai class. As mentioned earlier, the eighth shogun, Tokugawa Yoshimune, instituted the Kyōhō Reforms in an attempt to resolve a severe fiscal crisis during a period of economic turmoil. These reforms included increases in the annual rice tax, budgetary austerity and fiscal restraint, and price controls implemented through the merchant associations known as *kabunakama*—all measures that ran counter to the development of the market economy.

Yet criticism of Yoshimune's policies arose, grounded in the genuinely affirmative attitudes toward commerce that had spread so widely among the urban population. As an element in Yoshimune's reforms, an attempt was made to involve ordinary people in the policymaking process by permitting them to submit their ideas and opinions through a petition box placed in front of one of the gates of Edo Castle. In the twelfth month of Kyōhō 6 (1721), a scholar of military science signing himself Yamashita Kōnai submitted a petition in which he argues for the importance of the free circulation of money throughout the realm. If this flow were to be stifled by austerity measures, then just as when the circulation of blood in the human body is impeded, the health of the entire realm would suffer, and all the people would fall into economic distress. Here, he employs the same mode of thought that inspired other townsmen to grasp the mechanisms of the market in terms of the rhythms of human life. Yoshimune himself took note of this appeal and had it circulated among the senior shogunal officials, but it does not appear to have had an effect on policy.

As mentioned in chapter 4, Ogyū Sorai was a Confucian scholar whom Yoshimune looked to for guidance in the implementation of the Kyōhō Reforms. His policy proposal *Seidan* (Discourse on Government) is believed to have been written for submission to Yoshimune in 1726. In it, the policies Sorai develops, based on the ideal political system he believed existed in ancient China, are oriented toward a concerted effort to inhibit trade and commerce—at a time when the great cityscape of Edo that spread out before his eyes was in the process of even greater expansion due to the influx of population from rural areas.

> How far does Edo extend? Where does the countryside begin? There is no boundary, and as the people have been building houses willy-nilly, the sprawl of Edo increases year by year. Without anyone's permission, and without any of the magistrates or other officials paying any attention, at some point the area from Senju in the north to Shinagawa in the south has become a continuous expanse of buildings.[10]

In *Seidan*, Sorai criticizes the situation of the samurai in the Tokugawa period as being like that of "travelers at an inn": separated from their fiefs, living in castle towns, purchasing the necessities of daily life, and in some cases living in houses rented from commoners. And it was the townsmen who determined commodity prices and rents, which the samurai had no choice but to accept.

As a result, the samurai, who were originally of superior status to the merchants and other townspeople, found themselves in a subordinate position economically. As Sorai puts it, "the merchants have been amassing profits for the last hundred years, creating a situation that has never before existed since the origins of the cosmos, either in Japan or other lands."[11] Sorai had acutely perceived that the economic prosperity he was seeing was a change unprecedented in human history. This "world in which nothing can be accomplished without money" was "a paradise on earth"—not for the samurai, but for the merchants.[12]

Against this, Sorai advocates an unrelenting anti-commercialism as a means for implementing the ideal institutions of Chinese antiquity in the present day. In addition to thorough enforcement of frugality and austerity, like Kumazawa Banzan, Sorai proposes that the practice of making the samurai live in towns and cities should be abandoned in favor of a policy of returning them to rural fiefs. Moreover, the shogunate and daimyo should induce the common people to make a variety of necessary tools and utensils and provide them to the samurai as tax in kind.

Yamashita Kōnai's petition, as reproduced in *Nihon keizai sōsho* (Library of Japan's Economy), edited by Takimoto Seiichi.

If this were done, the proliferation of luxury and excess would naturally come to an end, the samurai would have more intimate contact with the people of their domains, and by overseeing them directly would restore their own confidence and authority as rulers. The direction Sorai wished to take was to freeze the development of the commercial economy and return, as much as possible, to an economy of autonomy, self-sufficiency, and barter. This vision was certainly diametrically opposed to that of Nishikawa Joken's *Chōnin bukuro*, published seven years earlier.

It is difficult to concretely assess the extent to which Sorai's advice was actually incorporated into Yoshimune's policies. But it is interesting that Sorai's student Dazai Shundai (1680–1747), while inheriting much from Sorai's discourses on policy, expresses a somewhat different perspective than his master with regard to the development of trade and industry.

Shundai was a leading student of Sorai, demonstrating particular talent in exegesis of the classic texts and in deliberations on policy. Yet while Sorai's disciples were famous for their freewheeling and unconstrained behavior, Shundai was known as an exceptionally scrupulous personality who led a life strictly regimented by the rules of Confucian etiquette—to the point that this alienated him from his mentor Sorai and made him a lonely presence among his fellow students.

Shundai's treatise *Keizairoku* (Discussions on Political Economy) was published in ten volumes in 1729. The word *keizai* is used in modern Japanese as a translation of "economics," but in Shundai's time it was an abbreviated form of the phrase *keisei saimin* ("governing the realm and aiding the people"), and was commonly used as a general term for the operations of government in works written in classical Chinese.

Dazai Shundai, from *Sentetsu zōden* (Illustrated Biographies of the Great Scholars, 1845).

The main thrust of Shundai's argument in *Keizairoku* is fundamentally similar to Sorai's advocacy of restraint of commerce, austerity, and rustication of the samurai. But in an addendum to *Keizairoku*, he expresses opinions differing from those of his mentor.

> Thus it is that we find ourselves in today's world of money.
>
> Grain is viewed simply in terms of its adequacy for morning and evening meals. And fabric is similarly seen only in its relation to clothing needs. Beyond these considerations, everything is money. Large and small expenses are all paid for from one moment to the next so that the people of today value money 100 times more than in ancient times. Indeed, though one may have adequate food and clothing today, one will find it difficult to make his way in society if short on money. Not only is this true for poor commoners, but also for the aristocracy, including the daimyo.[13]

In the "present" defined by the advent of Tokugawa rule, people had come to use "money" to secure the necessities of daily life—a decisive difference from the world of antiquity. As a result, the surplus rice and textiles they produced were not held in store, but sold to acquire currency. And the samurai were not exempt from involvement in this world. Like Sorai, Shundai notes that the samurai had become like travelers staying at an inn; but unlike Sorai, he tells them to adapt to these present-day customs.

Shundai makes the following proposal to the shogunate and the daimyo. These rulers should order the peasants and artisans of their domains to produce specialized regional products, to be collected by the government and sold to other regions to raise the revenues needed to restore fiscal health. Shundai cites Tsuwano and Satsuma as examples of domains that had successfully enriched themselves by the introduction of such policies. The teachings of Sorai offer an incisive insight into the differences between antiquity and the present, and among the customs and institutions prevailing in different periods of history. And what Shundai found to be a novel characteristic of his present is none other than the advent of a "world of money."

CHAPTER 6

The Age of Economics

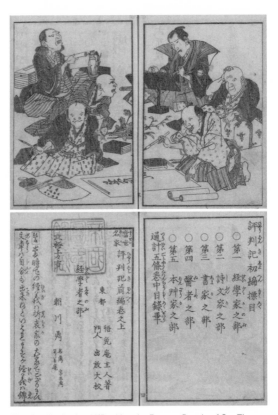

Tōsei meika hyōbanki (Ranking the Famous People of Our Time, 1835), a guide to scholars and men of letters.

Yamagata Bantō, Confucian merchant

The Tokugawa period was not only a time of unprecedented economic growth, but also one in which the arts and sciences flourished. This long period of peace and economic expansion permitted people to turn their attention to scholarly pursuits. In the late eighteenth century there was a vogue for publishing catalogues rating a variety of popular things and famous people. In addition to themes pitched to popular tastes—nature (insects, fish, etc.), music, popular literature, sumo wrestlers, and the women of the pleasure quarters—catalogues of scholars and men of letters were also published.

In contemporary terms this would be like publishing ranked listings and critiques of university professors, writers, and pundits. As noted earlier, there was considerable interest in intellectual pursuits among the more affluent strata of both the urban and rural populations. Just as they sought instruction in hobbies and pastimes, wealthy townsmen and farmers might frequent the private academies operated by independent scholars. The catalogues of scholars and men of letters would offer guidance on which of these schools to consider attending.

As we have seen, the eighth shogun, Yoshimune, initiated the Kyōhō Reforms and set up a public petition box outside one of the gates of Edo Castle. In 1720 (Kyōhō 5), as one aspect of his reform program, Yoshimune relaxed the ban on importing Western books in Chinese translation, provided they contained no explicitly Christian content. He realized that encouraging the assimilation of Western scientific knowledge was essential if the shogunate wanted to make use of advances in astronomy, geography, and other fields.

A recent study by Kazu Tsuguto, a historian of science, provides us with a detailed demonstration of how Yoshimune's policies gave major impetus to the development of astronomy in Tokugawa Japan.[1] Yoshimune wanted a more accurate calendar, and to lay the groundwork he ordered scholars to study the Western literature on astronomy. He also had an observatory set up within the precincts of Edo Castle, where he personally participated in making measurements and observations.

Yoshimune's efforts at calendrical reform ended in failure, frustrated by opposition from the Tsuchimikado family of Kyoto, who had established over many generations a virtual monopoly on matters related to the official calendar. But Japanese scholars' access to works of Western astronomy in Chinese trans-

"Mount Fuji at Torigoe," from Katsushika Hokusai's *One Hundred Views of Mount Fuji* (c. 1834–40), depicting the astronomical observatory established in Asakusa in 1782.

lation resulted in significant advances in that science during the Tokugawa period. According to Kazu, Japanese astronomers had previously been exposed only to traditional Chinese astronomy. Now, knowledge of Western astronomy began to be assimilated, and not merely by specialists in the shogunate or the imperial court, but by independent scholars with no official ties or positions.

A representative example of this is Asada Gōryū (1734–99), an astronomer who grew up in the Kitsuki domain on the Kunisaki Peninsula in Kyushu. Gōryū read the astronomy books being imported from China and also drew on his own observations as he worked to develop a new method of calendrical calculation. After moving to Osaka, he became acquainted with the Confucian scholars Nakai Chikuzan, then head of Kaitokudō, and his brother Nakai Riken, and trained a number of students of his own.

One of the men who studied astronomy under Gōryū was someone we have already encountered—the merchant and innovative Confucian thinker Yamagata Bantō (1748–1821). Yamagata left his home village of Kazume in

Harima province (now part of the city of Takasago in Hyōgo prefecture) at the age of thirteen and went to Osaka where he became an apprentice at Masuya, a large merchant house in the Dōjima area. Around the same time, he was adopted by an uncle who had previously served with the Masuya house and later established an independent branch of the family; he inherited his uncle's personal name, Kyūbei. Masuya was one of the five major brokers dominating the Dōjima rice market, but at that time their operations were shifting toward moneylending on a massive scale, with many of the country's daimyo indebted to them. The young apprentice Kyūbei, in addition to the training he was receiving in the ways of the merchant houses, was also sent to Kaitokudō, where he studied under Nakai Chikuzan and Riken. The motive for this was probably in part to give him

Nakai Chikuzan (top) and Nakai Riken (bottom).

the cultural sophistication that would aid him in his interactions with other well-educated merchants and the daimyo and their representatives.

Eventually Kyūbei rose to the position of head clerk of the main Masuya house, and in 1783 he masterminded a loan to the daimyo of Sendai that succeeded in rebuilding the domain's finances. Masuya had by this point expanded its moneylending transactions to more than fifty of the country's daimyo houses. In 1805, the main Masuya house honored him with privileges equivalent to kinship and by allowing him to use the family name of the house—Yamagata. He subsequently took the name Yamagata Yoshihide.

Meanwhile, he continued his study of astronomy with Asada Gōryū, and in 1802 began writing *Yume no shiro* (In Place of Dreams), a multivolume compendium of his knowledge and ideas, which would not see completion for another eighteen years, until 1820, when he reached the age of seventy-three. Bantō, the pen name he chose for his scholarly work, was a literary allusion to a mythical giant peach tree said to grow in the land of the immortals—but he also likely chose it because it is a homophone for "chief clerk."

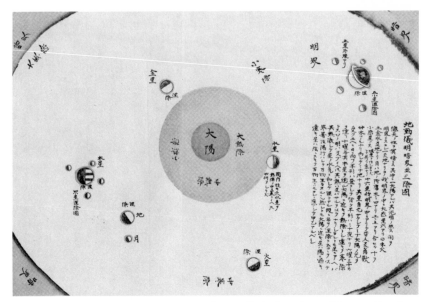

Heliocentric astronomical theory is explained and illustrated in the first volume of Yamagata Bantō's *Yume no shiro* (In Place of Dreams, 1820).

In the editorial notes at the beginning of *Yume no shiro,* Bantō credits Nakai Chikuzan and Riken as his teachers. In this regard, he positions himself as a Confucian thinker, unlike Tominaga Nakamoto, who proclaimed his own "Way of Truth" and criticized Shinto, Confucianism, and Buddhism. Yet even if Bantō premised this thinking on the idea that the truth was contained in the classic Confucian canon, *Yume no shiro* demonstrates that he shared with Tominaga Nakamoto a lively critical spirit.

The tenth and eleventh volumes of this work are devoted to a discourse on atheism (*muki*). In it, Bantō uses "gods and spirits" (*kishin*) as a generic term for all spiritual existences transcending human understanding—from spirits immanent in the natural world and the ghosts of the dead to the Shinto deities, the buddhas, and other spirits and supernatural beings of myth and legend. He then labels as heretical superstitions all teachings acknowledging such beings, arguing that Confucius and Mencius would have rejected such notions. So the stories in the eighth-century chronicle *Nihon shoki* relating the "miraculous events" of the Age of the Gods—what we would now describe as the mythology of Japan—are considered to be nothing more than fallacies produced by a primitive culture. In Yamagata's view, it was also erroneous to anthropomorphize the central Confucian concept of Heaven into a Lord of Heaven possessing a conscious will and ruling over the world and its fate, when its true nature was "a congregation of the minds of all people." In other words, the phenomenon driving social change was the collective mentality of the people.[2]

In this way Bantō denies the existence of the miraculous in this world and also rejects any talk of gods and buddhas as fallacious. Clearly, his study of Western astronomy with Asada Gōryū served to support his commitment to rationalism. By this time Shizuki Tadao had already published *Rekishō shinsho* (New Writings on Calendrical Phenomena, 1802), which contains the first full introduction of Copernican theory to Japan. Bantō cites this in *Yume no shiro* as the "theory of the earth's rotation" and explains it with detailed illustrations. He is also scathing in his criticism of Hattori Nakatsune's *Sandaikō* (Thoughts on the Three Great Realms), published as an appendix to volume 17 of Motoori Norinaga's *Kojikiden* (Commentary on the *Kojiki*), a text that builds on Shinto beliefs about the creation of the universe as "three realms": heaven (the sun), earth, and the land of the dead (the moon). Bantō attacks this work as "a theory unequaled in its strangeness by any other, past or present."

Undergirding Bantō's forceful denunciation of a variety of conventional theories was his confidence in the superiority of Western astronomy, based as it was on careful and systematic observation of the natural world: "Never in any country, past or present, has there been anything to match the precision of Western astronomy. Its discoveries are based on the direct observation of various parts of the world. It has no rival." Moreover, Western science was making steady progress. "Since astronomy and geography expand with each passing year, one should not become bogged down in outdated theories. The detailed understanding by Westerners of the various arts and sciences is unsurpassed by anyone in Japan or China." Here, Bantō is speaking of the pursuit of natural laws in the field of astronomy and, more broadly, in the natural sciences as a whole, rather than articulating a progressive view of history in general. Yet he is also clearly conscious that understanding of the natural world is growing with the passage of time, and that the theories and opinions recorded in the texts of the past are unreliable.

For Bantō himself, fundamentally educated in Confucian thought, the canonical texts transmitted from ancient China were still the first thing to be mastered, for the truths they contained concerning a broad range of natural and human phenomena. But to apply these truths to the concrete tasks of government in the present day, he argues that it was essential to design institutions that responded to contemporary needs.

> Viewed in this way, the political institutions of the Three Dynasties suited the people of the Three Dynasties, and the institutions of the Six Dynasties suited the people of the Six Dynasties. The institutions of the Song and Ming dynasties suited the people of the Song and Ming dynasties. The laws of our country in remote antiquity suited the people of that time; the institutions of the Heian period suited the people of that period; the institutions of the Kamakura and Muromachi periods and the eras of Oda Nobunaga and Toyotomi Hideyoshi suited the people of those times; and our present government should suit the people of today.[3]

In other words, the manners and customs of remote antiquity, as idealized by the Confucians, and those of the present are so completely different that government policies must be altered accordingly. This insight, which we have already seen in the writings of Ogyū Sorai, was shared by Bantō. At the same time, an awareness of the principle by which knowledge, of the natural world in particular, grows more extensive (or enlightened) with each generation was becoming more widespread. A consciousness of history was emerging in which the key image was one of unidirectional, cumulative, progressive change. We can sense this development in the unfolding of Bantō's argument.

Nor was Bantō comfortable with traditional Confucian policies that responded to the development of the market economy of the eighteenth and nineteenth centuries with stern warnings against luxury and extravagance and efforts to suppress the expansion of commercial activity. Bantō proclaims, "It is the Osaka rice market that consolidates the intelligence of the realm, causes its blood to circulate, and brings it great prosperity." Market prices resulted from the engagement of numberless individuals in the process of trading. This was an "aggregation of demand" (*jinki no atsumaru tokoro*) that might be likened "to the will of heaven, or the will of the gods."[4]

Thus, policies that attempted to constrain or depress prices were unfree, and undesirable.[5] Rather, officials should limit truly egregious consumption of wealth but otherwise leave prices to the market, with the understanding that they will eventually settle to an appropriate level. As a concrete economic policy, Bantō was proposing a laissez faire approach to the market rivaling that of Adam Smith. This was in the sixth volume of *Yume no shiro*, titled *Keizai*, and was almost entirely concerned with matters of fiscal administration for the daimyo. The word *keizai* in this context probably meant something close to what it does in modern Japanese: economics. In this sense, Bantō was a true economist of Tokugawa Japan, writing scholarly discourses on economics while simultaneously serving as a managing director of a major trading and financial firm.

"Esoteric teaching"

As we have seen, in *Keizai* (volume 6 of *Yume no shiro*) Yamagata Bantō proposes that, as concrete guidelines for contemporary economic policy, it was appropriate to permit free trade among merchants and leave matters of pricing to the self-regulating market. This argument is essentially limited to the context of a discussion of the sale of tax rice collected by the daimyo and the question of price controls. If anything, the tone of this text is established by Bantō's introduction, at the beginning of the volume, of a passage from his teacher Nakai Riken, which may be summarized as follows.

With the growth of the economy, a "culture of excess" infects the country. Government officials, merchants, artisans, court aristocrats, and others who live in urban areas, consuming but not producing food, proliferate while the rural farming population declines. Further development of commerce produces a situation in which goods are sought and purchased not only from other regions of Japan but also from distant lands such as Holland, and these are preferred even as articles of daily use. "The blessings of peace and prosperity notwithstanding, there is too much freedom." So in order to curb these tendencies, rulers "must make it their first priority to implement policies that suppress the people of the cities and towns and support the rural population and encourage crop production." What we see here is the classic Confucian stance, which regarded agriculture as the foundation of the nation and held the moral value of commerce in very low regard. In stark contrast to Bantō's criticism of the overly restrictive nature of price controls, Riken complained that, in a prospering economy, "there is too much freedom."[6]

Even so, in the first chapter of this volume on "economics," rather than offering a critique of his teacher's statements, Bantō chooses instead to cite this argument and follow it with his own opinion that if the "culture of excess" was allowed to proliferate, the rulers would resort to increases in the annual agricultural taxes to maintain their finances, which might result in the ruin of rural villages. He continues:

> Eventually the distress of the peasantry becomes the basis for civil disorder. Therefore, in order to govern the country, the peasants must be encouraged and the artisans and merchants suppressed, with the cities and towns allowed to decline. When urban areas prosper, the countryside declines. When rural areas prosper, the cities and towns decline. This is only natural.[7]

Bantō was himself a merchant active in the Osaka rice market and a scholar who welcomed the "enlightened" scientific knowledge of the West, but here he is advocating for the suppression of artisans and merchants and the weakening of urban areas. In those days, criticism of the policies of the Tokugawa shogunate could incur severe penalties. This did not mean that all publications that presented commerce in a positive light were liable to be banned by the shogunate. A profusion of self-help books for aspiring businessmen and merchant success stories were published, including *Nippon eitai-gura* (The Eternal Storehouse of Japan, 1688) by the popular writer Ihara Saikaku (1642–93). So it seems unlikely that it was fear of action by the authorities that drove Bantō to use language complicit in the suppression of the merchants.

In an article entitled "How to Begin to Study Medieval Philosophy," the twentieth-century German-American political theorist Leo Strauss argues that special techniques were necessary in the interpretation of writings by the medieval Jewish philosopher Maimonides, who was active in the Islamic world of his day, and those of the Islamic philosopher Al-Farabi.[8] In order to transmit their philosophical ideas and avoid censorship in a society that did not acknowledge the independence of philosophy from theology, these thinkers adopted a method of "esoteric teaching" that worked to conceal their true meaning. With this in mind, modern scholars reading these texts have learned not to take them at face value, but instead adopt interpretive strategies that allow them to discern the authors' hidden intentions.

Yamagata Bantō did not find himself in an environment so harsh that merely praising the development of commerce would likely engender persecution, so it is unlikely that he took the meticulous care that Strauss describes to strategically conceal his true intent. But like most of his contemporaries, Bantō was working within a Confucian framework that had traditionally been critical of commerce. In light of this, we should try to read this text in a way that might give us a glimpse of the "esoteric teaching" underlying his superficial critique of commerce.

After the passage criticizing commerce at the beginning of volume 6 of *Yume no shiro*, Bantō writes that it is important for rulers to make efforts to guarantee the livelihood of their people: "For enriching the people is itself a primary good." He then continues,

After this year's great flood in Kawachi, the wealthy merchants of Naniwa [Osaka] competed with one another to deliver rice and other necessities to aid the victims. Not one of them hesitated to participate in giving this relief, as appropriate to their station. . . . And this was simply because there is truly so much money in Naniwa. From this we can see that the people there are not greedy for wealth, and though it is said that manners and customs are deteriorating at present, it would be quite easy to reverse this trend.[9]

The "great flood in Kawachi" refers to a natural disaster in the summer of 1802 in which many parts of Japan experienced heavy rains and flooding, with Kawachi province in the vicinity of Osaka being especially hard hit. The merchants of Osaka (known also as Naniwa) distributed food and supplies to the people of the area. This reflected Osaka's affluence and also a merchant tradition of providing aid to those in distress. In other words, Bantō suggests here that the pursuit of wealth through commercial activity could also support an ethic of providing assistance to others. The harsh argument we saw earlier for "allowing the towns and cities to decline" may be understood as aimed at the "deteriorating manners and customs," which acknowledged no such morality and allowed people to ignore the plight of rural areas hit by disasters of this kind.

The rather involuted, "esoteric" line of argument that Bantō deploys here is an excellent example of how difficult it was to legitimate the pursuit of wealth and the development of commerce within the framework provided by Confucian thought. But as with his discussion surrounding "freedom" in the economic realm, a logic affirming the validity of the pursuit of profit within Confucian constraints was quietly spreading and growing.

Kaiho Seiryō, the itinerant Confucian

Seven years younger than Yamagata Bantō, and a child of Edo, the Confucian thinker Kaiho Seiryō (1755–1817) would come to adopt an even more positive stance toward encouraging the pursuit of wealth. An excellent recent study by Tokumori Makoto will serve as our reference for an investigation of the outlines of Seiryō's thought.[10]

Seiryō studied with Usami Shinsui, one of Ogyū Sorai's most prominent disciples. Thus he falls within Sorai's intellectual lineage, and shared with its founder a concern with "governing the realm" (keisei). But the content of Seiryō's thought was completely different, and unique. From his thirties onward, Seiryō traveled throughout Japan, serving as a sort of policy consultant to various daimyo. The principal theme he addressed was the fiscal crisis that many of them faced, and the issue of how to rebuild their finances and enrich their domains.

In one of his policy treatises, *Keikodan* (Lessons of the Past, 1813), he relates an anecdote concerning Yamagata Bantō (as Masuya Shōemon, his merchant name). At one time Masuya was in charge of the shipment of tax rice from the Sendai domain to Edo. These were quite large shipments of rice and required the stationing of staff to manage the shipments in Sendai, the port of Chōshi, and in Edo itself, at considerable expense. The daimyo of Sendai was already suffering financial difficulties, and Masuya reasoned that the daimyo would be unlikely to honor a request to pay for these managerial expenses.

Masuya noted that the samurai officials were "uneducated and unskilled," "blind to profit and unfamiliar with the laws of nature." So he requested of the daimyo that he be allowed to collect the cup or two of rice that spilled from each straw bale when they were punctured with a bamboo tube during the process of inspection of their contents on delivery. The daimyo and his officials agreed to this, thinking that the rice collected in this manner would not amount to much, but since the number of bales being inspected was so large, when it was converted into cash it put about 6,000 *ryō* per annum into Masuya's hands—quite enough to cover his staff expenses. Seiryō praises the wisdom of this, citing it as an example of knowledge adapted to contemporary realities: "Learning is not limited to a mastery of matters of the past. Good scholarship also means a mastery of the matters of the present day."[11]

In *Keikodan*, Seiryō also writes, "Bringing forth plentiful produce from the land should be considered the best strategy for enriching the country."[12] "It is the nature of the land to bring forth produce. It is not depleted by harvesting it."[13] The daimyo should encourage a variety of agricultural production on the part of the peasants, collect taxes in kind, and sell the produce through the nationwide market to domains across the country. Seiryō strongly advocates using the development of the market economy as a means for enriching the individual domains. His claim that crops would grow more abundantly rather than be depleted by harvest

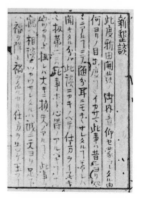

Kaiho Seiryō wrote many policy proposals. This is a page from *Shinkondan* (On Opening New Lands, 1813).

conveys an intuitive sense that Japan was in the midst of an economic transformation that was preparing the way for affluence.

Seiryō believed that the reason the samurai were so inept at fiscal management and daimyo houses were in financial distress was that they were pervaded by an ethos that "held money in contempt" and disrespected merchants (calling them *shōkonin*, "traders"). Seiryō is scathing in his criticism of this mentality:

> If they are to sneer at traders, one might well ask whether they themselves do not engage in trade. First of all, the great daimyo of the land sell rice year after year to convert it to cash, which they use for a variety of public works and other needs and purposes. Selling rice is trading. Everyone from the great daimyo on down is engaged in trade. To be engaged in trade and yet to hold it in contempt is to act in contradiction to one's station. No wonder they are so poor.[14]

Seiryō is essentially saying that insofar as the samurai class must sell their tax rice on the open market in order to acquire the cash they need to fund both their living expenses and their rule, they are really no different from merchants. In *Keikodan*, he also describes the relationship between the daimyo and their retainers as "transactional" (*urikai*): the retainers provide service to the daimyo and in return the daimyo pays them rice-denominated stipends. But since they officially advocated a Confucian morality that regarded the pursuit of profit as unethical, they had convinced themselves that they in no way resembled the merchants they looked down upon.

Seiryō does not argue against the class system of Tokugawa Japan, which accorded the samurai the hereditary responsibility for governing the land. In *Keikodan* he advocates "enriching the domain" (*fukoku*) and sees ensuring the livelihood of the people as a central goal, but the perspective he brings is exclusively that of the ruling elite. "Loving the people is the same as loving a small child. To spoil them is most harmful."[15] He expects the daimyo houses to take the lead in enriching their domains, while arguing that commerce and the merchant class could play an important role in this process. It is only within this context that Seiryō advises the samurai to acknowledge the reality of themselves as "participants in trade" and to equip themselves with the knowledge of commerce.

From Seiryō's viewpoint, the society of Tokugawa Japan was one of economic competition, with the daimyo houses vying with one another to enrich themselves and their domains.

> In today's world one cannot be careless regarding neighboring domains, and must cultivate vigilance regarding one's own. To say that one cannot be careless regarding neighboring domains means . . . that when the land of neighboring domains appears to be especially productive, one's own domain must exercise its ingenuity; otherwise one's neighbor would prosper and one's own domain would decline. And if one's neighbor prospers and one's own domain declines, money will flow only to the prosperous.[16]

For Seiryō, the land was capable of bringing forth a boundless supply of produce, so the competition he perceived was not a struggle for limited resources. However, if a daimyo was "careless" his domain could still fall quickly into poverty while its more clever and attentive neighbors siphoned off its wealth to enrich themselves. Seiryō proposes to the daimyo that they should treat "wealthy families" (fuka)—major merchant houses—with respect, because these merchants would "suck up money from neighboring and nearby domains" and make a major contribution to the enrichment of their own.[17]

In this age of "economics" (keizai) the samurai had to become conversant with money matters and approach governing with the sensibility of merchants. It was an era in which the peasants were also producing goods other than rice, and selling the products of their households on the open market. Seiryō was presumably able to see the reality of a world in which samurai, peasants, and townsmen alike would all be transformed into "traders." And in this sense, the economic growth of his time had introduced a decisive break with the past.

Moreover, this competitive arena was not limited to domestic economic competition among the daimyo houses of Japan. During Seiryō's lifetime, in

1792, the Russian envoy Adam Laxman arrived at the port of Nemuro, attempting to negotiate the opening of trade relations with Japan; twelve years later, Nikolai Resanov appeared in Nagasaki making similar overtures.

Probably with such events in mind, Seiryō wrote in *Yōshindan* (On Cultivating the Mind, c. 1803), "The shogun also has neighbors; from a broad perspective they include China, Korea, and Russia." Like Yamagata Bantō, who praised the advanced scientific knowledge of the West, Seiryō's perspective had widened to a global scale—and his vision was one of a global economy in which nations competed vigorously with one another.

Sketch by a Japanese artist of the Russian envoy Adam Laxman after his arrival at Nemuro.

Seiryō placed a high value on modes of life and thought that exhibited "freedom" (*jiyū*) or "freedom and independence" (*jiyū jizai*). He declares that "intellect" (*chi*) was essential to government, and describes its operations as "the free and independent use of the mind."[18] He later recalls the years he spent traveling throughout Japan as ones in which he had been "in a position of freedom and independence."[19] As we have seen, Seiryō did not reject the class system of his time. But his thought, which saw the samurai and townsmen alike as engaged in a form of "trade," embodied a certain type of egalitarianism. And his sense of "freedom" was one that corresponded to an expanding economy and a global perspective on economic freedom and the pursuit of affluence.

CHAPTER 7

Another Side of Motoori Norinaga

Utagawa Hiroshige, *Ise Pilgrimage: Crossing the Miyakawa River* (1855).

Yoshida Ken'ichi and Motoori Norinaga

The Kokugaku (National Learning) scholar Motoori Norinaga (1730–1801) is frequently mentioned even today in discussions of classical Japanese literature. During the Word War II era, Hirata Atsutane (1776–1843) was praised alongside Norinaga for developing the concept of the "Japanese spirit." After the war, however, the reputations of these two thinkers starkly diverged.

Since World War II, Hirata Atsutane has generally been described as a fanatic nationalist, and his works, though published before the war in popular editions such as Iwanami Bunko, are no longer readily available. It is safe to say that, outside of scholars specializing in intellectual history or Shinto, he has largely been forgotten. Motoori Norinaga presents quite a contrast. While fewer people now have direct experience of his writings than before the war, his reputation remains as a leading commentator on the classical Japanese canon, especially the *Kojiki* (Record of Ancient Matters, 712) and the *Tale of Genji* (early eleventh century). Almost all Japanese have encountered his name at one time or another in their school textbooks.

Moreover, prominent postwar writers and literary critics treat Norinaga's thought with great respect. *Motoori Norinaga*, a critical study by Kobayashi Hideo written in the latter years of his life, was serialized in the journal *Shinchō* beginning in 1965 and published in book form in 1977. The novelist Ishikawa Jun edited a selection of Norinaga's writings for which he provided a modern Japanese translation of the text *Uiyamabumi* (First Steps into the Mountains) and a brief interpretive assessment of Norinaga's work.[1]

Kobayashi and Ishikawa had been active in literary circles before the war, resisting both the I-novel and proletarian literature movements popular with their contemporaries to pursue work that stressed an aesthetic grounded in the play of language itself. While adopting some of the techniques of modern

Western literature, they also strove to immerse themselves in the Japanese classics. For writers such as these, Norinaga was appealing not merely as a great interpreter of the Japanese classics, but also as a prose stylist equipped with a unique critical consciousness.

Hasegawa Ikuo's recent biography of Yoshida Ken'ichi (1912–77)[2] informs us that this unusual literary figure, like his contemporaries Kobayashi and Ishikawa, also published work related to Motoori Norinaga. Although

Yoshida Ken'ichi (1912–77).

it has escaped standard chronologies and catalogues of Yoshida's literary output, volume 21 of *Nihon no koten* (The Japanese Classics), published by Kawade Shobō Shinha in 1972, is devoted to works by Arai Hakuseki and Motoori Norinaga, and contains Yoshida's translations into modern Japanese of Norinaga's *Hihon tamakushige* (Secret Book of the Precious Comb Box) and selections from the essay collection *Tamakatsuma* (The Precious Basket). Yoshida's old friend Kawakami Tetsutarō contributed modern translations of Norinaga's *Ashiwake obune* (A Little Boat among the Reeds) and *Uiyama-bumi* (First Steps into the Mountains) to the same volume.

Among the five members of the editorial committee for this *Nihon no koten* series, it was probably Yamamoto Kenkichi who masterminded the selection of Yoshida and Kawakami as contributors to this volume. A map of the contemporary literary scene would have placed Yamamoto and Kawakami in proximity to Kobayashi and Ishikawa, with whom they had friendly relations. And while Yoshida left very little writing connected to the Japanese classics, he shared a common sensibility with this circle of writers. His work as a critic, beginning with *Eikoku no bungaku* (British Literature, 1949), gives the impression that he was oriented almost entirely toward the West, but reading his translations of Norinaga make one realize how closely Norinaga's writing resembles Yoshida's in tone and style.

Hihon tamakushige is an opinion paper on government policy written by Norinaga in 1787 in response to a request from Tokugawa Harusada, daimyo of the Wakayama domain in Kii province who also ruled the Matsusaka domain (in Ise province), where Norinaga lived. *Hihon* (secret book) was added to the title because the treatise was concerned with the policies of the domain's ruling house; it remained unpublished during Norinaga's lifetime, and for fifty years after his death.

When a literary figure—especially one with a prose style as unique as Yoshida's—turns his hand to translation, it is perhaps to be expected that the rhythm of the translation should resemble that of the literary figure's own work. But a comparison of the translated passage with the original leads to the realization that the lengthy, meandering quality of Yoshida's sentences is fairly consistent with traditional Japanese style (as modeled on Heian-period prose).

As a son of the diplomat (and later prime minister) Yoshida Shigeru, Yoshida Ken'ichi spent much of his childhood overseas, and his family conversed in English, so learning to write Japanese required special effort. He struggled with the sense that there was a barrier between himself and his native language, and the style of prose he created, with conscious attention to the unique qualities of the Japanese language, is actually closer to the classical tradition than that of most of his contemporaries. At the same time, Norinaga's prose, though modeled on classical Japanese, is extremely logical. Perhaps it is this incorporation of logical argument into a classical voice that made Yoshida feel at home with Norinaga's writing. Or perhaps he first became acquainted with the works of Norinaga when, in his youth, he was struggling to develop his own style of writing.

The period in which Yoshida set his hand to these modern translations of Motoori Norinaga immediately followed one in which Yoshida had devoted himself to an objective reappraisal of the European civilization that he had up to that time embraced as his ideal. *Yōroppa no seikimatsu* (The Fin-de-siècle in European Intellectual History), the masterwork of his mature years, was published two years earlier, in 1970.

As the title suggests, the book's principal subject is the thought and art of late nineteenth-century Europe, but the discussion is largely devoted to praise for eighteenth-century European civilization, for its embodiment of universal significance while at the same time bringing the unique characteristics of

European culture to a high level of refinement. This civilization established the independence of the human spirit from both God and Nature, resulting in an acute self-awareness that never descended into self-involved introspection or rancorous ideological dispute, as it did in later periods. An elegant grace suffused high culture and society, accepting human complexity and tolerating social intercourse among a diversity of peoples.

In contrast, nineteenth-century European intellectual history was characterized by ideological conflict and the domination of the laws of the material world as revealed by science—a bleak era in which even free-spirited Romanticism tended to result in a rather predictable and stereotypical worship of the self. Yet finally, as the fin de siècle approached, the revival of a more nuanced awareness of the human spirit appears in the work of such poets and philosophers as Charles Baudelaire and Henri Bergson. This is the outline of Yoshida's argument, at least as far as the differences between the eighteenth and nineteenth centuries are concerned.

Yoshida also points out that in Edo-period Japan, as in eighteenth-century Europe, the glint of modernity may be discerned. In the second chapter, he lists three universal indices of civilization that typified the eighteenth century: "elegance," "consideration for the feelings of others expressed in attention to etiquette," and "a measured pursuit of happiness"—in other words, while pursuing one's own happiness, one should treat others humanely and seek to relieve suffering in the world. Despite superficial differences, this sense of liberty tempered by self-restraint was "something enjoyed similarly by the people of civilizations ranging from Edo Japan to Tang China to Rome under the rule of the Antonine emperors."

In chapter 9, Yoshida remarks on the influence of "Japan's ukiyo-e" on the Impressionist painters of fin-de-siècle Europe. According to Yoshida, while certainly Japanese, ukiyo-e also embodies certain universal characteristics of modernity, and this is what gained these Japanese woodblock prints ready acceptance in late nineteenth-century Europe—as artworks that exquisitely expressed "the precise workings of the spirit" in the attempt to convey "reality." Yoshida seemingly believed that by developing a high degree of self-awareness with regard to these "workings of the spirit," the culture of Edo Japan also represented a certain type of modernity and embodied elements of what could certainly be described as "civilization."

As Yoshida himself observes in *Yōroppa no seikimatsu*, what Japan adopted in the Meiji era was not the refined and elegant civilization of the eighteenth century, but contemporaneous nineteenth-century European culture. In that sense, Yoshida's work differs markedly from this book, which attempts to trace the prehistory of the adoption of Western "civilization" in Japan through the intellectual history of the Tokugawa period. But is it not true that the "elegance," "etiquette," and "liberty" that Yoshida detected intermittently in the Edo period existed in the thought of Motoori Norinaga? I feel that a sensitive perception of this fact is what must have drawn Yoshida to his experiment with translating Norinaga into modern Japanese.

The influence of merchant society

In *Hihon tamakushige*, Norinaga's concrete advice on policy begins by identifying the first issue of concern: how people of all ranks came to give undue attention to status, conducting themselves in a fashion inappropriate to their station. From the daimyo on down, samurai of all ranks, not only in their work as administrators but also in their behavior in everyday life, focused on enhancing their status. They spent money making their residences, clothing, and other appurtenances as grand as possible, and increased the number of their retainers and subordinates. Because such "extravagance" had permeated the samurai class as a whole, every domain in the land suffered from financial problems.[3]

Like Ogyū Sorai and Kaiho Seiryō, whom we have discussed previously, Norinaga did not see this epidemic of extravagance as simply the result of laxness or inattention on the part of the rulers.

Motoori Norinaga (1730–1801) at the age of forty-four.

In general, when the realm has been at peace a long while, worldly goods and affairs grow more lavish, and people gradually begin to over-emphasize their status. If this tendency is not periodically suppressed, but left unattended, it will only increase with the passage of time. Unrestrained, it will gradually bring poverty and trouble to the world, and a variety of unpleasant things will occur.[4]

In this work, Norinaga makes frequent mention of the development of commerce, so it is probably safe to assume that he was aware that underlying the epidemic of extravagance were societal changes in response to economic growth. At least in terms of his basic conceptual framework, his position on this was not, like Kaiho Seiryō, to praise commercial development and economic expansion.

In any case, there is no way to swiftly bring a halt to the lavishness and extravagance of society in general, which only grows with the passage of time. But all things have their limits; what rises to a peak must inevitably decline; and there will come a time for a return to the way things were originally.[5]

"The passage of time" is a phrase repeated in both of these extracts from Norinaga's text, suggesting his keen awareness that economic growth and material affluence were steadily increasing. But in his view, this growth could not continue indefinitely. After peaking, it must naturally begin to subside. Norinaga believed that the cumulative wealth of society followed cycles of expansion and contraction. And over time, a mechanism was always at work that tended to return wealth to a standard level, maintaining a balance between agriculture and commerce. We may think of this as a traditional perspective in economic thought grounded in Confucianism, such as we have seen in the work of Ogyū Sorai.

Yet if we examine the specific way in which Norinaga advances his argument in *Hihon tamakushige*, clearly he is not simply advocating restriction of commercial activity on the grounds that it is morally reprehensible. Norinaga was born and bred in Ise Matsusaka, a prosperous commercial center. His family members made their livelihood in the cotton trade, and at one time were successful enough to have opened a shop in Edo. Norinaga rejected the opportunity to inherit the family business and chose initially to pursue a career in medicine. After he became established as a

Former residence of Motoori Norinaga, relocated to the site of Matsusaka Castle.

Kokugaku scholar, he continued to receive financial support from the wealthy merchants of Matsusaka, many of whom became his students. In short, Norinaga's entire life was spent in the society of these merchants.

Norinaga does argue that the development of commerce instilled a taste for luxury among all classes, from the samurai to the peasantry, and that this taste for luxury was a source of fiscal difficulties for the domains and even bankrupted some individuals. But in his description of these problems, the tone is not one of wholesale condemnation of commercial activity.

> Trade cannot be conducted without merchants, and the larger the number of merchants, the more convenience [*jiyū*] the domain and its people enjoy. But generally speaking, the benefits of convenience are attended by equivalent drawbacks. As things become more freely available, expenditures increase; whereas restrictions on goods reduce expenditures. In our present world, people vie with one another in the pursuit of desirable things, and though enjoying free access to goods, want still more. So merchants and artisans, year after year, month after month, invent and produce a variety of convenient and useful things, and novel items, and sell them widely. As a result, year after year, month after month, many good and useful things are produced, and the expenditures of the people gradually increase.[6]

"Year after year, month after month, many good and useful things are produced"—this phrase conveys Norinaga's immediate sense of the steadily increasing production of a diverse range of new goods for sale on the commercial market. The word *jiyū* as employed in this passage has a different nuance than the Western concepts of "liberty" or "freedom" (which are translated as *jiyū* in modern Japanese); these Western ideas connote acting of one's own free will as a foundation for responsibility and ethics. As we see in the phrase "convenient and useful things" (*benri yoku jiyū naru koto*), *jiyū* is being used here to describe ready availability and ease of use. Norinaga argues that increased demand by society for an unlimited expansion of such availability and ease of use has resulted in a pursuit of luxury and increased expenditures—and, for an increasing number of individuals, financial ruin.

Norinaga's description of the process leading up to these ills is quite perceptive in tracing the psychology of people living in the midst of a market economy. Insofar as trade is essential to society, it is beneficial to both the domain (the ruling daimyo house) and the people (the ruled) for commerce to develop and the number of merchants to increase ("the benefits of convenience"). But as Norinaga points out, a mentality that endlessly seeks greater convenience eventually develops into a competitive mindset in which people "vie with one another." They compete in displays of luxury and pomp, and this competition drives further growth of the economy. Norinaga describes this mechanism based on his own experience.

From Norinaga's perspective, this competitive mentality was stronger among the townspeople than among the samurai. In comparison to the samurai class with its finely divided hierarchies, the townspeople were "all on the same plane" (*hira ichimai*). Yet precisely because they lived in greater equality, without the burden of hereditary rank, the gap between rich and poor was even more deeply felt. "Despite differences in circumstances as great as that of clouds and mud, everyone looks to the wealthy as models and envies them, and even those with very little imitate them, striving to live far beyond their means, such that many people end up being hard-pressed." Relative equality in terms of hereditary class or status produced even greater envy of those who were better off, and a deeply felt desire to catch up with them. This problem, frequently mentioned in Western political and social thought from the nineteenth century onward, was something Norinaga also grasped.

As a result, *Hihon tamakushige* does not recommend that the daimyo should issue sumptuary laws, visiting stern punishment on offenders as a means of dealing with the social problems associated with the epidemic of conspicuous consumption infiltrating all classes—samurai, townspeople, and peasants alike. "Even if efforts are made to regulate this, the tendencies of the times [*jisei no ikioi*] are difficult to resist, something beyond the reach of human capacity." People accustomed to seeking freedom and convenience are unlikely to obey sumptuary laws; they may make a show of obeying them while continuing to indulge privately in luxury. Norinaga's advice to "those above" is firstly for the daimyo himself to exercise self-restraint in terms of displays of wealth and luxury, thus serving as a model of behavior for his samurai retainers and the people below them to emulate. As a reform proposal, this may seem excessively modest, but Norinaga would probably argue that it was a method of governing that considered the hearts of "the people below" and was attuned to popular sentiment.

Mono no aware and tolerance

In a 2015 paper on *Hihon tamakushige*,[7] the intellectual historian Takayama Daiki draws attention to a passage in this text in which Norinaga discusses the prevalence of bribery—a common problem during the latter half of the eighteenth century. Norinaga concludes that this problem must be regulated, but before doing so, makes the following comment:

> Acquisitiveness is a common human feeling (*ninjō*) that almost no one can avoid, and because this is the case, and because delight in receiving things is a typical human feeling, it is also natural that gifts are given as an expression of intent. This is true past and present, in every land. And so it is that in all matters, a natural impetus arises at times to use bribes in an effort to ingratiate ourselves with others and achieve our goals.[8]

Setting aside moral judgments, Norinaga states that to desire things is a common human feeling. So it is also natural to assume that lavish gifts will delight others, and to please them with bribes. Norinaga speaks of this not as a phenomenon limited to the Japan of his day but as a universal aspect of human nature. It is also worth noting his use of the phrase "natural impetus" (*shikarubeki ikioi*). The above-mentioned "tendencies of the times" influencing society are born of the aggregate operations of a myriad individual human feelings—and thus almost impossible for anyone to control.

Manuscript of *Hihon tamakushige* in Norinaga's own hand.

Here, the operations of human feelings are understood as not being reducible simply to immediate demands such as the desire for material goods. Overlapping this is the capacity for intuiting the feelings of others—that they might be happy to receive a bribe—which can also be assessed as the workings of human feelings following natural principles. As Takayama observes, this way of understanding human psychology is connected to the attitude Norinaga speaks of as an essential condition for great poetry: *mono no aware o shiru*, or "a deeply sympathetic understanding of the things of this world."

Because poetry is the genuine expression of the deepest feelings of happiness and sadness as they naturally arise in the human heart, then when we read or hear it, even those things of which we have no personal experience penetrate our hearts and we may imagine the feelings of another person in a particular situation, what might delight them, what they might resent, perceiving and understanding them with great sensitivity. The sentiments of people everywhere are revealed more clearly than in the most spotless mirror, and because of this, the compassionate mind arises spontaneously within, and we come to feel that for the sake of others, it is wrong to behave badly. This is the virtue of *mono no aware*.[9]

Poetry expresses the workings of the human mind just as they are. Through it, we can come to understand the joys and sorrows of people in entirely different circumstances than our own, living in different eras. An accumulation of such experiences leads us to appreciate the way that others think and feel, and gives us a capacity for living with others in a way that does not disrupt the social order. This is the effect that "a deeply sympathetic understanding of the things of this world" has on social relations. In *Shibun yōryō*, his discourse on the *Tale of Genji*, Norinaga remarks, "This is the same as when people describe someone experienced in the ways of the world as being mellowed or seasoned."[10]

Norinaga has been described as a thinker who rejected foreign creeds such as Confucianism and Buddhism and who assigned absolute value to the Way embodied in the *Kojiki* and other works of the classical Japanese canon. In light of this, his respect for a "mellow" attitude of empathy and compassion for the feelings of others may seem somewhat surprising. But from Norinaga's perspective, such workings of the human heart and mind are precisely what is embodied so fully in the *Kojiki*, in classical Japanese poetry, and in the prose of the classical court tales, such as the *Tale of Genji*. We can assume that Norinaga's insights reflected the social relations among the townsmen of his day who, in a world in which competition and envy were rampant, still managed to restrain their own behavior and maintain relations with their neighbors by exercising empathy and compassion for one another.

In *Hihon tamakushige*, Norinaga was writing in the midst of the famines and recurrent peasant uprisings that swept many domains in the years of the Tenmei era (1781–88). He stresses that the daimyo must understand the desperate circumstances of the peasants and deal with them compassionately. He implores the daimyo and samurai living in urban areas a world apart from the sufferings of rural villages to empathize with the peasants, experiencing their

Corrected page proofs of Norinaga's *Kojikiden*, his extensive commentary on the *Kojiki* (712).

plight as if it were their own, and act to relieve their distress. He argues that such an attitude is consonant with "a deeply sympathetic understanding of the things of this world."

Such advocacy for tolerance of diversity may also be seen in Norinaga's writings on scholarship. While confining their use to the explication of the Ancient Way (*inishie no michi*) as recorded in the *Kojiki* and other classic Japanese texts, he argues that even the Confucian and Buddhist teachings imported subsequently might be studied with profit, as long as their shortcomings and errors were properly understood.

In an essay entitled "Nochi no yo wa hazukashiki mono naru koto" (On Becoming an Embarrassment in Later Ages) in the collection *Tamakatsuma*, Norinaga concludes a discussion of how far interpretive study of the *Man'yōshū* poetry collection (c. 759) had advanced since the time of Keichū (1640–1701), the Buddhist priest and Kokugaku scholar who produced the *Man'yō daishōki* (1687–90). Norinaga remarks, "So it seems that in all matters, we shall eventually become an embarrassment in later ages."[11] This is not precisely a progressive view of history, but at least in terms of a specific field of scholarship it does express a historical perspective that accepts the idea that the passage of time can eventually bring us closer to the truth. The essay mentioned in chapter 4, "Inishie yorimo nochi-no-yo no masareru koto" (Why the Present Is Superior to the Past), which discusses how economic progress brought new products into the world, probably had such developments in scholarship in mind too.

Tamakatsuma also contains an essay entitled "Oranda to iu kuni no manabi" (Dutch Learning), the main thrust of which is a critique of the popularity of Dutch studies and the scholars engaged in it for "having no respect for their own Imperial Land [*mikuni*]." Yet at the same time, Norinaga characterizes Holland as "a country that bestrides the world" in pursuit of trade, and is thus useful as a source of information to correct the errors of scholars who idealize China and its culture.[12] Conditional though it may be, we can see here an element of tolerance in Norinaga's attitude toward new ideas and new forms of scholarship.

Moreover, Norinaga was passionate about assimilating the knowledge of

Western astronomy being introduced to Japan at that time; he attempted to apply it to bolster his own theories about the interpretation of the *Kojiki*. But this effort would send Kokugaku down a different path.

CHAPTER 8

A New Cosmology and the Concept of *Ikioi*

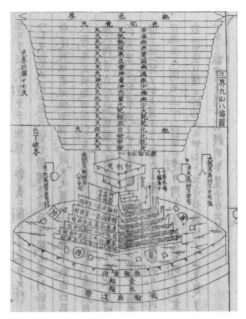

A depiction of the universe in Musō Monnō's *Kusen hakkai gechō ron* (1754). Following Buddhist cosmology, it placed at the center of the universe the immense Mount Sumeru, surrounded by an ocean in which floated four continents and above which were layered thirty-three separate heavens.

Motoori Norinaga and Dutch Learning

As mentioned in chapter 6, Yamagata Bantō's *Yume no shiro* (In Place of Dreams, completed in 1820) is devoted to a relentless pursuit of the Neo-Confucian universal principle, or *ri* (Ch. *li*). It rejects as fallacies all mystical doctrines preaching the existence of gods and spirits. The third fascicle of this work is entitled "Jindai" (Age of the Gods). Making reference to Motoori Norinaga's *Kojikiden*, an extensive commentary on the *Kojiki*, Bantō attempts a critique of the "myths" (*densetsu*) presented in the early sections of the *Nihon shoki* and the *Kojiki* concerning such ancient matters.

Bantō displays his characteristic critical attitude by declaring that the portions of the classic chronicles dealing with the Age of the Gods are no more than fictions, tales from the "primitive world" (*sōmai no yo*) of remote antiquity. The *Nihon shoki* and the *Kojiki* both claim to chronicle history "from the beginnings of the cosmos," but no one was there to observe this, he points out. Even if a witness had been present, they would not have possessed the written language with which to record their experience. Perhaps these ancient chronicles were orally transmitted before being written down, but they cannot be treated as factual.

For this reason, Bantō gives high marks to the canonical Chinese histories, which begin their narratives with the emperors Yao and Shun, without touching on legends concerning the Three Sovereigns (Fuxi, Nüwa, and Shennong) predating them. Such legends of the remote past are filled with "strange occurrences" that cannot be regarded as factual records, and therefore "one should not discuss the Three Sovereigns of China or the Age of the Gods in Japan, just leave them alone."[1] Since we have no reliable source material on the creation of the universe or prehistory before written language, he argues, we should accept our lack of knowledge, and leave it at that. As noted earlier, Bantō believed that human knowledge and learning advanced steadily with the passage of historical time—and that one should believe only those facts that could be solidly confirmed.

Bantō praises the Western nations of his day for having the most advanced knowledge and scholarship in specific fields such as astronomy, geography, and medicine. He recognizes that such scientific development was encouraged by systems of government that supported the arts and sciences. According to Bantō, in the West, someone who had "built a new device or invented a new technique" would report this to the government, and the government would respond by "giving the family of the inventor a stipend" to pursue his research and development. Such support might extend to the inventor's heirs as well, so that devices and inventions might be developed to completion, even if it took many years.

In contrast, what were the conditions in East Asia? "People in Japan and China might have such aspirations but are hard-pressed to make a living. Because of this, they are unable to achieve [success in their research]." Bantō mentions both Japan and China, but probably was thinking mostly of Japan. For scholars in the Tokugawa period, it was possible, if one was fortunate, to be employed as the retainer of a daimyo or the shogunate and given a stipend on which to live. But the vast majority of scholars had to eke out a living as neighborhood physicians or Confucian teachers, and consequently they had little leisure to advance their research. This passage clearly reflects these unfortunate circumstances and may express Bantō's own sense of frustration that, although he achieved success as a merchant, he might have accomplished more as a scholar had he been able to dedicate himself completely to his studies.

The image that Bantō presents of support for scholarship in the West is colored by his familiarity with the scholar-retainers of the shogun and daimyo. No doubt this knowledge of Japanese institutions was useful in making sense of his limited information about Western universities and academies. He also points to the role of international trade in stimulating economic growth and the development of science related to navigation:

In the countries of the West, the monarch is essentially a generalissimo of commerce. The reason they navigate around the world and gain a detailed knowledge of astronomy and geography is because of trade. If one navigates one cannot but be familiar with astronomy.[2]

Thus he describes the rulers in the West as captains of industry who work to promote economic development and international trade. One might read this as a veiled criticism of the Tokugawa system with its traditional bias against the market economy. Bantō believed that the early development of astronomy in the West had been driven by the necessities of commerce and navigation.

Toward the end of the Western Han dynasty, around 5 CE, the scholar Liu Xin revised the traditional calendar, modifying it with calculations of the movements of the planets and predictions of solar and lunar eclipses to produce the *San tong li* (Triple Concordance calendar). Bantō surmises that even at this early date the Western calendrical system must have been transmitted to China, which suggests the degree of his astonishment at the progress of Western astronomy in more recent times. The passage quoted above continues: "Since astronomy and geography expand with each passing year, one should not become bogged down in outdated theories." Here, Bantō suggests a practical response to rapid scientific progress in the West.

Bantō was deeply critical of the cosmologies of Buddhism and Shinto, regarding them as rigid and absurdly outmoded. Regarding Buddhism, he cites the treatise *Kusen hakkai gechō ron* (1754) by Musō Monnō (1700–1763), a Pure Land cleric who lived in Kyoto and Osaka, which attacked *Tianjing huowen* (1675), a work by the Qing-dynasty scholar You Yi incorporating Copernican heliocentric theory. Against this, Monnō reiterates traditional Buddhist cosmology, which placed at the center of the universe the immense Mount Sumeru, surrounded by an ocean in which floated four continents and above which were layered thirty-three separate heavens. The heaven in which the sun, moon, and stars revolved was conceived as an immense dome, like the lid of a serving dish.

In the case of Shinto cosmology, Bantō takes on Hattori Nakatsune's *Sandaikō* (Thoughts on the Three Great Realms, 1797). As mentioned in chapter 6, *Sandaikō* was published as an appendix to volume 17 of *Kojikiden*, by his teacher Motoori Norinaga. As Kanazawa Hideyuki's research on the original manuscript demonstrates, this brief work was brought to completion in the course of an exchange of opinions with Norinaga himself, and was appended to the first major section of *Kojikiden*, the commentaries concerning the Age of the Gods. It provides a unique interpretation of the text of the *Kojiki*, describing the process of the formation of the universe, dividing this into ten stages with illustrative drawings. According to this, through the actions of the gods, out of a "single thing" (*hitotsu no mono*) born into the cosmic void, three celestial bodies were created: heaven (the sun), earth, and the land of the dead (the moon).

According to Bantō, both the Buddhist and Shinto cosmologies were nothing more than "fallacies" (*mōsetsu*) that ran counter to scientific advances. He is especially scathing in his criticism of *Sandaikō*, saying it presents "a theory unequaled in its strangeness by any other, past or present. Others may equal its wisdom, but they cannot equal its stupidity."[3]

These religious cosmologies were based on ancient astrology, without referencing the *hun tian* cosmology supported by the Neo-Confucian scholars of Song-dynasty China, which conceived of a flat earth surrounded by a vast spherical universe with heavenly bodies moving above and below the earth. Compared with the "precision" of later Western astronomy, with a spherical earth orbiting the sun, these theories "are no better than the games of toddlers."[4] Bantō criticizes both Monnō and *Sandaikō* from the theoretical perspective of Western astronomy.

Yet Motoori Norinaga and Hattori Nakatsune were both acquainted with Western astronomy. As we have already seen, Norinaga believed in historical progress, at least as far as the ongoing development of new ideas in scholarship was concerned. At the

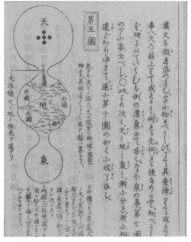

An illustration in Hattori Nakatsune's *Sandaikō* (Thoughts on the Three Great Realms, 1797), showing the "Imperial Land" of Japan directly connected to Heaven.

beginning of an essay entitled "Aratanaru setsu o idasu koto" (On Presenting New Theories) in *Tamakatsuma*, Norinaga writes: "In recent times, the paths of learning have expanded, and in dealing with all matters we are growing more perceptive and intelligent."[5] After this, he warns of the danger of getting carried away with strange new ideas in the pursuit of novelty or fame, saying that new theories must be advanced carefully and after thorough deliberation. Here we should note that Norinaga uses the same expression as Bantō—*hirakeru* (to expand, open up)—to describe the advancement of knowledge. Norinaga and Nakatsune saw themselves as living in a time when a variety of forms of scholarship—Confucianism, Kokugaku, Dutch Learning (Rangaku)—were all developing, expanding, and opening up new possibilities. This expansive sensibility was likely shared by many scholars and writers of their day.

In the essay "Oranda to iu kuni no manabi" (Dutch Learning, or Rangaku) mentioned in the previous chapter, Norinaga takes up the subject of the popularity "in recent years" of Rangaku in Edo and other parts of Japan. He sees the Rangaku scholars as superior to the Confucian scholars for abandoning the worship of Chinese thought, but also takes them to task for failing to realize "that our Imperial Land is superior to all others and worthy of respect." While making this criticism, however, he also notes that Holland is "a country that bestrides the world, voyaging to distant lands in pursuit of trade, and by studying its scholarship, we can learn much about these other countries."[6] Norinaga points to the role of commerce and navigation in advancing the knowledge of geography.

Norinaga uses his knowledge of Western astronomy to criticize Musō Monnō's *Kusen hakkai gechō ron*, declaring in a manuscript written in 1790 that Buddhist cosmology "is completely fictitious, without a grain of

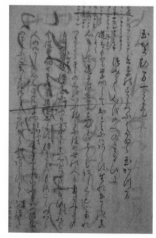

A page from the manuscript of *Tamakatsuma* (The Precious Basket), an essay collection by Motoori Norinaga.

truth."[7] Then, most likely referring to You Yi's *Tianjing huowen*, he writes, "In recent times the Westerners have traversed the earth, and their detailed knowledge of the world has gradually been spreading in China and Japan." Norinaga apparently shared Bantō's assessment that Western advances in geography and astronomy were directly related to experience with ocean navigation. But in this text Norinaga does not yet accept Copernican theory, premising his cosmology on a geocentric model in which the earth lies at the center of heavenly spheres, including the sun and moon.

Nakatsune's *Sandaikō*, completed the year after Norinaga's essay, clearly shows that they were aware that the spherical earth moved. Near the end of this work, Nakatsune writes, "According to a theory from the West, our earth as well is constantly revolving." Having introduced this idea, he insists that "even if the earth does in fact revolve," it does not conflict with "the essence of what has been transmitted to us from antiquity." Although the story of the creation of the universe as presented in *Sandaikō* is condemned by Bantō as absurd fantasy, it was developed by Norinaga and Nakatsune in the course of their own individual encounters with Western astronomy. Kanazawa Hideyuki's research shows that in the preface to a later work, Nakatsune reveals that he had only come to fully understand the Copernican model some time after the completion of *Sandaikō*.

The *Sandaikō* incident

Hattori Nakatsune's *Sandaikō*, written in collaboration with Motoori Norinaga, received criticism not only from Confucians like Yamagata Bantō. After Norinaga's death in 1801, a large number of Norinaga's disciples, along with Norinaga's adopted son and heir Motoori Ōhira as their spokesman, began to debate various aspects of *Sandaikō*, not only claiming that it conflicted with some of the opinions expressed by Norinaga in *Kojikiden*, but also raising doubts about Norinaga's understanding of the *Kojiki*. For instance, in *Kojikiden*, the afterworld is believed to be located beneath the earth; it is not equated with the moon, as in *Sandaikō*.

Yet such conflicts were the result of Norinaga and Nakatsune's attempt to reconcile the latest astronomical theories with the account given in the *Kojiki* of the origins of the world. The *Kojiki* states, "At the time of the beginning of heaven and earth, there came into existence in Takama no Hara [Plain of High Heaven] a deity named Ame-no-mi-naka-nushi-no-kami; next, Takami-musubi-no-kami; next, Kami-musubi-no-kami."[8] Thus the narrative commences with heaven and earth already in existence, as well as a region in heaven called the Plain of High Heaven, in which three deities appear, one after another. The stage prior to this, when heaven and earth themselves came into being, is neither described nor explained.

Yet Nakatsune speaks of what happened in this stage. At the beginning of *Sandaikō*, he cites the passage from the *Kojiki* quoted above, and explains it as follows: "At this time, neither heaven nor earth existed, and all was simply 'empty space' [*ōsora*]." The first of the text's ten illustrations shows a large circle with the three deities' names inscribed within it; the caption reads, "Within this circle is the void. But the circle has been drawn only for purposes of illustration. No such thing actually existed." He then states that the region called the Plain of High Heaven did not actually come into existence until a later stage, and that the first lines of the *Kojiki* simply use this term to describe the place where the three deities resided.

In other words, Nakatsune interprets the opening phrase of the *Kojiki* ("At the time of the beginning of heaven and earth") as referring to a period of pure primal void prior to the formation of heaven or earth. This totality was represented by a circle, a convenient way to present an image of the entire cosmos to the reader. What existed at the beginning of the cosmos was limitless space— *ōsora*—a pure void in which nothing at all existed. In an earlier text, *Tenmon zusetsu* (Astronomy Illustrated, 1782), Norinaga summarizes and provides

An illustration in Hattori Nakatsune's *Sandaikō*, depicting the cosmic void with the names of the three primal deities inscribed within it.

pictorial representations of his understanding of Western astronomy. An appendix, "Tengaku taii," provides a list of the principal ideas presented, the first of which is "Since heaven is empty, there is no way to know its movements. Because of this, it is through the movement of the various stars and planets that we may define the movements of Heaven."[9]

In *Sandaikō*, citing the opening section of the *Nihon shoki* on the origins of heaven and earth, Nakatsune posits that "one thing" (*hitotsu no mono*) appeared in the void and then gradually differentiated into three celestial bodies: heaven, earth, and Yomi (sun, earth, and moon). Living things came into being on earth—a process throughout which the "generative spirit" of Takami-musubi no kami and Kami-musubi no kami was at work. In other words, a procreative energy had begun to work within the limitless void of the universe. This energy, stirring at the very beginning of the universe, has continued to the present, eternally supporting the creation of all things.

In the vast expanse of the heavenly void float the spheres of the sun, moon, and earth. Nakatsune writes that the reason no other stars or planets are mentioned "in the transmissions from the antiquity of our Imperial Land" is that none were important enough to mention alongside these three bodies. The resulting cosmology is actually closer to that of contemporary Western astronomy than Yamagata Bantō's in *Yume no shiro*, which is partly premised on the Chinese *hun tian* theory of the universe itself being a sphere—and in

Illustrations 3 (left) and 10 (right) from Hattori Nakatsune's *Sandaikō*.

that sense a closed and finite space—within which the earth and other planets revolve around the sun.

The primary source Bantō cites for information on Western astronomy is *Rekishō shinsho* (New Writings on Calendrical Phenomena, 1798–1802), by a Rangaku scholar in Nagasaki, Shizuki Tadao (1760–1806). This book had its origins in a 1741 Dutch translation of a collection of introductory lectures on physics and astronomy, *Introductiones ad veram Physicam et veram Astronomiam*, written by John Keill, a Scottish physicist who had been a student of Isaac Newton. Shizuki translated this work, adding his own original commentary, and the result is *Rekishō shinsho*. Is the universe finite or infinite? When did time in this universe begin, and when will it end? Bantō quotes Shizuki's investigations of such questions verbatim.

The gist of Shizuki's response to these queries is that they are "immeasurable" (*fusoku*) by humankind and are thus difficult to determine. Yet the principle of the movements of the heavens and earth has been revealed through the law of universal gravitation. Just as each human being is equipped with a "mysterious and immeasurable spirit" that controls mind and body, each family has a patriarch that conducts its affairs, and each country has a government that unifies and rules it, so it is that the sun drives the "wondrous workings of heavenly and earthly creation."[10] This reference to a "mysterious and immeasurable spirit" residing in the human heart recalls the idea articulated by Neo-Confucian thinkers such as Yamazaki Ansai that a living, vital "principle" was at work within the human mind, identical in nature to that permeating all things in the universe.

In other words, Shizuki and Bantō believed that having a firm grasp of the principles governing our world was sufficient, and they were willing to abandon such "immeasurable" issues as the finiteness of the universe or the beginning and end of time. The adoption of the *hun tian* concept of the universe as a closed space was related to their attempt to grasp the order of nature by applying the similes drawn from human society.

But to this, the scientific revolution of seventeenth-century Europe counterposed the vision of an infinite universe. Earlier, Nicolaus Copernicus (1473–1543) had achieved the shift from a geocentric to a heliocentric model of the solar system, but had retained a sense of the cosmos as a closed system. Giordano Bruno (1548–1600) proclaimed a cosmology formed of particles continually coalescing and dispersing in infinite space. In the seventeenth century, Galileo Galilei (1564–1642) used observations with a telescope to suggest the possibility that fixed stars exist beyond the farthest reaches of human observation. And René Descartes (1596–1650) clearly articulated a concept of space as infinite (or as he termed it, indefinite) extension. In *Principia Philosophiae* (*Principles of Philosophy*), published in 1644, he writes:

René Descartes (1596–1650).

> We further discover that this world or the whole [universitas] of corporeal substance, is extended without limit, for wherever we fix a limit, we still not only imagine beyond it spaces indefinitely extended, but perceive these to be truly imaginable, in other words, to be in reality such as we imagine them; so that they contain in them corporeal substance indefinitely extended, for, as has been already shown at length, the idea of extension which we conceive in any space whatever is plainly identical with the idea of corporeal substance.[11]

The philosopher and historian of science Alexandre Koyré speaks of this shift in the paradigm dominating research in the natural sciences as being one from a closed world to an infinite universe, and sees it as leading directly to the establishment of modern science:

> This, in turn, implies the discarding by scientific thought of all considerations based upon value-concepts, such as perfection, harmony, meaning and aim, and finally the utter devalorization of being, the divorce of the world of value and the world of facts.[12]

Shizuki Tadao, and Yamagata Bantō after him, may have been able to comprehend Copernican theory, but did not arrive at the sweeping shift in cosmology that Koyré describes. This was also probably true of other Rangaku scholars. Their interest in astronomy was focused on better understanding the laws governing the movement of the heavenly bodies in order to arrive at a more accurate calendar. Such questions as whether the universe as a whole was closed or infinite were beyond the scope of such concerns, and could be set aside as "immeasurable." Moreover, as before, they probably felt that the premise of a self-contained cosmos allowed them to conceive of the human social order as a microcosm reflecting the heavenly order, rooted in the "principles" of nature and presenting a "Way" of life for humanity to honor and follow.

In contrast, Norinaga and Nakatsune grappled directly with the question of the origin of the universe and whether it was finite in extent. Since their knowledge of astronomy came through works by Rangaku scholars, their understanding of heliocentric theory was delayed, and they were probably unaware of the Western concept of the infinite universe. Nor did they suffer the distress Descartes felt in attempting to differentiate between the "infinite" nature of the transcendent God of Christianity on the one hand, and the "indefinite" extension in space of his Creation on the other.

These Kokugaku scholars presented a vision, following the opening passage of the *Nihon shoki*, that at the very beginning of the universe, "one thing" appeared in the infinite "void." In this cosmology, the primal "one thing" then divided into three heavenly bodies—sun, earth, and moon—privileged existences thoroughly suffused and animated by the flow of a "vital, generative spirit" from the gods. The Western notion of the infinite universe gave rise to a sense of humility at the minuteness of human existence in contrast to limitless space, but also a desire to carefully and accurately observe and record the movements of the heavens. Against this, the cosmology of the Kokugaku scholars privileged three heavenly bodies and an earth populated by humankind and ruled by emperors directly descended from the sun goddess Amaterasu Ōmikami, placing them at the center of an infinitely unfolding space.

Ikioi and the privileging of the "Imperial Land"

In the archives of the Museum of Motoori Norinaga in Matsusaka, there is a map of the world based on a Western source that was published in Japan in 1783. When the writer Ueda Akinari (1734–1809) claims that after looking at a world map it was absurd to argue that the tiny country of Japan was first-born and central among nations, Norinaga responds: "What is absurd is to act as if looking at a world map is such a rare thing and to make such a fuss over it." It was already common knowledge that, at least in terms of area, Japan was a small country. More important were Japan's qualities as a nation: its unbroken lineage of emperors, its bountiful harvests of rice, and the density of its population.[13] Norinaga was already well aware of the new world maps imported from the West. Even so, he proclaims that the Way inscribed in the *Kojiki* was "the True Way, extending to all the four seas and myriad nations."[14]

In point of fact, neither the *Kojiki* nor the *Nihon shoki* mentions the origins of any countries other than Japan, and both were written with no particular concern for the existence of other nations. But Norinaga and Nakatsune

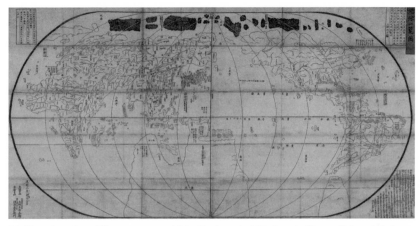

World map based on a Western source, published in Japan in 1783, from the library of Motoori Norinaga.

stepped in to fill this gap, reconstructing a narrative of the origins of the world. According to the caption of the fifth illustration in *Sandaikō*, the continents and islands of the rest of the earth were not born from the activities of the deities Izanagi and Izanami, as were the islands of Japan, but from the "generative spirit" of the two *musubi-no-kami* deities. As indicated by the ability of these two deities to travel back and forth between heaven and Ashihara no Nakatsukuni, the "Central Land of the Reed Plains" (referring to Japan soon after its creation), Ashihara no Nakatsukuni was positioned as "the crown of the great earth," with a direct connection to heaven (the sun), thus establishing from the very beginning a clear hierarchy with Japan at the apex of value. This is the interpretation set forth in *Sandaikō*.

The Way as recorded in the *Kojiki* and transmitted solely to Japan was believed to be something that all the nations of the world, the entire human race, should honor and practice. This variant of universalism would eventually be developed by late Tokugawa-period Kokugaku scholars into a notion that the international law conceptualized in the modern West was also in accordance with the Way of Japanese antiquity. In a treatise on international law published in 1867, Ōkuni Takamasa of the Tsuwano domain, a third-generation disciple of Norinaga by way of Hirata Atsutane, cites Western international law as expounded by Hugo Grotius as a "precursor" to "the true law of nations to be established by Japan," which would entail recognition by all nations that "the emperor of Japan is the universal sovereign of the world."[15]

With only limited knowledge of Western texts on geography and astronomy, Norinaga and Nakatsune had a much less detailed global awareness than Takamasa, who was writing at the end of the Tokugawa period, after the opening of Japan. Takamasa learned about international trade and international law from sources such as *Wanguo gongfa* (J. *Bankoku kōhō*), William Alexander Martin's translation into Chinese of Henry Wheaton's *Elements of International Law* (a reprint edition of which was published in 1865 by the Kaiseijō, the Tokugawa shogunate's official institute for translation and Western studies). Yet on the other hand, one might say that Norinaga's vision of an "Imperial Land" directly connected to the sun and looking out over (or down at) the entire earth was broad enough to support the intellectual leap made by Takamasa. At the foundation of this perspective was the cosmology pioneered by Kokugaku in which Japan occupied the summit of a globe floating in the midst of infinite space.

This perspective of Norinaga's—encompassing the entire globe against the background of an infinite universe—provided a unique vantage point for observing social conditions. The discourse on the epidemic of extravagance in *Hihon tamakushige* described in the last chapter is a good example of this.[16] He regards as inevitable that "when the realm has been at peace a long while," then "worldly goods and affairs . . . grow more lavish." And yet, "All things have their limits; what rises to a peak must inevitably decline; and there will come a time for a return to the way things were originally." We have already noted this awareness of cyclical patterns as a traditional way of thinking about economics based in Confucian thought—a line of reasoning suggesting that the age of extravagance should at some point "naturally" reach an end, giving way to an era of simplicity.

But Norinaga's discourse does not end with this. As he says, "The tendencies of the times [*jisei no ikioi*] are difficult to resist, something beyond the reach of human capacity." The conspicuous lavishness of the times was unprecedented in human history: "The degree to which extravagance has extended to the very lowest levels in our present world is unheard of at any time previously." The notion that this *ikioi*—the trend, or flow, or energy of the era—"would naturally shift in the direction of simplicity and frugality" was not to be expected, outside of a sudden "major change" such as a natural disaster. Therefore "those above" must do their utmost to carefully lead people in the direction of simplicity. Or so Norinaga argues.

Consciousness of the contemporary age as one of unprecedented economic development had cracked open the traditional perception of the world as governed by cyclical movement. Economic growth and the proliferation of luxury could not be tamed by leaving things to "nature"—the age seemed to be one of steadily accumulating progress. Therefore, the rulers must carefully examine the "*ikioi* of the times" and frame policies with reference to its current stage of development. Here, the "*ikioi* of the times" is conceived of as like a living being, pursuing its own path and pace of growth. This concept of *ikioi* likely overlapped with that of the Shinto "generative spirit," eternally at work since the beginning of the cosmos. Society as a whole possesses *ikioi*, a vital energy developing in a certain direction. Drawing on these concepts, Norinaga was able to develop a cosmic perspective, observing this process at work in society as if from the depths of space.

CHAPTER 9

Ikioi as the Motive Force of History

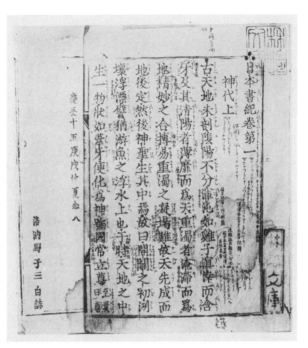

The opening passage of the *Nihon shoki,* from a 1610 edition printed
with wooden movable type, preserved in Jingū Bunko, the archives of
Ise Grand Shrine.

Maruyama Masao's "ancient strata"

In the previous chapter, we saw that Motoori Norinaga departed from the traditional understanding of history as a repeating cycle of order and disorder, articulating a perception that human history is driven forward in a particular direction by *ikioi*, a motive force embedded within society, and that the changes it inspires are irreversible. In a landmark essay, "Rekishi ishiki no 'kosō'" (The "Ancient Strata" of Historical Consciousness), originally published in 1972,[1] the historian Maruyama Masao (1914–96) points to the importance of this concept of *ikioi* in premodern Japanese historical thought.

"Underlying the diverse developments of historical consciousness leading to modern times there has been a persistent intellectual framework"—a framework that since ancient times has provided the *basso ostinato* of the history of Japanese thought. While the superficial forms of thought dominant in a particular era might change, beneath them all lay a common "conceptual pattern" or "intellectual framework" consistently sustained throughout Japanese history—this is what Maruyama believed, and describes with the term *kosō*, or "ancient strata." In contrast to the prewar ideologies of "national ethos" or "Japanese spirit," which proclaimed absolute loyalty to the emperor and reverence for harmony among the people as the main themes in the history of Japanese thought, Maruyama focuses not on these surface currents but on the "intellectual framework" submerged within them that sustained something quintessentially Japanese.

Maruyama's essay was published the year after he took early retirement from the University of Tokyo; he had been targeted during the student unrest then sweeping Japanese university campuses, and was stricken by serious illness. Because of this, some have interpreted the piece as an expression of disillusionment and defeat in the face of the student revolt. The interpretive essay was written for a volume devoted to historical thought, part of a twenty-volume collection of primary source material on the history of premodern Japanese thought published by Chikuma Shobō beginning in December 1968.[2] It is therefore reasonable to assume that the concept for Maruyama's essay had already begun to take shape before the outbreak of campus unrest.

As far back as 1956, Maruyama was speaking about the "primal thought patterns" of the Japanese people in his lectures on Japanese political thought at the University of Tokyo's faculty of law, revising this terminology to "archetypes" (*genkei*), beginning in 1963.[3] He would later refer to "ancient strata" and then *basso ostinato*. In any case, his discourse concerning "ancient strata" was not something suddenly arrived at in the late 1960s in the wake of the student revolt; it had already been gestating in Maruyama's thought for many years.

In this essay Maruyama argues that three key words—*naru* (becoming), *tsugi* (sequence), and *ikioi* (momentum), which could be linked in the phrase *tsugitsugi ni nariyuku ikioi* (roughly, "the momentum of continual becoming")—formed a "primal vocabulary" for grasping historical change that informed the narratives of Japanese mythology in the *Kojiki* and the *Nihon shoki*, and that this same "conceptual pattern" continued in the thought of later eras.

Maruyama's theory of "ancient strata" begins with the origins of heaven and earth, as expressed in the use of "naru" to describe the "birth" of gods; *ikioi*—vital energy or momentum—gave birth "one after another" to the beings and things of this world. This generative activity was understood to have value in and of itself, and was manifested in each era as an unshakeable reality, leading to a passive and conformist sensibility—one that has been passed down through the history of Japanese thought, even into modern times with the introduction of Social Darwinism, Marxism, and other Western ideas. Maruyama also remarks upon how difficult it was to cultivate in Japan a stance that sought to achieve, in the here and now, values that transcended historical reality.

But is Maruyama's theory convincing as a way of understanding the unique characteristics of Japanese myth as described in the *Kojiki*? Or is it really no more than an echo of the "Japanese mode of thought" proclaimed in works from prewar and wartime Japan celebrating the "Japanese spirit"?

Some of these works Maruyama mentions in his essay, such as Kihira Tadayoshi's *Naruhodo no tetsugaku* (The Philosophy of the Generative, 1941), and others that he does not cite were part of his personal library (now in the library of Tokyo Women's Christian University), such as Yamada Yoshio's *Kokugaku no hongi* (Fundamentals of National Learning, 1939) and *Hirata Atsutane* (1940). This criticism has certainly been leveled at Maruyama's theory of "ancient strata," but we will not debate it here.

Maruyama Masao (1914–96).

Of interest here is the source material Maruyama uses in this essay to point to the existence of these ancient strata of Japanese thought. To support an argument that attempts to tease out patterns of thought sustained since antiquity, he looks, as expected, to the mythology that marked the beginnings of Japanese intellectual history. The term "ancient strata" rested on a spatial metaphor, suggesting that atop an initial historical formation of "conceptual patterns," a succession of various layers of imported thought had accumulated through the ages. Given this manner of framing the discussion, an analysis of ancient Japanese mythology and the early classics was clearly required.

In pointing to the continuity of these "ancient strata" in later eras, Maruyama mentions classic texts such as the *Man'yōshū* poetry anthology, and historical chronicles such as *Ōkagami* and the Buddhist priest Jien's *Gukanshō*, but the majority of his references are to works by the Confucian and Kokugaku thinkers of the Tokugawa period. That he did not touch on any of the genres of modern thought was probably because, as mentioned above, his essay was written as an interpretive piece for *Nihon no shisō*, a multivolume collection of primary source materials on the history of premodern Japanese thought. Even so, why focus, as he did, on the Tokugawa period?

As noted in the previous chapter, it was Motoori Norinaga who saw, in the myths contained in the *Kojiki*, a process of creation in which the generative energy of *musubi* erupted in the infinite void to materialize in the earth. As Maruyama's essay relies heavily on Norinaga's *Kojikiden* for its interpretation of the ancient chronicle, naturally Maruyama's attention to the concept of *ikioi* overlaps significantly with Norinaga's worldview. This alone suggests how significantly the thought of the Tokugawa period colored Maruyama's understanding of the "ancient strata" of Japanese intellectual history.

Rai San'yō (1780–1832).

Also of importance to Maruyama was the work of Rai San'yō (1780–1832), the Tokugawa-period Confucian scholar and poet famous for his *Nihon gaishi* (An Unofficial History of Japan, completed in 1826). In section 3 of his essay, devoted to the concept of *ikioi*, Maruyama writes, "Consciousness of the irreversibility of history did not become established until the Edo period, when the phrase 'the overall momentum of the realm changed decisively' [*tenka no taisei ippen su*] began to see *concerted* use in historical writing in passages describing the period of transition from imperial rule to that of the military houses" (emphasis in the original). He then introduces Rai San'yō as the thinker responsible for this insight.

As an example of San'yō's perception of the irreversibility of history, Maruyama cites *Nihon seiki* (Chronicles of Japanese Government), a general chronological history of Japan that San'yō set his hand to after finishing *Nihon gaishi*; it was published posthumously, in 1845. A section of the tenth fascicle of this work is devoted to Emperor Go-Toba. Maruyama pays attention to San'yō's discussion in that section of the so-called Bunji Edict, issued in the eleventh month of the first year of the Bunji era (1185) by the retired emperor Go-Shirakawa, in which the imperial court acknowledged that Minamoto Yoritomo, who had established military control over the eastern provinces, had the right to appoint military governors (*shugo*) and estate stewards (*jitō*) to administer lands and estates throughout the country. Maruyama

quotes from San'yō's assessment of this edict, which was based on the popular views of his time as represented in the historical narrative *Genpei seisui ki*
(Record of the Rise and Fall of the Minamoto and the Taira), and differs from
the understanding of present-day historians.

According to San'yō, Yoritomo appealed to the court for permission to
appoint *shugo* and *jitō* "as a most urgent and pressing matter, and the court's
granting of this right was also compelled by the momentum of the times
(*jisei*)." In the *ritsuryō* system—the structure of centralized imperial rule as
originally established—local government was supposed to be controlled by
provincial governors (*kokushi*) dispatched from the imperial court. However,
the process of court appointments had become corrupted by greed and private interests, and it was common for members of the court aristocracy to
buy governorships and, without ever setting foot in the province they were
supposed to administer, enrich themselves even further on the taxes they
collected through deputies known as *mokudai*. Yoritomo, on the pretext of
reforming such abuses of local government, secured for himself the right to
appoint *shugo* as the de facto rulers of provinces throughout the realm.

San'yō saw the *shugo daimyō* of the Muromachi shogunate (1338–1573)
and the various daimyo of the Sengoku period (1467–1568) as essentially
inheriting this system. The system by which the imperial court had ruled the
country by appointing officials to administer the provinces had effectively
come to an end, and powerful warrior houses had divided the land among
themselves, ruling it by hereditary succession. San'yō described this shift as
one in which the imperial court "lost control of the realm, and in the end, the
momentum of the world [*tenka no ikioi*] had drastically changed, and there was
no turning back. How remarkable!"[4] San'yō is not upset by the imperial court's
loss of power and authority. Rather, he seems to be expressing the sense of
being present at a moment in which the protagonist in the historical narrative
has been replaced—a moment in which Yoritomo succeeded in "stealing the
realm" through a simple stratagem that starkly contrasted his skill and acumen
with the incompetence and ineffectuality of the imperial court. It appears that
Maruyama misread San'yō's "How remarkable!" as "How regrettable!" and
believed San'yō to be lamenting the loss of authority on the part of the court.

Rai San'yō and the *hōken/gunken* issue

From San'yō's perspective, the system of warrior rule implemented with the Bunji Edict had continued to his own era in the form of the hereditary rule of the Tokugawa shoguns and the daimyo. "In the end, the momentum of the world [*tenka no ikioi*] had drastically changed, and there was no turning back." Maruyama's understanding of this remark by San'yō as indicating "a consciousness of the irreversibility of history" is accurate, as far as it goes. But further investigation is probably needed to determine whether San'yō's use of the term *ikioi* is evidence that he perceived it as a force driving unidirectional historical change—something

Opening page of Rai San'yō's *Tsūgi* (Historiographical Reflections, posthumously published in 1840).

Maruyama does not explicitly spell out but which seems consonant with the overall structure of his argument concerning "ancient strata."

In this essay Maruyama also cites a text on political philosophy, *Tsūgi* (Historiographical Reflections), that San'yō was working on during the same period he was writing *Nihon seiki*.[5] The first fascicle of this work has a section entitled "Ikioi o ronzu" (On Momentum), which begins:

> The disintegration and unification of the realm, political order and disorder, and the security or insecurity of the state are all based on *ikioi*. *Ikioi* is a matter of things changing gradually and coming to completion gradually. It is not something that is within the power of human beings to control. However, when changes are beginning to take place and the change has not yet come to completion, it is within human power to act so as to direct the process of change, as long as one relies on that momentum. Even though it is not possible for human beings to go against the momentum of affairs, the momentum of affairs is also sometimes brought to completion by human beings.[6]

The momentum of the realm changes gradually and is not ultimately determined by human will. Yet if the ruler carefully observes these changes and implements policies skillfully aligned with the circumstances of this momentum, it is possible for human action to influence the workings of *ikioi*. In the latter part of "Ikioi o ronzu," San'yō compares the efforts of the ruler to influence the course of *ikioi* to those of a helmsman steering a riverboat downstream. Failing to steer, leaving everything to the momentum of the river, will eventually result in the boat capsizing when it encounters changes in the current. The ruler must instead adopt an attitude of "impartiality," carefully studying changes in *ikioi*, and making measured and deliberate responses after weighing the various possible options. He must possess the wisdom to judge the direction and speed of the changes in the *ikioi* and adjust and balance his policies accordingly.

In "Ikioi o ronzu," San'yō says of the Zhou dynasty in ancient China, "The Zhou relied upon the *ikioi* of the Xia and Shang dynasties, dividing the land among the various lords, controlling old and new alike. Thus did the Zhou rule the land." Here, *ikioi* seems to be used to speak of the institutional framework of the entire country. When the Zhou supplanted the Shang as rulers of the land, they inherited from the earlier royal dynasties a *hōken* (Ch. *fengjian*) system in which the king delegated regional and local government to members of a hereditary nobility. Yet the Zhou did not simply confirm all of the former Shang nobility and allow them to continue in place; they also created and enfeoffed new noble houses, and sought through this balance of power between old and new to secure the stability of their ruling order. Eventually, however, the royal house itself would decline, and some newly enfeoffed feudal lords grew powerful enough to secede and compete with one another for dominance.

San'yō's perspective on *ikioi* is clear from this example from the Zhou dynasty. The Zhou premised their rule on the *ikioi* of the preceding dynasties, but in devising an institutional order surrounding the new royal house, they created a system in which both new and old noble houses coexisted. But because the Zhou neglected to appropriately regulate the effects of this system, the power of newly enfeoffed lords metastasized to a degree that threatened to destabilize the entire political order. San'yō argues that the quintessential element in government was skill in reading *ikioi* as the ever-changing momentum of the country as a whole, and the judgment required to ensure that this momentum did not lead to a disintegration of the political order.

Thus, *ikioi*, as it appears in San'yō's discourse, primarily means the state or situation of the entire country as it confronted the ruler at any given time. As the metaphor of the river suggests, this sense of the word *ikioi* also overlapped with one that encompassed larger spans of time and changes so vast that no single ruler could hope to control them. But San'yō's emphasis is on the necessity for humanity to make the effort to read the currents of *ikioi* and attempt to navigate them in order to achieve stable government.

In "Hōken ryaku" (Strategies for Decentralization), the first fascicle of *Shinsaku* (New Policies, 1806), a text on government that might be seen as a precursor to *Tsūgi*, San'yō attempts to understand the transition from the *ritsuryō* system to the establishment of *shugo* and *jitō*. In his discussion of the *shugo* and *jitō*, San'yō borrowed the traditional Chinese classification system that distinguished between *gunken* (Ch. *junxian*, "prefecture and county") and *hōken*—or, between centralized and decentralized systems of government.[7] At the end of this section, San'yō draws a comparison between Japanese and Chinese history in terms of their development along this axis: "Japan went from governors to lords, while China went from lords to governors."

In other words, from the time of the sage kings Yao and Shun through to the Three Dynasties of Xia, Shang, and Zhou, a decentralized *hōken* system prevailed, in which noble houses ("lords") were invested with hereditary local power. This system was eventually replaced by one of centralized rule (*gunken*) in which the emperor dispatched scholar-bureaucrats to serve as regional officials ("governors"). In contrast, San'yō saw Japan as having instituted a *gunken* system during the reign of Emperor Tenji (r. 668–72), but that "momentum toward decentralization" (*hōken no ikioi*) began gradually with the Bunji

First page of the "Hōken saku" section in Rai San'yō's *Shinsaku* (New Policies, 1806).

Edict of 1185, matured during the Muromachi period (1333–1568), and reached its definitive form under Oda Nobunaga, Toyotomi Hideyoshi, and the rule of the Tokugawa shoguns.

San'yō is also critical of *Fengjian lun* (J. *Hōken ron*), a well-known text by the Tang-dynasty scholar Liu Zongyuan (773–819) that discusses the various merits and demerits of the *hōken* and *gunken* systems. According to Liu, under the *hōken* system the supervision of the Son of Heaven did not fully extend to the domains controlled by his vassal lords, and as a result, the local people might suffer from despotic rule. Liu states that this *hōken* system was the product of a momentum (Ch. *shi*; J. *ikioi*) that predated Yao and Shun and the Three Dynasties and "did not represent the will of the sages." He argues that to construct a public order in which all the people of the realm might live in peace, the *gunken* system was superior. But San'yō counters this by claiming that the historical circumstances of Japan were different. "In contrast, the momentum of our land actually had its origins in Ōe. I say that the *hōken* system was created by this momentum, and what controlled this momentum was people. We can only look back upon the nature of the stratagems they employed." The "Ōe" mentioned here is Ōe no Hiromoto, head of the Mandokoro, the administrative offices of the Kamakura shogunate, who proposed to Minamoto no Yoritomo the appointment of *shugo* and *jitō* given imperial approval in the Bunji Edict. San'yō is arguing that what is most important is not the conditions dictated by *ikioi* but the skill with which certain people are able to construct "stratagems" for "controlling *ikioi*."

Thus, when San'yō wrote in *Nihon seiki*, "In the end, the momentum of the world [*tenka no ikioi*] had drastically changed, and there was no turning back," these words were an affirmation of the Tokugawa shogunate as a continuation, with some modification over the years, of the Japanese *hōken* system that had been initiated with Ōe's proposals—though this argument placed no particular stress on the irreversibility of history. It was more or less conventional wisdom among contemporary intellectuals that a return to the emperor-centered *ritsuryō* system from the regime headed by the Tokugawa family was impossible. In 1672 the Confucian scholar Kumazawa Banzan wrote, "We really cannot return" to a "realm governed by court nobles" from a "realm governed by warriors."[8] Yamaga Sokō (1622–85), another innovative and influential Confucian scholar, offered a similar opinion, declaring in 1668, "The momentum of the noble families cannot be restored, even with the power of ten thousand oxen pulling backwards into the past."[9] For Rai San'yō, the continuity of Japan's *hōken* system for more than six hundred years, and the stability of rule achieved under the Tokugawa shoguns, was also one of the most admirable aspects of Japanese history.

San'yō's thinking represents a deviation from the traditional Confucian point of view, which held that an ideal world existed in Chinese antiquity, and which sought a return to the institutions, customs, and manners of that time. Liu Zongyuan had been forced to adopt the rather awkward explanation that at the dawn of human history the *hōken* system had existed as the result of a momentum predating the sages of antiquity, who then had no choice but to accept it. This blinkered perspective reflects how deeply entrenched was the belief in a golden age of Yao, Shun, and the Three Dynasties.

In contrast to this, San'yō's answer to the question of whether the Japanese state had begun, in the time of Emperor Jinmu, with a *gunken* or *hōken* system, was that the emperor himself had "aspired" to a *gunken* system but had been unable to fully realize it institutionally.[10] Since the historical processes in China and Japan were fundamentally different, there was no need to emulate ancient China. And even in Japan, it was not necessarily the case that an ideal social order had been established in remote antiquity.

It was an obvious premise for San'yō that the *hōken* system as administered by the current shogunate be given high marks. At the same time, his historical understanding led him, in his discussion of the Ōnin War (1467–77), to touch upon an "endemic ill" of the *hōken* system, which was the fact that when "those above" lost their authority, an anarchic struggle among the vassal lords could swiftly arise.[11] Moreover, like Liu Zongyuan, San'yō points to the merits of a *gunken* system as one that was easier on the common people.[12]

We have mentioned earlier that in Tokugawa-period thought there was a gradual shift in progress away from the historical perspective that sought a return to antiquity. Rai San'yō was studying and commenting upon history in the midst of this shift. Thus his works could later be read in a way that went beyond his own intentions, conceiving them in terms of a debate over the merits and demerits of the *gunken* and *hōken* systems and determining which would be better suited to Japan's future.

明治維新と郡縣思想

浅井 清著

巖南堂書店

Title page of Asai Kiyoshi's *Meiji ishin to gunken shisō* (The Meiji Revolution and the Concept of Centralization, 1939).

In his classic study of the *gunken/hōken* issue in Japanese intellectual history, Asai Kiyoshi relates the following fascinating episode.[13] In his later years, Itō Hirobumi, a principal architect of the Constitution of the Empire of Japan (1889), recalled the decision to abolish the domains and replace them with a centralized system of local government based on prefectures (*haihan chiken*) in the following terms:

> From an early age, I loved reading San'yō's *Nihon seiki*, and in addition to inspiring me with his imperial loyalism, it also left a deep impression on me that during the glory days of the imperial court what we would now call a *gunken* system had been practiced, and that in fact this system was the vital essence of imperial rule. Then a bit later, when I went to study in England, I saw for myself how the nations of Europe had prospered as a result of their implementation of the *gunken* system, and became increasingly convinced of the necessity of abolishing the *hōken* system.[14]

We can probably discount Itō's recollection of being impressed by San'yō's "imperial loyalism" as late-in-life faulty memory. But what rings true is the sense that the historical narrative of *Nihon seiki* prepared the way for thinking of a European-style "*gunken* system" as a potential replacement for the *hōken* system in Japan.

A history boom and memorializing the ancestors

Rai San'yō's most famous historical work is *Nihon gaishi*. In contrast to the rather dry chronicle style he employed in *Nihon seiki*, it treats the history of the rise and fall of the great families—Taira, Minamoto, Ashikaga, Oda, Toyotomi, and Tokugawa—in a narrative focused on figures and personalities. Like *Nihon seiki*, it was published after San'yō's death, around 1836–37, but it had gained popularity well before that, circulating in manuscript copies. Tokutomi Sohō's critical biography *Rai San'yō* (1926) describes how popular the book became:

> Even before it was published, *Nihon gaishi* was already highly regarded among intellectuals throughout the land, and was soon being praised in every quarter. It is clear from [San'yō's] own correspondence that he sent copies to [Neo-Confucian scholar and calligrapher Shinozaki] Shōchiku, [the poet] Ono [Rekiō] of Nagao in Bitchū, and a variety of others, including even Ōshio Heihachirō [leader of an 1837 rebellion]. Copies were also distributed to various daimyo houses: the Sakai family of Himeji, the Ii of Hikone, the Uesugi of Yonezawa, and the Asano of Aki, rulers of [San'yō's] home domain. Even the likes of Kyokutei Bakin [the famous novelist], a contemporary, but one born earlier and who lived longer than San'yō, made copies for their own use. So from this it goes without saying that even prior to its publication this book had already spread widely throughout the country.[15]

Why did *Nihon gaishi* achieve such popularity? One reason was the scarcity at the time of easily readable general histories of Japan. But there was more to it than this. Shimada Hideaki has written an interesting article pointing to other characteristics of this work that attracted a wide readership.[16]

According to Shimada, San'yō intentionally used two quite different styles for *Nihon gaishi* and *Nihon seiki*: the former was framed as a historical panegyric (*shisan*) offering a standard evaluation of historical figures; the latter, a strictly historiographic treatise (*shiron*) attempting to deliver an original argument by its author. But both texts significantly changed the emphasis of their narratives from that of the traditional Confucian histories, whose stern judgments regarding good and evil sought to demonstrate to readers that the former would be rewarded and the latter punished.

San'yō's historical works, particularly *Nihon gaishi*, eschewed such moral orientation, presenting vivid portrayals of the psychology and personalities of figures confronting the *ikioi* of a particular historical moment, and discussing the merits of their policies. Readers are encouraged to project their own dreams of what it would be like to participate in politics at the level of these heroes of the past, and indeed San'yō himself takes this stance. His discourse in *Shinsaku* entitled "Strategies for Decentralization," mentioned earlier, concludes with the following passage: "I have written of strategies for decentralization. I regret that I cannot show Liu [Zongyuan] the present in which we live, just as I regret that I cannot arouse Ōe [no Hiromoto] to discourse with me of this scheme."

From Rai San'yō's *Nihon gaishi* (An Unofficial History of Japan, completed in 1826).

San'yō is saying that he would have liked to be able to show Liu Zongyuan the stability and order achieved by the *hōken* system in nineteenth-century Japan, and revive Ōe no Hiromoto to discuss with him effective strategies for maintaining it—in his imagination living alongside these heroes of the past and taking part in their great achievements. For San'yō and his readers, this is the appeal of history. As Shimada observes, the popularity of San'yō's works during this era encouraged a number of other literary figures to turn their hands to this type of writing, producing a flood of historical discourses.

This sudden interest in history was rooted in a consciousness that produced another widespread social phenomenon of that era, one that became the subject of a monograph by the historian Haga Shōji.[17] Haga shows that in the nineteenth century, prominent samurai houses and even rural notables put considerable effort into memorializing their ancestors and individuals who had made significant contributions to local communities. For example, at the beginning of the Bunsei era (1818–31), Satomi Yoshitake, senior councillor of the Manabe family and daimyo of Sabae, donated a memorial stele to Enmyōji, a Buddhist temple in Awa province, where his ancestral fief had been located, praising his family's founder, Tadayoshi, and the continuity of the family.

Memorializing ancestors in this way—identifying with them and seeking to recreate their achievements by carrying on the family business—might be seen as a product of the same mentality that drove the history boom and its encouragement of identification with heroes of the past. Two centuries of peace under Tokugawa rule seems to have turned people's attention to the continuity of their own families and houses. Of course, as Yamamuro Kyōko has pointed out in her 2015 empirical study of merchant life in Edo, continuity over a century or more in the same trade or profession was largely restricted to the high-ranking warrior houses or great merchant families.[18] However, this must have contributed to a further strengthening of the desire to commemorate one's ancestors for the sake of family continuity. And this value system likely spread, at least to a certain extent, even among the classes of people not fortunate enough to expect their houses to endure for long.

Interestingly, during the same period that the practice of memorializing ancestors became widespread and people developed an imaginative identification with the heroes of the past through reading historical works, a theory emerged that, if bloodlines were traced back far enough, all Japanese families and houses were related to one another. In a recent study of Shinto and Kokugaku in early modern Japan, Maeda Tsutomu cites a 1795 work by the Shinto scholar Matsumoto Rokuroku that makes the following argument in a criticism of adherents of the Jōdo Shinshū (True Pure Land) sect of Buddhism:

> They do not realize that everyone born in Japan is a member of the same ancestral house, and so not respect the various gods that are ancestors of each one of us, nor do they think of their majesties, our present emperor and shogun, as the heads of the main houses that have clearly continued the bloodlines from these ancestors of us all.[19]

This perception of all Japanese families sharing the same hereditary origins as the emperors and shoguns was at the time probably limited to Shinto adherents such as Matsumoto. But a renewed interest in family continuity and identification with ancestors seems to have coalesced in the idea of the nation as a type of family. This notion of all Japanese being "descendants of the gods" (*mitane*), belonging to the same bloodline, was taken up by the Kokugaku scholar Hirata Atsutane (1776–1843) and passed on by his disciples as a teaching of the Hirata school.

Shifts in the momentum of history

The Kokugaku scholar Date Chihiro (1802–77), who was also a highly placed samurai official in the Kii domain, which was ruled by a major branch of the Tokugawa house, is famous for a unique historical work, *Taisei santen kō* (A Study of Three Changes in the Momentum of History), written in 1848. The collection of historical writing edited by Maruyama Masao mentioned above reprints the complete text of this work, along with interpretive notes and a translation into modern Japanese.[20] It was no doubt selected as a text that brilliantly portrayed something akin to Maruyama's "ancient strata" in the form of "successively evolving *ikioi*" (*tsugitsugi ni nari-yuku ikioi*).

Date Chihiro studied with Motoori Norinaga's adopted son Ōhira, and became known for his scholarship in the fields of classical poetry and studies of court ceremony and etiquette. At the same time, he enjoyed the patronage of Tokugawa Harutomi, then daimyo of Kii, and rose with unusual swiftness through the ranks of the domain's retainers. He demonstrated particular skill when placed in charge of reforming the domain's finances. *Taisei santen kō* was written for his own reference while he was serving in the post of *ōban-gashira* (captain of the great guards). After the Meiji Revolution, his adoptive heir (by marriage) Date Muneoki, and his sixth son, Mutsu Munemitsu (who would later serve as foreign minister at the time of the First Sino-Japanese War of 1894–95), urged him to make the work public, and it was eventually published in 1873.[21]

The foreword written for this occasion by Fukuba Bisei (1831–1907), a Kokugaku scholar of the Tsuwano school (the followers of Ōkuni Takamasa), states, "To deal with current affairs requires understanding the overall momentum of the realm [*tenka no taisei*]. And to understand this momentum, it is necessary to understand historical developments since ancient times." In the body of the work, Chihiro himself draws attention, in speaking of this historical momentum, to the role of institutions (*seido*; he also uses the term *daiseido*, "great institutions"), which rulers used to organize their subordinates and govern the people. In the following passage, Chihiro argues that there were three institutional frameworks that permit Japanese history to be divided into three major periods: "In earliest times, the realm was ruled through the clans [*kabane*]; in the middle ages, offices of the court [*tsukasa*] were used to govern; and in later times, the

Title page of Date Chihiro's *Taisei santen kō* (A Study of Three Changes in the Momentum of History, 1848).

'names' [*na*] were used to bring order to the realm."

In other words, from the time of the founding emperor Jinmu, the institutions of the earliest Japanese state centered on the *kabane*, powerful clans under the control of the emperor who granted them hereditary "domains and posts" that combined a local or regional place name with a title—Totori (Tottori) no Miyatsuko (governor of Totori), for example. The place name with a title was passed down from the clan chieftain as a hereditary family name. However, from the time of Prince Shōtoku through the reign of Emperor Tenmu (the latter half of the seventh century), there was a major transition to institutions based on "offices" (*tsukasa*) within the imperial court. With the implementation of the *ritsuryō* system modeled on the government of Tang-dynasty China, a court bureaucracy was created, with positions awarded to at least some degree on the basis of individual merit, and officials dispatched from the imperial capital to serve as provincial and local governors. Eventually, times changed, and in turn this system was supplanted by the era of "names" ushered in by the Bunji Edict (1185) and the appointment of *shugo* and *jitō* by the Kamakura shogunate. This was an institutional system in which local rule was hereditary, and concentrated in the hands of "warrior houses" headed by daimyo (literally, "great names") and minor lords (*shōmyō*, or "lesser names")—a state of affairs, Chihiro writes, that continued to the present "era of peace and security."

It should be apparent that the eras of "offices" and "names" in Chihiro's terminology correspond exactly to what Rai San'yō describes in *Shinsaku* and *Nihon seiki* in terms of the transition from centralized (*gunken*) to decentralized (*hōken*) systems. Moreover, it was fairly common in the Tokugawa period to conceive of the period from Emperor Jinmu to before the implementation of the *ritsuryō* state as an example of the *hōken* system, as Yamagata Bantō does in his discussion of institutions in fascicle 5 of *Yume no shiro*. Before he became a Kokugaku scholar, Date Chihiro studied the Chinese canon, probably from a Neo-Confucian perspective. His periodization of "clans," "offices," and "names" was, in a sense, merely a Kokugaku-style rephrasing of the *hōken/gunken/hōken* succession that contemporary Confucians were employing in their discussions of Japanese history.

Additionally, with regard to the shift from "clans" to "offices," Chihiro praises the "great courage and determination" displayed by Prince Shōtoku and his associates in resolutely pursuing their reform program in the face of the "momentum of the times" (*jisei no ikioi*), which appeared to be favoring the power of the Soga clan. This way of framing the situation is exactly like that employed by Rai San'yō. It also probably reflects Chihiro's personal experience in undertaking the fiscal reform of the Kii domain.

But it is also important to note that he did not see the transition from "offices" to "names" as some sort of return to the "clan" system that had prevailed before. No doubt this is because in the era of "names" it was the "warrior houses" that were responsible for local government, and they did not receive family names from the emperor based on their domains or official positions. But even more importantly, it is because he saw history as unidirectional, irreversible, and moved by great forces that are ultimately beyond the capacity of individuals to predict or control. Chihiro wrote of the thinking behind the imperial court's implementation of the system of "officials" as follows:

Giving serious consideration to the changing momentum of the times, whether or not it is an inherent principle of the cosmos, or the will of the gods, it is something beyond our humble abilities to calculate; ultimately, it is something neither human wisdom nor human power can reach. Yet with the passage of five hundred years or so, certain fortunes will arise spontaneously in the course of such changes, and at such times exceptional individuals will appear, riding the momentum of fate to achieve great things.

No doubt this recalls Motoori Norinaga's perception of "the momentum of the times" (*jisei no ikioi*) discussed in the preceding chapter. Chihiro thought that changes in the momentum of the times were an expression of the energy of society as a whole and therefore difficult for people to completely predict or control. Yet it was possible to be aware of the nature of these changes and to construct institutions that accorded with new social realities, as, for example, the imperial house demonstrated when it established the institutions of the *kabane* period. Moreover, Chihiro saw such changes in the momentum of the times as overlapping with economic development.

During the generations of Emperor Jinmu's successors, the country developed greatly [*ōi ni hirake*], the people flourished, and soon this momentum was such that money became a necessity. Nor was money alone sufficient; without a teaching, it was difficult for the emperor to rule. With the establishment of relations with the continent, the Confucian and Buddhist teachings came to our country. That these were reverently adopted by our sovereigns was also inevitable, and we must be grateful for this as the sacred intent of the deities.

The transition to the system of "offices" was the result of a perception of the momentum of society arising out of the development of the economy and the refinement of the culture. Chihiro does not comment on the social developments influencing the transition from "officials" to "names." However, the adoption of the institutions of the *ritsuryō* state was led by the imperial court, whereas Chihiro writes that "the transition from 'offices' to 'names' arose from below and gradually gained strength, gaining an irresistible momentum." This probably refers specifically to the spontaneous phenomenon of the growth of the samurai class, but underlying this he likely saw economic development (for which he uses the term *hirake*) operating as a force at work regardless of the era.

An essay by the intellectual historian Watanabe Hiroshi points out that use of the word *hirake* (noun) or *hirakeru* (verb) was common in the works of Tokugawa scholars and literary figures.[22] Frequently it was used in a positive sense, as Motoori Norinaga and Kaiho Seiryō had done, to connote the proliferation of new goods and material affluence, accompanied by a greater refinement of culture and the arts and sciences. Date Chihiro took a similar perception and developed it into the image of a momentum (*ikioi*) that had been consistently at work in the background of history, from ancient times to the present.

Thus, if the historical perspective of other late Tokugawa-period intellectuals resembled that seen in *Taisei santenkō*, then they were only a small step away from the perspective offered in the following:

When heaven and earth first gave birth to the human race, this creation endowed humanity with a spirit. As this spirit grew, it developed intelligence; at first only the slenderest of shoots, but becoming more refined with the passage of time. As this intelligence grew, its discoveries became more extensive; encountering a variety of situations and things, it became able to reflect on its past and future course. With concerted, painstaking effort and difficulty, over the centuries and millennia, great results were achieved, and we have arrived at the present, in which our realm has been transformed and a civilized world has come into being.

This passage, written in classical Chinese by Mitsukuri Genpo (1799–1863), a renowned scholar of Western Learning, is from a preface to *Taisei daiji saku*, a history of the Western nations compiled from his own translations of a variety of Western sources.[23] Interestingly, Mitsukuri began writing this book in 1848, the same year Date Chihiro was writing *Taisei santen kō*.

Of course the argument that Genpo develops is based on what he had learned from his reading of Western histories of civilization. But that did not mean it was completely foreign to other intellectuals of his day who had not been engaged in Western studies. The image of progress toward "civilization" simply gave clear expression and an indication of future prospects to their own immediate experiences of a changing world, and a view of history they had embraced in response.

CHAPTER 10

A Farewell to the *Hōken* System

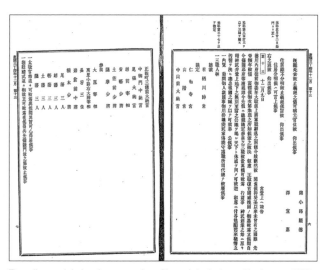

The edict proclaiming the restoration of imperial rule, issued in January 1868.

The reorganization of government

The prototype of the current system of regional and local government in Japan was established in 1871 (Meiji 4) with the abolition of the domains and the establishment of prefectures (*haihan chiken*). The edict announcing the restoration of imperial rule, issued in January 1868, eliminated the shogunate and established a new governmental organization with the emperor at its apex. Initially, the institutions of local government were divided into three levels: *fu* (major cities), *han* (domains), and *ken* (prefectures). Landholdings expropriated from the Tokugawa house and the daimyo that had supported it in the Boshin Civil War of 1868–69 (making them "enemies of the imperial court") were organized into *fu* and *ken* and administered by governors and other officials appointed by the new central government. But the rest of the domains were left in the hands of the daimyo houses that had traditionally ruled them. (The use of the word *han* to designate the daimyo domains was an informal one, popularized by Confucian scholars in the late Tokugawa period; its first official use was in the text of the restoration edict.) To this extent, the traditional decentralized *hōken* (feudal) system was permitted to live on, with the daimyo serving as direct vassals of the emperor, while at the same time a centralized *gunken* system was introduced in the newly created *fu* and *ken*. One might call the arrangement a hybrid *hōken/gunken* system.

As a result, aside from the areas under direct administrative control of the new government, a system permitting continuity of rule by the daimyo temporarily persisted. In July 1869, *hanseki hōkan* was implemented: the daimyo surrendered their domain registers to the new government, which in turn appointed them as governors of their old domains (but made the post non-hereditary). This enabled a de facto continuity of daimyo rule within the *han*, and the maintenance of lord-vassal relations between the daimyo and his retainers. Thus, until the *haihan chiken* order of August 29, 1871, which officially abolished the entire hereditary organization of the daimyo houses and their networks of vassals, rule under the *hōken* system continued.

An assessment of the institutional reforms just described—the establishment of the *fu-han-ken* system of regional and local government, the return of domain registers, followed by the abolition of the domains and creation of a nationwide prefectural system (*haihan chiken*)—would suggest a con-

The ceremony proclaiming the abolition of the domains and creation of prefectures. Mural by Kobori Tomoto in the Meiji Memorial Picture Gallery, Tokyo.

sistent intent on the part of the new government to rapidly centralize political power and establish a solid military and financial foundation for itself. Seen from a present-day perspective, the process of the Meiji Revolution appears to have been somewhat inevitable. It is easy to get the impression that the restoration of imperial rule and the abolition of the domains and establishment of a centralized prefectural system were part of a unified reform. Consequently it is often stressed that Japan's present prefectural system is a legacy of the Meiji era, a system that was determined at the very beginning of modern Japan.

The majority of the 271 daimyo houses nationwide favored a system in which they maintained their hereditary authority and participated in a policymaking assembly within the new government. But the new government, backed by the military power of the domains of Satsuma and Chōshū, pushed ahead with *haihan chiken* and the establishment of a *gunken* system. In a recent book on *haihan chiken*, the historian Katsuta Masaharu writes that it was not until August 19, 1871 that the abolition of the domains began to be openly debated in government circles.[1] If young bureaucrats such as

Yamagata Aritomo, Inoue Kaoru, and Saigō Takamori had not united to spearhead this effort, the *hōken* and *gunken* systems would likely have coexisted for a longer period. For contemporaries, the restoration of imperial rule and the aboltion of the domains in favor of a centralized government were not necessarily linked; the future of the national polity seemed open to a variety of options. As mentioned in chapter 2, Fukuzawa Yukichi's remarks on "antipathy to hereditary power" clearly express this. In the course of his discussion on how the degree of development of human intelligence determines the progress of civilization in chapter 5 of *Bunmeiron no gairyaku* (Outline of a Theory of Civilization), Fukuzawa makes the following observation:

> Only recently we Japanese saw the feudal *han* abolished and prefectures established. The nobles and samurai lost their political powers and their feudal stipends. Why did they not dare to complain about it? Some people maintain that the Imperial Restoration was due to the influence of the Imperial House and that the setting up of prefectures in place of the *han* system was the result of decisive steps by those in government. These are mere conjectures, by men who know nothing about the momentum of the times.[2]

It is worth noting that here again we see the "momentum of the times" (*jisei*) perceived as representing irreversible change, discussed in the previous chapter as *ikioi*, or the momentum of history. For Fukuzawa, social change could not be controlled by a handful of people in positions of power; it was a product of this vast temporal force. But *jisei* was not some abstract notion of fate or fortune; rather, it drew its substance from the level of "intellect and morality" (*chitoku*) exhibited by society as a whole. Viewed as individuals, the people of a particular era would no doubt possess a disparate range of intellect and morality. But the aggregate intellect and morality of society as a whole steadily progresses, albeit more rapidly at some times than others, and this progressive change is the reality of *ikioi*, the momentum of history.

By dividing the changes taking place in the early Meiji period into two phases—the restoration of imperial rule, followed by the abolition of domains and creation of prefectures—Fukuzawa is able to attack the conventional wisdom that it was the influence of the imperial house and "decisive steps by those in government" that brought about these reforms. At the same time, he expresses his opposition to the idea that it was the anti-foreign movement (*jōiron*) that had toppled the shogunate. If the influence of the imperial house was so strong, and the reverence of the people for the emperor so great, then more than two centuries of rule by the Tokugawa shogunate would have been impossible. And since the new government immediately implemented policies oriented toward continuing the opening of the country, clearly the intention of "expelling the barbarians" was not what had overthrown the shogunate. If the slogan "revere the emperor and expel the barbarians" (*sonnō jōi*) had been the motivation behind the change in regime, then it would have been highly unlikely that the attendant reforms would have gone beyond restoring imperial rule to initiate the radical dissolution of the hereditary status system of the daimyo and samurai.

In Tokugawa society, despotism based on lineage was a constant. Even "intellect and morality" were of no avail to those without hereditary status. "But," Fukuzawa observes, "the creative powers of the human intellect are irrepressible." As time went on, people became disenchanted with the hereditary system, and "antipathy to lineage" grew. Finally, at the end of the Tokugawa period, prompted by "the ideas of Western civilization" but at the same time spurred on by an anti-foreign fervor, people's disenchantment exploded, which resulted in the imperial restoration. In large part motivated by antipathy toward the hereditary class system, reform did not end with a simple shift of power from the shogun in Edo to the emperor in Kyoto; it proceeded more or less immediately to the abolition of the domains and the creation of a new centralized government, which brought about the dissolution of the samurai class itself.

Fuzukawa's belief that intellectual and moral progress in the general populace was the force driving history derived from, as we saw in chapter 3, the works of European historians, notably François Guizot's *History of Civilization in Europe* (1828) and Henry Thomas Buckle's *History of Civilization in England* (1857–61). While these works portray the consistent progress of human civilization leading to an enhancement of the material conditions of life, they also argue that "moral development" (Guizot) and "intellect and morality" (Buckle) were equally important. Tokugawa-period intellectuals straining under the strictures of the hereditary class system probably found such ways of thinking about history to be relevant to their situation.

Henry Thomas Buckle (1821–1862).

The fact that it took three years to move from the restoration of imperial rule to *haihan chiken* is evidence that the transition from *hōken* to *gunken* systems had not been thought through, nor was it accepted without protest. Even for Fukuzawa, who saw both antipathy to the *hōken* system and support for it from the hereditary lineages as central to the momentum that brought about the restoration of imperial rule, the rapid implementation of *haihan chiken* must have come as an unexpected development.

Why did the daimyo not resist the shift to a completely centralized system of state power? Even among the *sonnō jōi* activists at the end of the Tokugawa period, there were those who argued for the necessity of maintaining the feudal system after the overthrow of the shogunate. Maki Yasuomi (1813–1864, also known by his court title, Izumi no Kami)—a Shinto priest in the service of the Kurume domain who joined with activists from Chōshū to mount the unsuccessful rebellion known as the Kinmon Incident (Kinmon no hen) in 1864—wrote the following passage in a discourse on politics, *Keii gusetsu* (My Opinions on Recent Events), presented to the anti-foreign court noble Nonomiya Sadaisa in 1861:

In antiquity there was a *hōken* system, in the middle ages this became the *gunken* system, and then again the *hōken* system that has persisted for nearly a millennium to the present day. Our country stands alone amidst the seas, and even if threatened from all sides, the various lords could be relied upon to defend their own domains; a system whose excellence remains unchanged for generations. Is it not the will of heaven that things should naturally be this way? Even the emperor could not change that situation, though the imperial court might prefer a *gunken* system. But there were also naturally remaining customs from the earlier *hōken* system, such as the use of hereditary precedent to determine positions held by noble families. In any event, the topography of our realm and the sentiments of its people make the *hōken* system the norm. To determine ranks [among daimyo] it would be best to create a graded system of five ranks of nobility.[3]

Here, too, we detect a perspective on Japanese history that sees it as passing through three distinct phases: from *hōken* to *gunken* and then back to *hōken*. Maki's contention that it was natural to entrust the various daimyo with rule over their domains because the country as a whole was protected by the sea probably reflects the sense of crisis with regard to coastal defenses that arose toward the end of the Tokugawa period. Because the topography of Japan lent itself naturally to a *hōken* system, even when the imperial court instituted the centralized *ritsuryō* state and adopted the *gunken* model, its institutions were inevitably intermingled with "remaining customs" from the *hōken* system, such as inherited court rank and office among noble families. Maki believed that during the long period of rule by the warrior houses the *hōken* system once again became the norm, so even if the shogunate were to be eliminated and replaced with a government centered on the imperial court,

it would be necessary to allow the daimyo to continue to hold power within a decentralized political structure—though Maki was proposing to reorganize them into a new system of five ranks of nobility.

This suggests that, for people who had lived during the long era of peace guaranteed by the *hōken* system, even after a restoration of imperial rule it would seem quite natural for the emperor to delegate regional and local govern-

Maki Yasuomi (1813–64).

ment to the daimyo and to continue to make their authority hereditary. The daimyo did not resist the abolition of the domains that took place in the fourth year of Meiji (1871), owing in part to fear of the military strength of the Satsuma-Chōshū coalition protecting the new government. The fiscal crisis that many of the daimyo houses were facing at the time was another contributing factor. Finally, the transformation in consciousness that was taking place regarding the nature of the national polity supported these changes.

"The emperor's land and subjects" and the Mito School

In the tenth month of the first year of Meiji (November 1868)—as the Boshin Civil War was drawing to a close and military support for the former shogunate had dwindled to a band of Tokugawa loyalists under the command of Enomoto Takeaki that had occupied part of what is now Hokkaido, the northernmost island—the new government promulgated an official message proclaiming the legitimacy of "the imperial restoration" (ōsei isshin) to the people of Kyoto, and contemplated its wider distribution nationwide in the coming year. In it, we find the following statement: "We owe a vast and limitless debt of gratitude to the Imperial Land [gokokuon]. Reflect well upon this. It was founded by descendants of the gods, and thus all things in this land, without exception, belong to the emperor."[4]

Not only the land, but everything in Japan belongs to the emperor—the "son of heaven." All living beings drink the emperor's water and feed themselves with what grows upon the emperor's land. In gratitude for the grace thus bestowed upon them for many generations, the people must obey the emperor's edicts and work to "fulfill their duties to him." In other words, institutional arrangements such as centralized or decentralized systems aside, all of Japan belongs to the emperor, and the people owe their existence to his benevolence. This concept is forcefully articulated in Shinron (New Theses, 1825) by Aizawa Seishisai (1782–1863), a treatise read enthusiastically by sonnō jōi activists such as Maki Yasuomi and Yoshida Shōin. Shinron is a comprehensive set of policy proposals directed toward the daimyo of the Mito domain and the Tokugawa shogunate concerning how to deal with not only the fiscal crisis in Mito and a perceived decline in the morale and morals of both the samurai and commoner population in the country but also the foreign policy crisis brought on by the increasingly frequent appearance of British and Russian vessels in Japanese waters. *Shinron* was not officially published until 1857, but it circulated in manuscript copies long before that and was widely read throughout the country.[5]

Aizawa Seishisai (1782–1863).

The first three chapters of *Shinron* (after a brief preface) are entitled "Kokutai" (meaning the national polity). The "heavenly ancestress," the sun goddess Amaterasu Ōmikami, decreed that her divine descendants should "carry out the divine tasks hitherto accomplished naturally through the operations of heaven"— that is, the work of nourishing and guiding the people. Thus, the position of emperor could not be ceded to any other lineage: "the distinction between ruler and subject was established, and the greatest virtue of all, loyalty of subject for ruler, was made manifest." Originally the word *kokutai* signified the general state or condition of any country, but here Seishisai uses it to refer specifically to the unique polity of the Japanese nation. This concept of *kokutai*, along with the "unity of loyalty and filial piety" preached by Seishisai, Fujita Tōko, and other members of the Mito School, would later be inherited by Meiji-era moral and patriotic education. According to the Mito School, however, the ultimate authority for governing the realm had been delegated by the emperors to the Tokugawa shogunate. In this sense, their writings were intended as a renewed legitimation of a political order centered upon the shogun.

It is unsurprising that Seishisai, in the first chapter of *Shinron*, expresses an understanding of Japanese history that sees it as beginning with a *hōken* system in the reign of Emperor Jinmu, shifting to a *gunken* system with the introduction of *ritsuryō* by Emperor Tenji, and then returning to a *hōken* system once again from the Kamakura period onward. Under the *gunken* system, Seishisai explains that "in the entire realm there is no land that is not imperial land [*ōdo*] nor a single person who is not an imperial subject [*ōshin*], and all under heaven enjoy orderly government." This conception of imperial land and imperial subjects would be echoed in the proclamation of the imperial restoration to the people of Kyoto in the first year of Meiji, and to the whole nation in the following year.

Title page of Aizawa Seishisai's *Shinron.*

Yet according to Seishisai, even under the *hōken* system of Emperor Jinmu's time, his enfeoffment of the local rulers known as *kuni no miyatsuko* "brought all the people of the land under the influence of the imperial court, and the entire realm enjoyed orderly government." Morever, under the later *hōken* rule of the military houses, particularly that instituted by Tokugawa Ieyasu, "Government of all the land and people of the realm was unified, with all revering the benevolence of the imperial court and submitting to the virtue of the shogunate." In short, Japan's land and its people were "imperial land and imperial subjects," and this made Japan's national polity—its *kokutai*—unique. *Hōken* versus *gunken* was merely an institutional selection that did not affect *kokutai* as a fundamental truth. The emphasis on the concept of "imperial land and imperial subjects" in the 1868 proclamation to the people of Kyoto, for example, was not necessarily directly linked to advocacy for a *gunken* system.

The logic of Seishisai's "imperial land and imperial subjects" relates to the importance accorded by the Kyoto proclamation to *gokokuon*—the debt of gratitude owed to the imperial land. As noted earlier, it was the duty of the emperors—their *tenshoku*, or divinely appointed task—to "carry out the divine tasks hitherto accomplished naturally through the operations of heaven" and carefully nurture and educate the people. It was also essential to cultivate among the people the proper feelings of gratitude for this benevolence. A 2015 article by Jiang Jianwei (J. Shō Ken'i) points to the significance of the idea of "the people's livelihoods" (*minmei*) in Seishisai's concept of *kokutai*.[6]

In Seishisai's thought, the entire land and people of Japan were inherently subject to the rule of the emperors; institutional matters such as the choice between *hōken* or *gunken* systems were secondary. But this did not mean that the sovereign could arbitrarily abuse the people, or exploit their labor solely for the benefit of the imperial house. Far from it: the ruler was under a heavy moral obligation to ensure the people's livelihoods and welfare.

The last of the three chapters of *Shinron* dealing with *kokutai* begins with the following passage: "Because Amaterasu attached great importance to Her people's livelihoods, She provided them with the source of life—food and clothing. The rice and silk that now abound in the realm all originate from Her august rice field and loom; we, Her subjects, continue to enjoy her blessings even today."[7]

In the section of the *Nihon shoki* treating the Age of the Gods, Amaterasu Ōmikami is said to have cultivated two divine rice fields and woven her own vestments from silk. Seishisai uses this passage as the basis for asserting that one of the most important commands the "heavenly ancestress" had given to the successive generations of emperors was for them to ensure that the people of the land were adequately provided with food and clothing.

Jiang Jianwei's research suggests that the phrase employed by Seishisai concerning the importance of the people's livelihoods and welfare signified more than simply attending to their material well-being. In another work, *Dokusho nissatsu* (A Reading Diary, 1851), Seishisai writes, "Heaven and the people are inseparable," elaborating on this as follows: "When the people obey, this is due to the mandate [of heaven]. When they disobey, this means the mandate has been withdrawn." The mandate of heaven, passed down from the "heavenly ancestress," expresses itself in the will of the people. In a typically Confucian notion of government for the people, if the people willingly follow the ruler, this is a sign that he holds the mandate of heaven, which legitimizes his rule. On the other hand, if the people turn their backs on him, this is evidence that he has lost the mandate.

Of course Seishisai does not, like Mencius, use this idea to legitimize a revolutionary change of dynasty. In Japan it was unthinkable that the emperor might be replaced by someone from another lineage, as this would violate the sacred vow of the "heavenly ancestress" Amaterasu Ōmikami. But this was not to say that one could achieve rule in accordance with her will without making any special effort. The Japanese emperor and those who governed as his ministers and officials were charged with an important duty and responsibility: to sensitively read and give due consideration to popular sentiment as they worked to support the lives of the people. When Seishisai urges that serious attention be paid to the people's livelihoods, this idea also includes respect for the will of the people. Before the choice of *gunken* or *hōken* systems even arises, this duty—essential to the purpose of government—must be engaged. For those involved in governing, this was the practical implication of the declaration that all of the land and its people were "imperial land and imperial subjects."

The policies Seishisai outlines for caring for the people's livelihoods in the context of current conditions indicate a keen awareness of the realities of the development of the market economy in the Tokugawa period. In the third chapter of *Shinron*, Seishisai complains that "cunning, tight-fisted profit-mongers manipulate the great lords of the land like so many puppets-on-a-string. Clearly the realm's wealth has fallen into the merchants' clutches."[8]

Despite rising commodity prices fueled by economic development, daimyo and samurai were selling such large quantities of tax rice to supplement domain finances that the price of rice remained low. This led to the impoverishment of the daimyo and samurai, who began to resort to loans from the great merchants to support themselves, and also brought misery to the peasants. To Seishisai it seemed clear that only the urban merchants were being enriched.

Suffering from a fiscal crisis, the Mito domain raised the annual rice tax, which, combined with poor harvests, touched off frequent peasant unrest. On the other hand, many farming villages in the domain had developed sidelines in various types of commodity production, such as firewood and charcoal, so this image of city people being the only ones prospering may come from an overemphasis on the suffering of the peasantry encouraged, as in the case of Ogyū Sorai, by a perspective on society shaped by traditional Confucian values. In any case, the policy Seishisai proposes for ensuring the people's livelihoods in this chapter of *Shinron* is a reactionary one: to keep rice off the commodity market as much as possible so that daimyo, samurai, and peasants could stockpile it.

If, by this plan, the living conditions of the peasants could be improved, then they would have the opportunity to cultivate a stable and harmonious mentality (what Mencius calls *hengxin*, a "fixed" or "constant" heart). Only then might they "be induced to stand in awesome veneration of Amaterasu's will, bring forth the richest possible harvests that the soil will yield, and partake of Amaterasu's gifts, derived as they are from the bounties of Heaven and Earth."[9] In other words, Seishisai expects the populace to be grateful for the debt they owed to rulers modeling themselves on the "heavenly ancestress," and in worshipful reverence for the mandate of heaven, apply themselves wholeheartedly to their allotted labors and productive activities.

As an important means to lead the people to reverence for the mandate of heaven, Seishisai points to the Daijōsai, a ritual of thanksgiving performed by successive generations of emperors ("sons of heaven") since antiquity. The hallmark of Ogyū Sorai's discourse on policy was the establishment of institutions consonant with Confucian ideals as a means to forestall social disorder, stressing the importance of "rites"—that is to say, the elaboration of a body of ritual and etiquette based on the Confucian canon that could be used to instruct and guide the people. Seishisai envisioned the establishment of a ritual system centered on the Daijōsai that would unify the various practices and ceremonies that people followed in venerating their ancestors. In part this may have been a response to the contemporary interest in commemoration of ancestors touched upon in chapter 9.

Seishisai characterizes the Daijōsai as a ritual in which the newly enthroned emperor thanked the "heavenly deities" (Amaterasu Ōmikami and the other deities) for a bountiful harvest, symbolically making an offering of new grain to them and, afterward, consuming it with the people. Of course only a small number of people served directly in the Daijōsai ceremonies, but it was a ritual that received support and participation from people of all stations, from the artisans who made the ceremonial clothing and ritual implements to the farmers who grew the grain offerings. Through it, the hearts of the people throughout Japan could be unified and "induced to stand in awesome veneration of Amaterasu's will, and bring forth the richest possible harvests that the soil will yield."

At the same time, as is frequently pointed out in discussions of the Mito School, Seishisai argues that the Daijōsai would also serve as a device for focusing the loyalty of the people on the person of the emperor as the "son of heaven," the "heavenly descendant" of Amaterasu Ōmikami. In the first chapter of *Shinron*, mentioned earlier, Seishisai writes that through people's participation in the Daijōsai and rituals venerating the ancestral lineages of their own houses or families, the "relationship of ruler and subject" is confirmed and an order in which "loyalty and filial piety are synonymous" is maintained. This vision is premised on the idea that if the ancestral lineages (*uji*) of all Japanese are traced back to their origins, they will be found to have been direct retainers and servants of the emperors of antiquity—and that the true practice of the virtues of loyalty and filial piety is to faithfully carry out the allotted duties (*shoku*) of one's lineage, thus fulfilling the intentions of one's ancestors in service to the present emperor, under the guidance of the shogun.

When, through the Daijōsai and rituals honoring the ancestors of their own lineages, people of all stations "are taught simply to revere Amaterasu and Her Divine Imperial line, their allegiances are undivided and they are blind to all heresies."[10] In the logic of *Shinron*, this was seen as the bulwark defending the unity and independence of Japan against the threat of encroachment by the Western nations. If the Western "barbarians" perceived that the hearts of the Japanese people were without a lord and master, they would attempt to spread Christianity among them.

The people, enticed by fear of the supernatural and a doctrine that promised them a joyous afterlife—in Seishisai's words, "seeking personal advantage and awed by the spirits"— might be induced to become Christians, which

Commemorative postage stamp for the enthronement of Emperor Shōwa in 1928, depicting the Daijōkyū, a structure specially built for the Daijōsai.

he was convinced would weaken their loyalty to Japan. Seishisai believed that it was the unified popular mentality achieved through Christianity that had made the modern Western nations such a formidable force. And to combat this indirect incursion, he felt that Japan must establish a similar unity of government and religious teaching through a revival of Japan's ancient rituals.

In the first chapter of *Shinron*, Seishisai consistently adopts an anti-foreign stance, accusing scholars of Dutch Learning of becoming enamored of "the far-fetched theories of the Western barbarians" and possibly enticing the people to give their allegiance to the West. In a later chapter, "The Barbarian's Nature," he speaks of the cunning with which Christianity was being employed to win the hearts and minds of Asian peoples. Seishisai observes: "By occasionally performing small acts of charity they acquire a reputation for benevolence, which they use to enhance their teachings, fooling people with their busy tongues and filling their ears with specious nonsense." He accuses the Christians of engaging in charitable activities to lend an appearance of kindness and benevolence to their heretical creed and thus win new converts.

The Western nations were not trading and deploying military force the world over simply in their desire to expand their power and influence. Seishisai observed that with their ability to give the impression of treating other peoples with benevolence and charity, they could also appeal to the common people, who appeared to be relatively indifferent to the virtue of loyalty. Believing that the guarantee of the people's welfare was a basic tenet of government, Seishisai was alarmed by the Western nations precisely because they at least made a show of taking the welfare of the people as seriously as he did.

In 1862, after the Tokugawa shogunate had signed commercial treaties with the major Western nations and effectively abandoned its earlier stance of "expelling the barbarians," Seishisai wrote a brief text entitled *Jimusaku* (A Plan for Tasks at Hand) altering his earlier stance, lending his support to the opening of the country, and winning the antipathy of the anti-foreign activists. One of the main reasons he gives for this change in position is "the concern of his sacred majesty, the emperor, for the welfare of his people." Having seen first hand the military might of the Western nations, he believed that if the shogunate aligned with the anti-foreign radicals and chose to fight "without any expectation of victory," it would result in great suffering and would force the emperor himself "onto a path devoid of benevolence." Here the choice between a closed or open country is seen as something that must be determined in response to the current situation, using protection of the people's livelihoods as the standard of judgment. The welfare of the people is certainly an important goal of government, and in this regard, the Western nations appeared to have been achieving better results than Japan or China. In *Shinron*, we catch a glimmer of such a perception.

"Benevolent government" and "public discussion" in the West

Among Aizawa Seishisai's contemporaries, diffusion of knowledge of the West was widening the perception that it was the Western nations that were actually achieving the Confucian ideal of "benevolent government" (*jinsei*). As Watanabe Hiroshi demonstrates in considerable detail in an essay on Western modernity and the Confucian tradition, from the end of the eighteenth century onward, what Confucian scholars and other Japanese intellectuals noted in particular when discussing European manners and customs was the prevalence of institutions such as hospitals, orphanages, and poorhouses.[11] Providing assistance to orphans, the disabled, the elderly, and others in need was seen as a hallmark of benevolent rule—and one that the West, rather than Japan, was making a reality. This assessment was not limited to the Dutch Learning (Rangaku) scholars; it was also broadly shared among intellectuals whose patterns of thought were grounded in Confucian teachings.

Moreover, unlike China and Korea, there was another issue for Japanese intellectuals in their assessment of the West. Both China and Korea consistently held to an ideal that promised that anyone, regardless of birth, who acquired a Neo-Confucian education sufficient to allow him to pass the civil service examinations could become an official and demonstrate their talents in governing the country. In Japan, however, even in the late Tokugawa period after Confucian teachings had permeated society, there was no attempt to introduce a system in which government officials were selected through open public examinations. Officials serving the shogunate and the daimyo houses were samurai who owed their positions to hereditary rank and office, and it was extremely difficult for anyone to attain a post above their allotted station. As Fukuzawa Yukichi observed, by the late Tokugawa period, these restrictions had come to feel like a heavy yoke.

The Western nations presented a noticeable contrast. Yokoi Shōnan (1809–69), a Neo-Confucian scholar from Kumamoto, had been an ardent reader of *Shinron* and a supporter of the "expel the barbarians" rhetoric, but knowledge of politics and society in the Western nations gained through Wei Yuan's *Haiguo tuzhi* (Illustrated Treatise on the Maritime Nations), a Chinese work on world geography reprinted in a Japanese edition in 1854, led him to change his position and advocate opening Japan to the outside world. In his treatise *Kokuze sanron* (The Three Major Problems of State Policy), written in 1860, Yokoi gives the following assessment of the West:

In America, three major policies have been set up from Washington's presidency on: First, to stop wars in accordance with divine intentions, because nothing is worse than violence and killing among nations; second, to broaden enlightened government by learning from all the countries of the world; and third, to work with complete devotion for the peace and welfare of the people by entrusting the power of the president of the whole country to the wisest instead of transmitting it to the son of the president and by abolishing the code [of obligation] in the relationship between ruler and minister. Based on these policies, the Americans have adopted all of the best political institutions and administrative and other tools and techniques from throughout the world and made them their own, implementing a truly benevolent government.

In England the government is based entirely on the popular will, and all government actions—large and small—are always debated by the people. The most beneficial action is decided upon, and an unpopular program is not forced upon the people. [...] Furthermore, all countries, including Russia, have established schools and military academies, hospitals, orphanages, and schools for the deaf and dumb. The governments are entirely based on moral principles, and they work hard for the benefit of the people, virtually as in the three ancient periods of sage-rule in China.[12]

Yokoi Shōnan makes frequent use of the phrase "Yao, Shun, and the Three Dynasties" to express the Neo-Confucian ideal of government, and here he is saying that the nations of the West have achieved something comparable in the present age. As noted earlier, the "hospitals, orphanages, and schools for the deaf and dumb" he mentions are emblems of benevolent government. Japanese intellectuals of this era were quite taken with the idea of "schools and military academies" in Western countries that gave people the opportunity to cultivate their talents and participate in government regardless of birth or station.

This recognition was connected to the high esteem in which they held Western parliamentary politics and the American presidency. Shōnan believed the presidency to be an institution in which virtuous men were selected for office according to the will of the people. Essentially, even the ruler of the nation was entrusted with his position on the basis of wisdom rather than inheritance, and hereditary relationships of ruler and subject had been abandoned. Aizawa Seishisai's *Shinron* also calls for government "based on the will of the people," but Shōnan regards the British parliamentary system as an even better reflection of the popular will in the affairs of state. In private correspondence, he describes it as government through "public discussion" (*kōron*)—debate among equals, rejecting all discrimination on the basis of class or birth.

Political decision-making should not be monopolized by a small group at the center of power, but should be conducted through debate in which a range of people might participate— through what was termed at the time "public discussion" (*kōron*), "public deliberation" (*kōgi*), or "popular opinion" (*yoron*). In *Keii gusetsu*, Maki Yasuomi calls for "opening the pathways of discourse so that not only great lords and officials but even the most humble farmers and rustics

Yokoi Shōnan (1809–69).

might be permitted to express their thoughts fully, without fear or inhibition, and have them heard." From *sonnō jōi* activists like Maki to the daimyo supporting plans for a "union of court and shogunate," and even the more progressive factions within the shogunate itself, represented by figures such as Katsu Kaishū, implementation of a politics grounded in public debate was a slogan adopted by many forces in the political maelstrom of late Tokugawa Japan.

Based on this ideal of public discussion, Shōnan gave the parliamentary systems of the West high marks, and was one of the earliest to propose their introduction to Japan—an idea that was inherited by the new Meiji government. The first article of the Charter Oath (Gokajō no Seimon) issued by the new government in April 1868 (Keiō 4.3) reads: "Deliberative assemblies shall be widely established and all matters decided by public discussion." This reflects the fact that Yuri Kimimasa, who had taken the initiative in reforming the government of the Fukui domain with Shōnan, was involved in drafting this document. The task of establishing the institutions that would enable government through "public discussion" took a variety of twists and turns before arriving at the promulgation of the Constitution of the Empire of Japan and the convening of the Imperial Diet in 1890, with a lower house made up of popularly elected representatives.

At the same time, if one had to place the political institutions of the modern West within the *gunken* versus *hōken* framework, they would obviously be examples of a centralized *gunken* system. Research by the legal historian Asai Kiyoshi has introduced us to examples of late Tokugawa Dutch Learning scholars and other intellectuals who explicitly addressed this issue.[13] Among them, the case of Tsuda Izuru (1832–1905), a samurai from the Wakayama domain and a student of both the Sorai School and Western Studies, is particularly interesting. Following the restoration of imperial rule he was appointed to lead the Wakayama government in a variety of political reforms as it moved to adopt the *gunken* system well before many of the other domains.

Moreover, Tsuda saw this as significant, not merely in terms of changing the form of local government, but in following the Western countries in deconstructing the hierarchy of hereditary classes. In his posthumously published autobiography, *Tsubo no ishibumi* (The Stone Urn, 1917), he relates that in the twelfth month of the first year of Meiji (1868), Date Chihiro's son Mutsu Munemitsu asked him how the "framework"(*kumitate*) of Japan should be reformed in the coming years. Here is Tsuda's response:

> Well, to begin with, in the times of the ancient emperors we had a *gunken* system. From the Kamakura period onward we had *hōken* rule under military governments that took advantage of the decline of the imperial house and usurped its authority. Setting aside for a moment this talk of the past, once the world has become civilized we do not find this *hōken* government anywhere—not in Japan, in China, or in the nations of Europe and America. So it should not be that difficult to abolish militaristic *hōken* rule and construct a *gunken* system that can stand alongside those of Europe and America, if we administer it properly.[14]

This is a memoir from the late Meiji period, decades after the conversation actually occurred, so we cannot be certain that Tsuda's thinking on this subject was as well defined as it is presented here. But as Asai's research points out, in the second volume of *Seiyō jijō* (Conditions in the West, 1868), widely read in the early Meiji years, Fukuzawa Yukichi engages in a discussion entitled "National Laws and Customs." According to Fukuzawa, the "hereditary feudal system" (in this work, Fukuzawa uses the Japanese term *hōken* to translate the term "feudal") of medieval Europe represented the institutions of an age whose "customs were barbarous," and as these countries advanced toward civilization, the "remnants of feudal law" were abolished and "protections" and "freedoms" established for the people. In this analysis, feudal institutions are completely rejected as pernicious customs of the past, to be abandoned in the process of history's advance toward civilization.

By treating all the land and people of Japan equally as "imperial land and imperial subjects," the constraints of "hereditary feudal law" could be abolished and the livelihoods of the people guaranteed and confirmed, and a path opened to a system in which the individual was "free" to engage in debate and participate in politics. The shift to a *gunken* system of centralized government as a result of the return of domain registers to the emperor, and the abolition of domains and creation of a prefectural system were also seen as supporting such hopes. It might be said that these ideals were merely window-dressing, something the new government was offering for public consumption. But because they were being proclaimed in tandem with such real and irreversible changes as the imperial restoration and the abolition of the domains, the historical consciousness of the people registered them as decisive steps along a direct pathway from feudalism (the *hōken* system) toward civilization.

CHAPTER 11

The Advent of "Civilization"

Famous Places of Tokyo: Horse-Drawn Trams on the Streets of Ginza, woodblock print by Utagawa
Hiroshige III, 1882.

A limitless universe of unlimited progress

Toward the end of his life, Fukuzawa Yukichi wrote an introduction to his collected works, published in five volumes in 1898.[1] In it, he looks back over his life, providing brief commentaries on the works included in the collection. For example, he discusses the role of his bestseller *Seiyō jijō* (Conditions in the West; published in three successive volumes, in 1866, 1868, and 1870), whose appearance more or less coincided with the restoration of imperial rule.

Fukuzawa remarks that the "activists from the various domains" who propelled the movement for "revolution" (*ishin*) were full of martial spirit but not very well-read, and that, "regarded from the lofty heights of a Confucian education, one would have to call them ignorant." He continues:

> This unlettered crew succeeded in the great work of the Revolution, but when it came to the next step, even though they had seen the foolishness of trying to keep the country closed and expelling the barbarians, they hadn't any notion of how to go about opening the country to civilization. What happened to catch the bemused eyes of these activists at this juncture was the recently published *Seiyō jijō*. No sooner did one of them get hold of it and say, this looks interesting, I bet it would be a good reference for our plans for civilization—than he was joined by ten thousand more, and suddenly both in and out of government circles there wasn't a soul among those chattering about Western civilization and arguing for the necessity of opening the country who did not have a copy of *Seiyō jijō* at their side. *Seiyō jijō* was like a bat in a birdless village, providing guidance to an ignorant society, with even some decrees and ordinances of the new government taking their cues from these slender volumes.[2]

Fukuzawa all but claims that *Seiyō jijō* set the course for the mentality of the Japanese people as a whole and provided the major impetus for the policies of the Meiji government. In this same introduction, Fukuzawa claims that the 1866 volume of *Seiyō jijō* reached a circulation of 200,000 to 250,000 copies (including pirated versions). In 1870 the population of Japan was recorded as being between 32 and 35 million. The current population (in 2017) is 126.8 million, so this

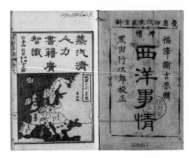

Cover and title page of a pirated edition of Fukuzawa Yukichi's *Seiyō jijō* that was published, with unauthorized revisions, by Kuroda Kōjirō in 1868.

would be equivalent to selling about a million copies today. Considering that the literacy rate in early Meiji Japan was significantly lower than it is today and the number of published titles fewer, Fukuzawa's book must have had an immense impact on the reading public.

In his influential book *Nihon yuibutsuron shi* (A History of Japanese Materialism, 1936), Marxist philosopher Nagata Hiroshi describes the Western-influenced intellectuals in the Meirokusha (Meiji 6 Society), referring to them as the "Meiji Enlightenment" and naming Fukuzawa as their leading representative. Nagata's characterization of Fukuzawa and company as enlightenment thinkers was part of a conscious effort to conceive of the early Meiji as a period during which bourgeois society was established, similar to what occurred in eighteenth-century Europe, with the Meirokusha playing a role similar to that of the enlightenment thinkers of Britain, Germany, and France in working to "demolish feudal ideology."

According to the intellectual historian Sakagami Takashi, the English word "enlightenment," the source of the Japanese word *keimō*, connotes "the effort to create a more just society by exposing established ills to the light of reason."[3] Nagata Hiroshi, while critical of the limitations of "bourgeois liberalism" in the thought of Fukuzawa and company, still saw enough of its virtues to christen the period the Meiji Enlightenment. Yet *keimō*, the classical Chinese compound chosen to translate "enlightenment" into Japanese, signifies the edification of the ignorant masses by wise men and sages. In the postwar period, leftist intellectuals criticized Fukuzawa and Meiji Enlightenment thought as being indifferent to the lives and mentality of the common people—a criticism still prevalent today. This was partly because the term "enlightenment thought" became established in Japanese as *keimō shisō*, with the connotations just mentioned, and also because Fukuzawa himself could give the impression of being a rather snooty elite reformer, evident in the passage cited above. (The historian Maruyama Masao, who valued Fukuzawa and his colleagues highly, might be called a victim of this negative assessment of the Meiji Enlightenment, as he was frequently derided for being a member of the "Postwar Enlightenment" [*sengo keimō*] himself.)

In any event, in the early Meiji years Fukuzawa exerted himself tirelessly to introduce and foster in Japan the philosophy, scholarship, and institutions of the "civilized" nations of the West. In the introduction to his collected works, Fukuzawa also comments on *Kunmō kyūri zukai* (Illustrated Course in Science), which was published in the autumn of 1868. Fukuzawa recalls his motivation for writing it:

> In the early days of the opening of the country, our most fervent vow as scholars of Western Learning was to somehow enlist the majority of the people to support a genuine opening of the country and serve as hosts to Western civilization in the Orient, aiming on the one hand to sweep away the hidebound conservatism of Chinese Learning while at the same time demonstrating the practical value of Western Learning. As I racked my brain, considering every possible way of accomplishing this, it occurred to me that there could be no more powerful method than to introduce people to the laws of science and let them master this for themselves.[4]

From the late Tokugawa period onward, Fukuzawa came to believe that the way to introduce Western civilization to the people of Japan was to begin with the principles of natural science (*butsuri*). In traditional Neo-Confucian language, *butsuri* referred to the phenomena of both the natural and human realms, but in Fukuzawa's use of the term it has become divorced from human society, connoting the principles (*ri*) inherent in material phenomena (*butsu*) as elucidated by the natural sciences of the modern West. *Kunmō kyūri zukai* is an illustrated primer of scientific concepts, using familiar natural phenomena as examples to explain the basics of physics, meteorology, and astronomy.

Page from *Kunmō kyūri zukai* (Illustrated Course in Science, 1868) by Fukuzawa Yukichi.

In his preface to *Kunmō kyūri zukai*, Fukuzawa writes that the study of science will enhance the intellect, and that encouraging this pursuit among its readers is the goal of the book. He argues that, in order to completely fulfill our duties as human beings, we must not only develop ethics and morality but also refine the intellect.

Interestingly enough, it is here that the modern Western conception of an infinite universe was first introduced to Japan. As we saw in chapter 8, knowledge of Western astronomy had already begun to enter Japan during the Tokugawa period, largely through the Dutch Learning scholars associated with the shogunate's astronomical institute. But their introduction of the principles of Western astronomy stopped with the concept of the earth as a globe rotating around the sun and the principles of movement of the other planets in the solar system. Instead, it was the Kokugaku scholars, taking their cues from the opening passage of the *Nihon shoki*, who developed a cosmological concept close to that of the Western infinite universe, describing a void enfolding innumerable heavenly bodies.

In contrast, Fukuzawa's book *Kunmō kyūri zukai* makes no reference whatsoever to Tokugawa-period astronomical works, relying instead on a number of British and American textbooks for information on natural philosophy and geography that he edited and adapted in his own way. The seventh chapter deals with gravity, introducing the theory of universal gravitation and its effect on the orbits of the planets, and then turns to a discussion of the vastness of the universe.

The immensity of Creation is beyond human measurement. Think about it for a moment: though the sun and moon seem high and distant, as we said earlier, our sun is not the only sun; we cannot know how many millions of others exist. Nor is there anything we can compare to this vastness. The nearest of the fixed stars, if we calculate in *ri* [1 *ri* = 3.9 km], is not a million, ten million, or a hundred million *ri* from us, but 785 billion *ri*. If we think of this in terms of the rows on an abacus, it would be fifteen rows above single digits. And when it comes to the distance of things like the Milky Way, even our billions and trillions are insufficient to measure it. One may call it vast, one may call it limitless—in any case, it is enough to make the head swim.[5]

While he does not explicitly state that the universe is infinite, his description of its vastness and immeasurability, and the vertigo we experience when thinking of such distances, evokes the primal feeling of awe (and even terror) that humans feel in confronting such infinite spaces.

This perception of the infinite expanse of the universe surrounding our planet was accompanied by a historical sense that the human society living upon it is progressing in a unilinear fashion. We see this in the second volume of Fukuzawa's *Seiyō jijō*, published in the summer of 1868. This work was compiled by Fukuzawa from a translation of a textbook by John Hill Burton, *Political Economy: For Use in Schools and for Private Instruction* (Edinburgh, 1852), supplemented by selected translations from a variety of other sources. Fukuzawa mistook the name of the publishers—William and Robert Chambers—for that of the author, and describes it as "a book on *keizai* compiled by the Englishman Chambers." Here Fukuzawa uses *keizai* not as "economy" or "political economy" but as "governing the realm and helping the people" (*keisei saimin*; abbreviated to *keizai*), as we discussed in chapter 6.

The fourth chapter of Fukuzawa's translation corresponds to the chapter entitled "Civilization" in Burton's original text. Fukuzawa begins by declaring that the progress of humanity from "savage" or "barbarous" states toward "civilization" (*bunmei* or *bunmei kaika*) is a universal law, and gives the following overview of its history:

Examining history, we find that humanity begins in a barbarous state, and gradually progresses toward civilization. In barbarous and unlettered times, the higher moral qualities are not yet developed, and people are unable to restrain their passions or control their desires. The great abuse the small, and the strong tyrannize the weak. The married woman is like a slave to her husband; the father has complete power over his child. As a result, there is little trust among members of society, and social intercourse is restricted, making it difficult to construct institutions that would advance the general welfare. As the world advances towards civilization, this state of affairs is gradually ended; moral feelings are honored, desires are curbed, the small are aided by the great and the weak protected by the strong; institutions for the general benefit flourish.[6]

Here, as in the writings of Nishi Amane that we examined in chapter 3 and of Mitsukuri Genpo in chapter 9, is a moment in which a new historical vision—of the past, present, and future progress of human society—is clearly articulated. Later in the same chapter of *Seiyō jijō*, Fukuzawa describes the population growth attendant upon the development of agriculture, livestock farming, and handicrafts as part of the transition from humanity's original "barbarous" state (in Burton's terminology) toward a "civilized" one, and also observes that "as the teachings of civilization flourish, society becomes more affluent." Economic affluence in turn supports the development of learning, and people are given more leeway to develop compassion and tolerance for one another. The perception of historical change that we have glimpsed in the writings of Tominaga Nakamoto, Kaiho Seiryō, and Motoori Norinaga is thus more clearly and explicitly formulated.

Moreover, Fukuzawa does not see "civilization" as a product of Western culture alone. As noted in chapter 3, his classification of countries as "primitive" or "civilized" was predicated on an assessment of their degree of progress or development and was no more than a relative measure. It represents a general standard for humanity transcending cultural differences, and while in the nineteenth century the Western countries were the most advanced on this scale, they had not yet achieved this ideal either. Thus, while Fukuzawa made Western civilization the goal of Japan's present efforts, the quest for civilization in the sense of enhancing the people's intellect and morality was not, in principle, to be equated with westernization.

The choice of *bunmei* or *bunmei kaika* to translate the word "civilization" was itself based on the awareness that this connoted something desirable from the perspective of traditional East Asian values. As the lexicographer Satō Tōru has pointed out, although the expression *kaika bunmei* (with the words reversed) makes an appearance in 1865 in the short-lived early newspaper *Nihon shinbun*,[7] it was probably the second volume of Fukuzawa's *Seiyō jijō* that popularized the four-character phrase *bunmei kaika*.[8]

However, as we may see from its use as an era name (*nengō*) for the years 1469–87 during the reign of Emperor Go-Tsuchimikado in the Muromachi period, *bunmei* originated in the Confucian classics. In the "Canon of Shun," chapter 2 in the *Book of Documents* (*Shujing*), the phrase *bunmei* is used to praise the everlasting virtues of Shun, the epitome of the ancient Chinese sage king. And in the *Book of Changes* (*Yijing*), the commentaries on the first hexagram, *qian*, describe the stability of the realm under the influence of a virtuous ruler as "'Dragon appearing in the field.' Through him the whole world attains beauty and clarity [*tenka bunmei*]."[9] In short, *bunmei* is a phrase originally used to describe the ideal government of ancient China under Yao, Shun, and the Three Dynasties, and thus carries a strong moral and ethical connotation.

In addition, in a commentary on the *Book of Documents* by the Song-dynasty Neo-Confucian scholar Cai Shen, *bunmei* is explained as the process by which humans appropriately restrain their darker passions, allowing the "principle" inherent in their hearts and minds, as in the universe as a whole, to express itself, thus achieving harmony with all people and things. Arriving at this ideal state, the world is brightly illuminated. The word *bunmei* is used to capture this brilliant beauty. Fukuzawa's use of it to translate Burton's "civilization" is an expression of both the high esteem and sympathy he felt for this concept.

Of course the perspective on society seen in the chapter on "Civilization" in the second volume of *Seiyō jijō*—taking the inalienable rights of the individual as its point of departure and preaching the equality of parents and children, men and women alike—would have been unfamiliar to Tokugawa intellectuals. But Burton's discussion of "civilization" (especially as translated by Fukuzawa) centers on the idea that the human race was leaving behind its former "barbarous" state, "honoring moral feelings and restraining the passions," and working to create a harmonious society. Fukuzawa renders the "higher moral qualities" and "moral feelings" in Burton's original text as *reigi*, an innate human aspiration to treat others with respect and fairness, not a superficial attention to manners. The argument that an ideal society is one that enables the most complete realization of this aspiration was one consonant with the Neo-Confucian conception of humankind. For those living in the Tokugawa period, the vision of history—and the future—as one of progress toward "civilization," or *bunmei*, seemed convincing, both from the perspective of their own direct experience of a changing society, and from the Neo-Confucian system of values that served as the basis of their understanding of the world.

Gunken and *kaika*

Like *bunmei*, *kaika* was frequently used as a translation of "civilization" (as was the expression *bunmei kaika,* which is often rendered into English as "civilization and enlightenment"). It also has its origins in the Chinese classics, where it is used to signify the commencement of the process by which the ancient kings created institutions to instruct and transform the people (*kai* meaning "opening" or "beginning"; *ka* meaning "transformation" or "change"). In the *Nihon shoki,* the ninth emperor, Wakayamato Neko-hiko Ōhihi no Mikoto, appears with the posthumous Chinese-style name of Emperor Kaika, but the account of his reign is terse, and nothing is given concerning his personality or accomplishments. The posthumous name Kaika probably signifies little more than a desire to solidify his position as one of the earliest emperors. Read with the pronunciation *kaike,* the same kanji are used in Japanese Buddhist terminology as a term meaning "to instruct the people in the truth and lead them to goodness; to dispel delusions with teaching and guidance."[10]

In the sense of instructing and transforming the people, *kaika* was associated with *bunmei*, as in the phrase from the *Book of Changes* cited above, *tenka bunmei* ("the whole world attains beauty and clarity"). But even more than in this somewhat special sense, *kaika* was used as a more refined version of the popular expression *hirakeru*, which as noted in chapter 9 suggested development or progress—in scholarship, in the flow of information and social intercourse, in the economy and the proliferation of consumer goods. As a way of expressing this, *kaika* also served as an appropriate translation for "civilization."

Inaugural issue of *Meiji gekkan*, a monthly journal published by the Osaka Prefectural Government beginning in 1868.

We also have an example from the early Meiji period in which *bunmei* and *kaika* are distinguished from one another, with *bunmei* accorded a higher status. The Osaka Prefectural Government began publishing the *Meiji gekkan* (Meiji Monthly) in the early autumn of 1868. In its second issue is a brief article entitled "Jin'un kaika no kōge" (Rating Human Development),[11] which divides the progress of human societies into five levels determined by "the quality of their customs and institutions." At the bottom are the "savage" (*yaban*), and then the "barbarous" (*izoku*) peoples. In third place are the "half-civilized countries" (*hankai no kuni*), in which agriculture, technology, and scholarship have developed to a significant degree, but "distinctions between high and low" in social status are severe; they are unaware of "how to enrich and strengthen themselves through intercourse with other nations," thus "new inventions" and "innovative teachings" are rare, and their technology and scholarship are stagnant. China, India, Persia, Turkey, and the North African states are cited as contemporary examples of this level.

The author of the *Meiji gekkan* article then turns to the most advanced nations of Europe and America, which he subdivides into *kaika no kuni* ("developing nations") and *bunmei no kuni* ("civilized nations"). The top-ranked *bunmei no kuni* are the same as those mentioned by Fukuzawa in the works discussed in chapter 3: Britain, France, Switzerland, Germany,

Belgium, Holland, and the United States. In contrast, the *kaika no kuni* "have not completely rid themselves of the pernicious customs of the past; education is completely inadequate and the common people ignorant, and an immense gulf divides high and low." Without proper educational systems or representative assemblies, government and people are alienated from one another. Placed in this group are Russia, Italy, Spain, Portugal, and the countries of South America.

In a 1965 article analyzing early Meiji publications on the subject of *bunmei kaika*, the sociologist Mita Sōsuke observes that *kaika* is probably positioned as inferior to *bunmei* because in the early Meiji era, the "progress" or "development" represented by *kaika* or the more vernacular expression *hirakeru* was welcomed mainly as a liberation of basic human desires.

> The image conveyed by *hirakeru* was one of being liberated from a confined space into one that is bright and open. The concrete components of this sense of liberation were (1) liberation from the cultural solipsism of Japan's closure to the outside world; (2) liberation from the regional constraints of the institutional system of the shogunate and domains; (3) liberation from ignorant and irrational customs and conventions; and (4) liberation from the fixed station in life assigned to individuals by the feudal class hierarchy. In turn this might give rise to a fresh and simple curiosity with regard to Western culture, encourage the impulse of ambitious youth from the provinces to move to Tokyo, spawn a rash and obsessive desire to imitate fragments of "civilization," or foster the illusion that limitless social advancement was possible for anyone.[12]

In contrast, under the strict class system of the Tokugawa period there were severe restrictions on travel and the economy. Rutherford Alcock, who served for three years as the British consul-general and diplomatic representative in Edo, wrote perceptively of this:

> [T]he policy attributed to the Bourbons and petty sovereigns of Italy, of seeking to discourage locomotion, internal and external trade, and

almost every branch of industry, except the ordinary operations of agriculture, exactly represents the policy of the Japanese rulers. In trade, especially foreign trade, they see the elements of wealth and growth of a middle class, which could not long be retained in a state of serfdom. What took place in Europe by the same development of wealth and intelligence, among the mercantile classes, enabling these to break the chains of a feudal tenure, and create free cities as centers of resistance, would follow here. Foreign trade and intercourse do carry with them inevitably the germs of a social revolution to these Eastern states.[13]

Alcock wrote this passage in 1863, before the restoration of imperial rule, and before the popular enthusiasm for "civilization and enlightenment" had even begun. At the time, Alcock saw the severe restrictions on travel, commerce, and trade imposed by the Tokugawa shogunate as forestalling the social revolution that might come from the growth of a middle class and the development of free cities. However, the actual course of historical events following the opening of the country and the collapse of the Tokugawa political order was not the creation of "free cities as centers of resistance." It ushered in instead a chaotic situation in which people actively vied with one another as they sought to fulfill their individual desires.

The painter Kaburagi Kiyokata (1878–1972) recalls the following episode in his essay "Usagi to omoto" (Rabbits and Lilies), originally published in 1939.[14] In the early years of Meiji, "when everything was changing," there was a fad for buying and selling rabbits. Many people began raising fancy breeds and selling the prodigious number of offspring, and for a time "the sky was the limit" in terms of the prices they would fetch. This craze ended, however, almost as soon as it began. It was followed by a similar boom in potted Japanese lilies (*Rohdea japonica*), and a similar round of speculative investment. Speculation, gambling, and prostitution flourished, with people's avarice on full display.

Rutherford Alcock (1809–97).

Such were the realities of the era of "civilization and enlightenment."

As we saw in the introduction, works by present-day historians frequently assess the *bunmei kaika* phenomenon of the early Meiji years as a movement of top-down westernization forcibly promoted by the government, which the common people experienced as little more than a nuisance. But this grasps only part of the reality. The collapse of the shogunate and the launch of the new government was experienced initially by the people as a liberation from the constraints imposed on every aspect of their lives. The importation of Western institutions and cultural artifacts was welcomed as part of that process.

The political commentator Taguchi Ukichi (1855–1905), editor of the economic journal *Tōkyō keizai zasshi*, wrote in his 1885 book *Nihon kaika no seishitsu* (The Nature of Japanese Civilization):

> Gentlemen, there is but one humanity. Therefore the original elements that led the Europeans and Americans to invent today's civilization must also certainly exist within the people of our nation. It is simply that they must be developed. I believe they can be seen in our own working-class society. Think for a moment of the clothing traditionally worn by our workers—such garments as the *momohiki, haragake, tekko, hanten,* and *jōi* all resemble the trousers, vests, capes, and overcoats of the contemporary West. Permitted a proper process of development, these garments would no doubt have arrived at something nearly identical to today's Western clothing.[15]

Taguchi is surmising that the common people of Japan, who had to engage in physical labor for their livelihoods, would invent work clothes easier to move about in and would eventually arrive at Western-style dress. Before the opening of the country and the encounter with *bunmei kaika*, the evolution of work clothes had stopped with the traditional *momohiki* and *hanten* without developing into even more convenient and efficient garments. This was because in Tokugawa society with its strict class system, those working people who became more affluent merely imitated "upper-class society" or became servants in "noble houses," abandoning the clothing they had previously worn for their work.

Taguchi's idea—that, if unfettered by the class system of Tokugawa times, the Japanese would have eventually invented something equivalent to Western dress—was an expression of his belief in a universal human nature. In the work that propelled him to fame, *Nihon kaika shōshi* (A Brief History of Japanese Civilization, 1877–82), he declares that all human beings wish to "preserve their lives and avoid death," and to that end develop the intellect to invent a variety of conveniences, amass money and

Taguchi Ukichi (1855–1905).

goods, and make "progress." Such progress is "the nature of society," and while it is repressed by a hierarchical class system, it cannot be stopped entirely. That Western-style clothing should gradually be adopted throughout the population during the age of "civilization and enlightenment" was merely part of the normal course of progress.

The transition from the *hōken* to the *gunken* system was similarly conceived by its proponents as a reform that would advance the cause of civilization. In the spring of 1869, three months before the formal return of the domain registers to the emperor, Tsuda Mamichi (1829–1903), who like Fukuzawa Yukichi would later become a member of the Meirokusha, published an article in the sixth issue of the newspaper *Chūgai shinbun* entitled "Gunken gi" (On Centralized Rule) that touched off a debate in later issues regarding the strengths and weaknesses of the *hōken* and *gunken* systems.[16] In it, he writes that in remote antiquity Japan had a "mixed *hōken-gunken* system"; that from the time of Emperor Tenji onward it had "a *gunken* government; and after the seizure of power by the warrior houses following the Hōgen (1156) and Heiji (1160) rebellions, it assumed "a feudal guise" (*hōken no sugata*)—expressing a historical view resembling that of Rai San'yō. Now, he continues, it was necessary to reintroduce a *gunken* system to "unite the entire country of Japan, make it grow even richer, stronger, and more civilized, and allow everyone from the emperor and great lords above to their vassals and subvassals and the common people below to gain a proper place for their abilities."

Tsuda believed that a new era of *gunken* rule would provide the best conditions for a unified nation to pursue its quest to grow "even richer, stronger, and more civilized [*kaika*]." This vision of Tsuda's did not lead directly to the abolition of the domains and creation of a centralized prefectural system of government. But at the time, when the *hōken* system was equated with the hereditary class system, the transition to a *gunken* system was probably perceived as something that would further *kaika* in its sense of a general liberation of desire.

Tsuda Mamichi (1829–1903).

In ways reminiscent of Jean-Jacques Rousseau's critique of civilization in eighteenth-century France, some Meiji intellectuals asked, if all that had driven the progress of civilization in the West in modern times had simply been vigorous economic activity and the proliferation of luxurious material goods to arouse people's passions and desires, would this not simply lead to dissipation and ruin? In the midst of a superficially affluent urban existence, would people not become driven by empty vanity, constantly worry about the opinions of others, and lose the resilient independence and individuality they previously possessed?

In a similar vein, the trend of *kaika* in the sense of liberation of desire came under sharp attack from certain quarters. Unrestrained *kaika* might have an effect opposite to that of fostering the "moral feelings" hoped for by Fukuzawa. In a 2011 study of the political thought of the Meirokusha,[17] Kōno Yūri brought attention to an essay by the former shogunal retainer and early Meiji journalist Narushima Ryūhoku (1837–1884) entitled "Bunji no hei o ronzu" (On the Decline of Language), published in 1875, the same year as Fukuzawa's *Bunmeiron no gairyaku* (Outline of a Theory of Civilization). The essay contains the following passage:

> Have we made progress toward development (*kaika*)? Yes, I say. But have we arrived at civilization (*bunmei*)? I say no. To those who might question why I have come to this strange conclusion, my answer is this.

Locomotives race, steamships sail, telegrams are delivered, gaslights shine. The intellect of the masses is at long last beginning to shed a small portion of its ignorance. What can we call this other than progress toward development? Yet in view of the decline of literature and corruption of language in today's world, where do we find anything worthy of being called "civilization"? Is not civilization that "complete and elegant" state of affairs in which the literature and scholarship of a country flourish and gentlemen regulate their own behavior and deportment and refine their language?[18]

Technology has advanced, everyday life has become more comfortable and stylish. Thanks to these developments, the nation might even become richer and stronger. But have literature and civility made similar advances? Can we pride ourselves on our civilization when all we really have is material progress? This is the question Ryūhoku is raising. In the same spirit, Fukuzawa, in *Bunmeiron no gairyaku*, proclaims that progress toward civilization must be a matter of enhancing not only "intellect," but "morality" as well. It is also interesting to note that in this book Fukuzawa does not use the phrase *bunmei kaika*, which he himself had popularized in earlier writings, preferring to use only *bunmei*; the word *kaika* appears only eleven times in the entire work. Such usage suggests Fukuzawa, too, felt deep unease at the way *kaika* was unfolding in the Japan of his day.

Narushima Ryūhoku (1837–84).

Freedom and progress

Rutherford Alcock was one of the first British diplomats stationed in Japan, and he recorded his impressions of his time there in his book *The Capital of the Tycoon*. In it he attempts to be fair in his treatment of Japan and even at times to praise Japanese customs and culture, at least partially succeeding in overcoming a strictly Eurocentric value system. He also raises objections to Jeremy Bentham's utilitarianism, and touches on the work of John Stuart Mill and Alexis de Tocqueville—suggesting an intelligence sensitively keyed to the issues confronting contemporary Western society. In chapter 13 of the second volume of this book, Alcock discusses "the civilization of Japan" and explains the enduring power of the institutions of Tokugawa rule. In his view, the Japanese social system corresponded to the feudalism of the medieval West, and though at that time it had given Japan a stable and prosperous society, "the hour seems approaching when even this Japanese stronghold of medieval and feudal institutions must disappear before the ever-advancing tide of European invasion and civilization."[19] Yet even after expressing this dire prediction, Alcock gives the following assessment of the durability of Japan's institutions and the magnitude of their effect:

> Looking forward to this impending future, the actual state of a people and their institutions, so long and successfully maintained in medieval forms, and with a fully developed feudalism, is worthy of careful study. This feudalism has left the nation, if not free in our estimate of freedom, yet in enjoyment of many blessings which all the boasted freedom and civilization of Western States have failed to secure for them in an equally long succession of centuries. National prosperity, independence, freedom from war and material progress in the arts of life—these are all among the possessions of the Japanese as a people, and the inheritance of many generations.[20]

Alcock points out that the social order maintained by the class system of the Tokugawa period produced a sustained peace and prosperity unknown even in Europe, but also notes that it is "not free in our estimate of freedom." A prosperous, comfortable society—but one without freedom. Such is his perspective. In previous chapters we have touched on how Kaiho Seiryō and Motoori Norinaga used the word *jiyū* to suggest a "freedom" associated with affluence and ease of fulfilling one's material desires, and how they observed the changes being wrought in Tokugawa society by the expansion of such "freedom." But this was a type of freedom that Alcock would likely consider different from what was meant by the word in Western countries.

At about the same time as Alcock, Fukuzawa Yukichi was coming to a similar conclusion— that Japan might have *jiyū* in the Tokugawa-period sense, but not "freedom." In a well-known passage at the beginning of the first volume of *Seiyō jijō*, published in

A JAPANESE SALUTATION

Illustration from Alcock's *The Capital of the Tycoon* (1863).

1866, Fukuzawa lists "six essential conditions" for "civilized government" seen in the European nations, the first of which is "freedom":

> Freedom [*jishu nin'i*]. The national laws are lenient and do not inhibit the people from individually doing as they please; those who wish to be civil servants become civil servants, those who prefer farming become farmers, no discrimination is made among the four classes of civil servants, farmers, artisans, and merchants; lineage does not matter; court ranks are not used to look down upon others; high and low, noble and base each have their place, and do not interfere with one another's freedom, so that each may exercise his naturally endowed talents. The distinction between high and low is observed only in the realm of official duties where government offices are respected. Otherwise, there are no distinctions among the four classes, other than that literate, reasonable, conscientious men are respected as gentlemen [*kunshi*] and unlettered manual laborers considered small or petty persons [*shōjin*].[21]

The ideal of civilization (*bunmei*) that Fukuzawa saw in the West was a society in which individuals could exercise their talents, unbound by hereditary status or lineage; the nucleus of this vision was the value of *jishu nin'i*—freedom. Upon close scrutiny, we can also discern issues concerning equality embedded in this passage. But rather than indicating that Fukuzawa was indifferent to the potential conflict or contradiction between freedom and equality as values, these suggest that he saw freedom as the fundamental value underlying civilized society, with equality as a norm directly demanded by it.

Fukuzawa provides a note explaining his translation of "freedom" as *jishu nin'i*. "The words *jishu nin'i* and *jiyū* as they appear in this text do not signify selfish indulgence or a lack of respect for the laws of the land. Rather, they mean that in all social relations in these countries one should do as one sees fit unhindered by reservations or concern for what others may think. In English, this is called 'freedom' or 'liberty.' We still do not have an apt translation for it." Fukuzawa clearly feared that translating "freedom" as *jishu nin'i* or *jiyū* would create the impression that it meant selfishness and license. But freedom does not mean simply gratifying one's own desires: "it must also not interfere in any way with the freedom of others." As long as this caveat is observed, one should be free to behave as one wishes, without reservation or hindrance.

In an essay by the historian Tsuda Sōkichi, "Jiyū to iu kotoba no yōrei" (The Word *Jiyū* and Its Usage, 1955), and in the autobiography of the folklorist Yanagita Kunio, *Kokyō shichijūnen* (1959), we are told that in premodern Japan, the word *jiyū* was used exclusively with the negative connotation of "selfish." Although these sources are frequently cited in discussions of the Japanese view of "freedom," this meaning is likely a misunderstanding derived from a somewhat careless reading of Fukuzawa's footnote. The use of "unfree" (*fujiyū*) in phrases describing physical disability has been part of everyday speech from premodern times, and, as we have seen earlier, there are examples in the writings of both Kaiho Seiryō and Motoori Norinaga in which *jiyū* is used in a positive sense.

Fukuzawa's point had more to do with how these premodern Japanese words inadequately expressed the seriousness that the word "freedom" possesses as a behavioral norm, or the centrality of its value as a political principle. Freedom does not merely enable people to do as they please; it also informs "all social relations in these countries." It is a core principle defining the social order itself. The Japanese word *jiyū* is inadequate to express the centrality and normative value possessed by the word "freedom." Fukuzawa's explanatory note indicates how viscerally aware he had become of the word's importance, a result of his study of Western thought and his experiences traveling abroad.

Yet if an apt translation for "freedom" could not be found in the Japanese tradition, was it then impossible for Japanese to truly understand and assimilate this concept? Perhaps Japan, which had thus far followed a completely different historical path from the West, might prove unable to set itself on the upward path toward civilization. As the historian Matsuzawa Hiroaki has pointed out, in *Bunmeiron no gairyaku* Fukuzawa addresses this question directly, arguing that Japan is already on a course of progress toward civilization, albeit one different from that of the West.[22]

For example, in "Western Civilization as Our Goal," the second chapter of *Bunmeiron no gairyaku*, he writes that in Japan, "by the late classical time [...] political power lay in the hands of the samurai; the most sacrosanct was not necessarily the most powerful, and the most powerful was not necessarily the most sacrosanct"[23]—referring to the sacred authority possessed by the imperial house and the political power wielded by the shoguns (recently, by the Tokugawa house). Fukuzawa saw this division as enabling the people to preserve a diversity of thought. Their mental processes were "manifold and multifarious," and what naturally emerged was "a spirit of freedom." In chapter 10, "A Discussion of Our National Independence," Fukuzawa argues that the loyalty felt by samurai toward their lords "back in feudal (*hōken*) times" should be preserved and expanded into a "patriotism" serving the entire nation of Japan. Of course, from a comprehensive historical perspective, the dominance of the hereditary class system of Tokugawa-period "feudal (*hōken*) lineages" would have to be abandoned in the early stages of progress toward equality. But Fukuzawa perceived that even in the midst of the *hōken* era there were embedded elements strongly associated with the progress toward civilization.

Here, Fukuzawa intentionally swims against the current of social change wrought by the shift to a *gunken* system after the abolition of domains and the creation of prefectures, and if anything pays tribute both to the diversity of thought that existed in "feudal times" (*hōken no jidai*) and to the samurai virtue of loyalty. He was attempting to chart a unique course toward civilization for Japan as a nation by making apt use of such elements of its tradition. Later, in a work entitled *Bunkenron* (On Decentralization, 1877), while he does not use the word *hōken*, he proposes the active engagement in local government of the Tokugawa-period samurai, and their "spirit of self-government" as something to be emulated in modern times. In that "feudal" age, Fukuzawa grasped the first stirrings of "freedom" and the "spirit of self-government" and sought to apply it to a new era. No doubt this perception is the product of the generation that experienced both the Tokugawa and Meiji periods in adulthood, an experience he thus describes in the preface to *Bunmeiron no gairyaku*: "We have lived two lives, as it were; we unite in ourselves two completely different patterns of experience."[24]

The generation that came of age after the Meiji Revolution and whose intellectual development was shaped by reading the discourse on civilization presented by Fukuzawa and others had already lost this inclination to grapple with a reevaluation of "feudalism." By the late 1880s, Tokutomi Sohō (1863–1957), whom we encountered briefly in chapter 2 as a colleague of Takekoshi Yosaburō in the Min'yūsha publishing company, depicts the "feudal society" (*hōken shakai*) of the Tokugawa period in his bestselling debut work *Shōrai no Nihon* (The Future Japan, 1886):

> In short, under Japan's feudalism, from the shogun on top to the village headman at the bottom, everyone was an unconditional slave to those of higher ranks and an absolute master to those of lower ranks. Social relations were therefore straight up and down; at no time was anyone ever allowed to be on the same footing as another. Whatever the circumstances, human relations were always vertical. This was indeed inevitable in military organization.[25]

Here, the word *hōken* has lost its sense as one side of the traditional *hōken/gunken* classification, and is now clearly a translation of the word "feudalism"—likely spurred by the frequency with which "feudalism" appears in Tocqueville's *Democracy in America*.

Fukuzawa's discussion of the merits and demerits of *hōken no jidai* came

a scant four years after the shift toward centralized government brought about by the abolition of
domains and creation of prefectures. In contrast,
what the twenty-four-year-old Sohō aimed at with
The Future Japan, with the promulgation of the
constitution and the establishment of a national
assembly already in sight, was the destruction of the
political dominance of the domainal cliques and
the establishment of a democracy whose backbone
would be the "common people" (*heimin*) engaged
in productive and commercial activities. Thus for
him, the "feudal society" predating the "new Japan"

Tokutomi Sohō (1863–1957).

to come was perceived in entirely negative terms as a society in which people were rigidly controlled by a hierarchical class system. He wanted to see a
gleaming Future Japan, cleansed of the remaining dark elements of its past and
promising the liberty and prosperity of its people. For Sohō, this was the pros-
pect offered by "inevitable principles" of "social progress" (*shakai shinka*).

But what did older intellectuals of the previous generation make of these
bold pronouncements by the young Tokutomi Sohō? The reaction of Nakae
Chōmin (1847–1901) is one interesting example. In February 1888, Sohō,
as editor-in-chief of the influential journal *Kokumin no tomo* (The Nation's
Friend), wrote an editorial entitled "Shizoku no saigo" (The End of the Samurai) in which he argues that the rough and violent "samurai spirit" (*shizoku
konjō*) remaining in the Freedom and Popular Rights Movement ran contrary
to the "momentum of the times" (*jisei*), which tended toward a "commoner
society" (*heimin shakai*), and must be "dismantled and dispersed" for the sake
of national progress. Chōmin responded to this with a vituperative blast published as an editorial under the pen name Nankai-sei (Mr. South Seas) in the
February 8 issue of the newspaper *Shinonome shinbun*:

> Why is it that what flows from the tip of his brush is something that
> only pleases people, rather than making them weep? Is it not because
> he simply stands as an innocent bystander, leaving everything up to the

visible and invisible gods of progress? But don't these gods of progress reside in our own hearts? If a writer is rich in feeling, outstanding in talent, how can he not rage and weep? And is not such raging and weeping what drives progress in the world?[26]

Chōmin is criticizing Sohō, who condemns the former samurai as the remaining "refuse" of the "feudal society" of the past. Chōmin will not accept an attitude that assumes the role of a passive bystander, abdicating personal responsibility to the impartial laws of the gods of progress. Recollecting past history, examining the present-day world, we rage and weep at the travails of others. And it is the vigorous operation of such empathy that engenders in our own hearts the ideas that propel genuine social progress. Such is Chōmin's criticism of Sohō.

Sohō's proclamations concerning the principles of social evolution were a new species, a hybrid born from the fusion of a unilinear consciousness of historical progress emerging in the Tokugawa period with progressive views of history imported from the West. But are these principles a golden rule enabling us to clearly divide and define past and present? Chōmin questioned this. There may be elements buried in the thought of the past that could serve as guides to future progress. Perhaps genuine progress comes as a result of a continuing dialogue with the past, full of stops and starts along the way forward. This critical stance of Chōmin's is worthy of our attention today, as we attempt to grasp our own history and chart a course toward a more refined civilization.

Nakae Chōmin (1847–1901).

NOTES

INTRODUCTION

1. Norbert Elias, *The Civilizing Process*, vol. 1 (Oxford: Blackwell, 1969).

2. Samuel P. Huntington, "The Clash of Civilizations?," *Foreign Affairs* 72, no. 3 (Summer 1993): 22–49.

3. Huntington later prefers the term Sinic. See his book *The Clash of Civilizations and the Remaking of World Order* (New York: Simon & Schuster, 1996).

4. Dieter Senghaas, *The Clash within Civilizations: Coming to Terms with Cultural Conflicts* (London: Routledge, 2002).

5. Niall Ferguson, *Civilization: The West and the Rest* (New York: Penguin Press, 2011).

6. Yamazaki Masakazu, *Kindai no yōgo* (PHP Kenkyūjo, 1994), 215–26.

7. Samuel P. Huntington, *The Clash of Civilizations and the Remaking of World Order* (New York: Simon & Schuster, 1996).

8. Michael Ignatieff, "Fault Lines," *New York Times*, 1 December 1996.

9. Huntington, *The Clash of Civilizations*, 105.

10. Tōyama Shigeki, "Public Education, Civilization and Enlightenment, and the Promotion of Industry," chap. 4, sect. 4 in *Meiji ishin* (Iwanami Shoten, 1951), 302.

11. Shiota Ryōhei, ed., *Meiji Bungaku zenshū 4: Narushima Ryūhoku, Hattori Bushō, Kurimoto Joun* (Chikuma Shobo, 1969), 180.

12. Tōyama Shigeki, "Mitogaku no seikaku," in *Kokumin seikatsushi kenkyū: Seikatsu to shisō*, ed. Nakamura Kōya et al. (Shōgakukan, 1944).

13. Tōyama Shigeki, "Bakumatsu seiji katei ni okeru kōshitsu," *Rekishi hyōron*, October 1946 (inaugural issue).

14. *Kōmei tennō ki* and *Iwakura-kō jikki*, both published by the Department of the Imperial Household, 1906. Tada Kōmon, ed., *Iwakura-kō jikki*, vol. 2 (Iwakura-kō Kyūseki Hozonkai, 1927).

15. Michael Ignatieff, *Blood and Belonging: Journeys into the New Nationalism* (London: BBC Books, 1993).

16. Michael Ignatieff, *The Warrior's Honor: Ethnic War and the Modern Conscience* (London: Chatto & Windus, 1998).

17. Huntington, *The Clash of Civilizations*, 320.

18. Michael Walzer, *Thick and Thin: Moral Argument at Home and Abroad* (Notre Dame, IN: Notre Dame Press, 1994).

CHAPTER 1

1. See Marius B. Jansen, *The Making of Modern Japan* (Cambridge, MA: Harvard University

Press, 2000); Andrew Gordon, *A Modern History of Japan: From Tokugawa Times to the Present* (New York: Oxford University Press, 2003); Watanabe Hiroshi, *A History of Japanese Political Thought, 1600–1901,* trans. David Noble (I-House Press, 2012); and Mitani Hiroshi, "Meiji Revolution" (*Oxford Research Encyclopedia of Asian History,* 2017), online.

2. *Naikaku Kanpōkyoku,* ed., *Hōrei zensho,* published in 1887 (written in 1867, Keiō 3), 6. Available through the National Diet Library at http://dl.ndl.go.jp/info:ndljp/pid/787948.

3. Francis Ottiwell Adams, *The History of Japan,* vol. 2 (London: Henry S. King, 1875), 80.

4. William Elliot Griffis, *The Mikado's Empire* (New York: Harper & Brothers, 1876), 291. Reprinted by Stone Bridge Press in 2006.

5. *Iwakura Tomomi kankei monjo,* vol. 1 (Nihon Shiseki Kyokai, 1927), 266.

6. Tada Kōmon, ed., *Iwakura-kō jikki,* vol. 2 (Iwakura-kō Kyūseki Hozonkai, 1927), 60.

7. *Meiji tennō ki,* vol. 2 (Yoshikawa Kōbunkan, 1969), 248.

CHAPTER 2

1. Takekoshi Yosaburō, *Shin Nihon shi,* 2 vols. (Min'yūsha, 1891–92). Reprint, Iwanami Shoten, 2005.

2. Takekoshi, *Shin Nihon shi,* vol. 2, 11–12.

3. *Shōsetsu Nihonshi* (Yamakawa Shuppansha, 2008; edited in 2006), 226.

4. Takekoshi glosses the kanji 乱世的革命 with the English words "anarchical revolution."

5. Takekoshi, *Shin Nihon shi,* vol. 2, 22.

6. Ibid., 27.

7. Raymond Williams, *The Long Revolution* (London: Chatto & Windus, 1961). The "long" revolution refers to the cultural revolution that occurred alongside the democratic and industrial revolutions.

8. Originally published in 1927, reprinted in 1930 in a volume with the same title.

9. Translation based on the original passage in Fukuzawa Yukichi's *Bunmeiron no gairyaku,* published in 1875. See *Fukuzawa Yukichi zenshū,* vol. 4 (Iwanami Shoten, 1959), 70–71. For a translation of the full text, see *Outline of a Theory of Civilization,* trans. David A. Dilworth and G. Cameron Hurst III (New York: Columbia University Press, 2009).

CHAPTER 3

1. Yoshimi Shun'ya, *Banpaku to sengo Nihon* (Kōdansha, 2011), 68–75.

2. Fukuzawa Yukichi, *Bunmeiron no gairyaku,* (1875), 41. The translation, used here with some modification, is from *Outline of a Theory of Civilization,* trans. David A. Dilworth and G. Cameron Hurst III (New York: Columbia University Press, 2009), 48. Dilworth and Hurst translate "refinement of human character" as "esteem for human refinement."

3. Ibid. Dilworth and Hurst use "man" instead of "humanity," and translate "intellect" as "knowledge."

4. Fukuzawa, *Bunmeiron no gairyaku*, 18; Dilworth and Hurst, *Outline of a Theory of Civilization*, 19. Dilworth and Hurst translate "the modern world" as "modern history."

5. "Fukuzawa zenshū shogen" (1897), in *Fukuzawa Yukichi zenshū*, vol.1 (Iwanami Shoten, 1958), 60.

6. Fukuzawa, *Bunmeiron no gairyaku*, 119; Dilworth and Hurst, *Outline of a Theory of Civilization*, 143–44. Dilworth and Hurst translate "authority" as "power and virtue."

7. Watanabe Hiroshi, *Kinsei Nihon shakai to Sōgaku*, rev. ed. (Tōkyō Daigaku Shuppankai, 2010), 23–29.

8. Masubuchi Tatsuo, *Rekishika no dōjidaishi-teki kōsatsu ni tsuite* (Iwanami Shoten, 1983), 181–87.

9. Sorai was Ogyū Sorai's pen name. The pen name is often the preferred usage for premodern artists, writers, and scholars.

10. Since the *Book of Music* was lost in the Qin (pre-Han) period, these early Confucian classics are referred to as the Five Classics in Western scholarship.

11. Ogyū Sorai, *Gakusoku*, in *Ogyū Sorai*, vol. 36 in *Nihon shisō taikei*, ed. Nishida Taiichirō (Iwanami Shoten, 1973), 192–93. The English translation is from Richard H. Minear, "Ogyū Sorai's *Instructions for Students*: A Translation and Commentary," *Harvard Journal of Asiatic Studies* 36 (1976): 5–81.

12. Unpublished at the time, this manuscript has been dated to 1721 by Hiraishi Naoaki in his chronological study of Sorai, *Ogyū Sorai nenpu kō* (Heibonsha, 1984), 229–37.

13. Sorai's influence on Nishi is given detailed treatment in Sugawara Hikaru, *Nishi Amane no seiji shisō: Kiritsu, kōri, shin* (Perikansha, 2009), 204–10.

14. Nishi Amane, "Suehiro no kotobuki," in *Meiji keimō shisōshū*, ed. Ōkubo Toshiaki, vol. 3 of *Meiji bungaku zenshū* (Chikuma Shobō, 1967), 30–32.

15. Ibid., 31–32.

CHAPTER 4

1. James B. Lewis, "Beyond *Sakoku*: The Korean Envoy to Edo and the 1719 Diary of Shin Yu-han," *Korea Journal* 25, no. 11 (November 1985): 22–41. This article provides an account of the 1719 mission and an English translation of portions of Shin's *Haeyurok*.

2. Translation of this passage is based on the modern Japanese translation of Shin Yu-han's diary by Kang Jeon, *Kaiyūroku* (Heibonsha, 1974), 116.

3. Hayami Akira and Miyamoto Matao, eds., *Nihon keizaishi 1 Keizai shakai no seiritsu 17–18 seiki* (Iwanami Shoten, 1988).

4. Saitō Osamu, *Edo to Ōsaka: Kindai Nihon no toshi kigen* (NTT Shuppan, 2002).

5. Miyagawa Yasuko, *Jiyū gakumon toshi Ōsaka: Kaitokudō to Nihonteki risei no tanjō* (Kōdansha, 2002).

6. The text of *Okina no fumi* cited here appears in Ishihama Juntarō et al., eds., *Nihon koten bungaku taikei 97: Kinsei shisōka bunshū* (Iwanami Shoten, 1966), 556. The English translation here is by Katō Shūichi, "*Okina no Fumi*: The Writings of an Old Man, by Tominaga Nakamoto," *Monumenta Nipponica* 22, nos. 1/2 (1967): 204. Katō's translation is based on a different Japanese edition of the text: *Nihon jurin sōsho, kaisetsubu II* (Tōyō Tosho Kankōkai, 1929).

7. Katō Shūichi, "Edo shisō no kanōsei to genjitsu: Kyōhō no nika ni tsuite," interpretive essay in *Nihon no meicho 18: Tominaga Nakamoto, Ishida Baigan* (Chūō Kōronsha, 1972).

8. Katō Shūichi, "*Okina no Fumi*," 200.

9. Ibid., 206.

10. Ibid., 197.

11. Ibid., 198.

12. Yoshikawa Kōjirō et al., eds., *Nihon shisō taikei 40: Motoori Norinaga* (Iwanami Shoten, 1978), 468.

CHAPTER 5

1. Mizutani Mitsuhiro, *Edo wa yume ka* (Chikuma Shobō, 1992), 125–32.

2. Gotō Yōichi et al., eds., *Nihon shisō taikei 30: Kumazawa Banzan* (Iwanami Shoten, 1971), 113–14.

3. This is James Legge's translation of a passage from the "Li Ren" chapter of the *Analects*.

4. This is the final line of James Legge's translation of *The Great Learning*.

5. Wen Yan Zhuan commentary on the hexagram Qian, *Yijing* (*I Ching, The Book of Changes*).

6. Nakamura Yukihiko, ed., *Nihon shisō taikei 59: Kinsei chōnin shisō* (Iwanami Shoten, 1975), 134.

7. Ibid., 101.

8. Ibid.

9. Nomura Maki, "Kinsei Nihon ni okeru 'kami no miezaru te'—Dōjima kome sōba no chōnin shisō," in *Hokkaidō Daigaku Hōgakubu Raiburarii 6: Fukusū no kindai*, ed. Ogawa Kōzō (Hokkaidō Daigaku Tosho Kankōkai, 2000).

10. Hiraishi Naoaki, ed., *Seidan: Hattori-bon* (Heibonsha, 2011), 25.

11. Ibid., 93.

12. Ibid., 108–9.

13. Dazai Shundai, "*Keizairoku shūi*: Addendum to 'On the Political Economy'," in *Tokugawa Political Writings*, ed. Tetsuo Najita (Cambridge: Cambridge University Press, 1998), 141–53; for the original text, see Rai Tsutomu, ed., *Nihon shisō taikei 37: Sorai gakuha* (Iwanami Shoten, 1972), 47.

CHAPTER 6

1. Kazu Tsuguto, *Tenmon gakusha-tachi no Edo jidai: Koyomi uchū kan no daitenkan* (Chikuma Shobō, 2016), 68–74.

2. Mizuta Norihisa and Arisaka Takamichi, eds., *Nihon shisō taikei 43: Tominaga Nakamoto, Yamagata Bantō* (Iwanami Shoten, 1973), 487. All subsequent citations from *Yume no shiro* are from this edition.

3. Yamagata, *Yume no shiro*, 446–47.

4. Ibid., 397.

5. Ibid., 382.

6. Ibid., 363–64.

7. Ibid., 364.

8. Leo Strauss, "How to Begin to Study Medieval Philosophy," in *The Rebirth of Classical Political Rationalism: An Introduction to the Thought of Leo Strauss*, ed. Thomas L. Pangle (Chicago: University of Chicago Press, 1989). Complete, unedited version published as "How to Study Medieval Philosophy," *Interpretation* 23, no. 3 (Spring 1996), 319–38.

9. Yamagata, *Yume no shiro*, 365.

10. Tokumori Makoto, *Kaiho Seiryō: Edo no jiyū o ikita jusha* (Asahi Shimbun Shuppan, 2013).

11. Tsukatani Akihiro and Kuranami Shōji, eds., *Nihon shisō taikei 44: Honda Toshiaki, Kaiho Seiryō* (Iwanami Shoten, 1970), 247.

12. Ibid., 226.

13. Ibid., 241.

14. *Zenchūdan*, in *Kaiho Seiryō zenshū*, ed. Kuranami Shōji (Yachiyo Shuppan, 1976), 490.

15. Tsukatani and Kuranami, *Nihon shisō taikei 44*, 227.

16. *Keikodan* in *Nihon shisō taikei 44*, 295.

17. Ibid., 237.

18. *Rōshi kokuji kai*, in *Kaiho Seiryō zenshū*, 813.

19. *Azuma no hanamuke*, in *Kaiho Seiryō zenshū*, 357.

CHAPTER 7

1. Ishikawa Jun, ed., *Nihon no meichō 21: Motoori Norinaga* (Chūō Kōronsha, 1970).

2. Hasegawa Ikuo, *Yoshida Ken'ichi* (Shinchōsha, 2014).

3. Ōkubo Tadashi, ed., *Motoori Norinaga zenshū*, vol. 8 (Chikuma Shobō, 1972), 333.

4. Ibid., 334.

5. Ibid., 349.

6. Ibid., 345.

7. Takayama Daiki, "'Mono no aware o shiru' setsu to 'tsū' dangi: shoki Norinaga no ichi," *Kokugo kokubun* 84, no. 11 (November 2015).

8. Ōkubo, *Motoori Norinaga zenshū*, vol. 8, 359.

9. Motoori Norinaga, *Isonokami sasamegoto*, fascicle 3, in *Ashiwake obune, Isonokami sasamegoto*, ed. Koyasu Nobukuni (Iwanami Shoten, 2003), 289–90.

10. Koyasu Nobukuni ed., *Shibun yōryō* (Iwanami Shoten, 2010), 66.

11. Yoshikawa Kōjirō et al., eds., *Nihon shisō taikei 40: Motoori Norinaga* (Iwanami Shoten, 1978), 359.

12. Ibid., 213.

CHAPTER 8

1. Mizuta Norihisa and Arisaka Takamichi, eds., *Nihon shisō taikei 43: Tominaga Nakamoto, Yamagata Bantō* (Iwanami Shoten, 1973), 273.

2. Ibid., 179.

3. Ibid., 196. The last sentence is an allusion to the "Gong Ye Chang" chapter of the *Analects* of Confucius: "The Master said, 'When good order prevailed in his country, Ning Wu acted the part of a wise man. When his country was in disorder, he acted the part of a stupid man. Others may equal his wisdom, but they cannot equal his stupidity.'"

4. Ibid., 200.

5. Yoshikawa Kōjirō et al., eds., *Nihon shisō taikei 40: Motoori Norinaga* (Iwanami Shoten, 1978), 33.

6. Ibid., 213.

7. Motoori Norinaga, "Shamon Monnō ga *Kusen hakkai gechō ron* no ben" (1790), in Ōkubo Tadashi, ed., *Motoori Norinaga zenshū*, vol. 14 (Chikuma Shobō, 1972), 163–64.

8. English translation from Donald L. Philippi, trans., *Kojiki* (Princeton University Press and University of Tokyo Press, 1969), 47; for a recent edition of the original text, see Kōnoshi Takamitsu and Yamaguchi Yoshinori, eds., *Shinpen Nihon koten bungaku zenshū 1: Kojiki* (Shogakukan, 1997).

9. Ōkubo, *Motoori Norinaga zenshū*, vol. 14, 163–64.

10. Mizuta and Arisaka, *Nihon shisō taikei 43*, 214.

11. René Descartes, *The Principles of Philosophy*, tr. John Veitch, part 2 "Of the Principles of Material Things," sect. 21, in *The Method, Meditations and Philosophy of Descartes* (Washington and London: M. Walter Dunne, 1901).

12. Alexandre Koyré, *From the Closed World to the Infinite Universe* (Baltimore: Johns Hopkins University Press, 1957), 2.

13. *Kagaika*, in Ōkubo, *Motoori Norinaga zenshū*, vol. 8 (Chikuma Shobō, 1972), 405–6.

14. *Uiyamabumi*, in Ōkubo, *Motoori Norinaga zenshū*, vol. 1 (Chikuma Shobō, 1968), 5.

15. Tahara Tsuguo et al., eds., *Nihon shisō taikei 50: Hirata Atsutane, Ban Nobutomo, Ōkuni Takamasa* (Iwanami Shoten, 1973), 497–500.

16. Ōkubo, *Motoori Norinaga zenshū*, vol. 8, 349.

CHAPTER 9

1. Maruyama Masao, "Rekishi ishiki no 'kosō'," in *Maruyama Masao shū*, vol. 10 (Iwanami Shoten, 1996).

2. *Nihon no shisō 6: Rekishi shisō shū* (Chikuma Shobō, 1972).

3. Hiraishi Naoaki, introduction to *Maruyama Masao kōgiroku*, vol. 6 (Tōkyō Daigaku Shuppankai, 2000).

4. Uete Michiari, ed., *Nihon no shisō taikei 49: Rai San'yō* (Iwanami Shoten, 1977), 280–82.

5. *Tsūgi* was posthumously published in 1840.

6. Translation by Barry D. Steben, in "Rai San'yō's Philosophy of History and the Ideal of Imperial Restoration," *East Asian History* 24 (December 2002): 140. The original text of *Tsūgi* may be found in Kizaki Aikichi and Rai Seiichi, eds., *Rai San'yō zensho*, vol. 2 (Rai San'yō Sensei Iseki Kenshō Kai, 1932).

7. The text used here is from *Rai San'yō zensho*, vol. 2.

8. Kumazawa Banzan, *Shūgi washo*, fascicle 8, 1672, in Gotō Yōichi et al., eds., *Nihon shisō taikei 30: Kumazawa Banzan* (Iwanami Shoten, 1971), 150.

9. Yamaga Sokō, *Takkyo dōmon*, fascicle 5, 1668, in Hirose Yutaka, ed., *Yamaga Sokō zenshū: shokō hen*, vol. 12 (Iwanami Shoten, 1940), 320.

10. See the section on Emperor Jinmu in Rai San'yō's *Nihon seiki*, in Uete, *Nihon no shisō taikei 49: Rai San'yō*, 11–12.

11. Ibid., section on Emperor Go-Tsuchimikado, 411.

12. Ibid., section on Emperor Kōtoku, 65.

13. Asai Kiyoshi, *Meiji ishin to gunken shisō*, rev. ed. (1939; repr., Gannandō Shoten,1968), 100–101.

14. Komatsu Midori, ed., *Itō-kō jikiwa* (Chikura Shobō, 1936), 208–9.

15. Tokutomi Sohō, *Rai San'yō* (Min'yūsha, 1926), 217.

16. Shimada Hideaki, "Keisei no yume, bunshi no yūgi: Rai San'yō ni okeru seiji shisō to shigaku," *Kokka gakkai zasshi* 127, nos. 7–8 (August 2014), 157–59.

17. Haga Shōji, *Shisekiron: Jūkyū seiki Nihon no chiiki shakai to rekishi ishiki* (Nagoya Daigaku Shuppankai, 1998), 160–65.

18. Yamamuro Kyōko, *Ōedo akinai hakusho: Sūryō bunseki ga tokiakasu shōnin no shinjitsu* (Kōdansha, 2015), 38–48.

19. Matsumoto Rokuroku, *Chōju yōjō ron* (completed in 1795, published in 1830), cited in Maeda Tsutomu, *Kinsei Shintō to Kokugaku* (Perikansha, 2002), 366.

20. *Nihon no shisō 6: Rekishi shisō shū* (Chikuma Shobō, 1972).

21. Citations to this work below refer to this edition: Matsumoto Sannosuke et al., eds., *Nihon shisō taikei 48: Kinsei shironshū* (Iwanami Shoten, 1974).

22. Watanabe Hiroshi, "'Shinpo' to 'Chūka'—Nihon no baai," in *Higashi Ajia no ōken to shisō*, rev. ed. (Tōkyō Daigaku Shuppankai, 2016).

23. Ozawa Eiichi, *Kindai Nihon Shigakushi no kenkyū: Bakumatsu-hen* (Yoshikawa Kōbunkan, 1966), 477.

CHAPTER 10

1. Katsuta Masaharu, *Haihan chiken: Kindai kokka tanjō no butaiura* (Kadokawa Sofia Bunko, 2014), 169–76.

2. *Fukuzawa Yukichi zenshū*, vol. 4 (Iwanami Shoten, 1959), 70; Fukuzawa Yukichi, *Outline of a Theory of Civilization*, trans. David A. Dilworth and G. Cameron Hurst III, rev. trans. (New York: Columbia University Press, 2009), 83.

3. Ogawa Tsunendo and Tokunaga Haruo, eds., *Maki Izumi no Kami zenshū* (Kurume: Suitengū, 1998), vol. 3, 29.

4. Tōyama Shigeki, ed., *Nihon kindai shisō taikei 2: Tennō to kazoku* (Iwanami Shoten, 1988), 24–27.

5. Citations to *Shinron* have benefited from Bob Tadashi Wakabayashi's complete English translation of the text in his monograph *Anti-Foreignism and Western Learning in Early-Modern Japan: The New Theses of 1825* (Cambridge, MA: Harvard University Press, 1986). The Japanese text used here is contained in Imai Usaburō et al., eds., *Nihon shisō taikei 53: Mitogaku* (Iwanami Shoten, 1973).

6. Jiang Jianwei, "Aizawa Seishisai no 'kokutai' shisō ni okeru 'minmei,'" *Nihon Chūgoku gakkai hō* 617 (October 2015).

7. Wakabayashi, *Anti-Foreignism and Western Learning*, 184.

8. Ibid., 190.

9. Ibid., 192.

10. Ibid., 158.

11. Watanabe Hiroshi, "Seiyō no 'kindai' to Jugaku," in *Higashi Ajia no ōken to shisō*, rev. ed. (Tōkyō Daigaku Shuppankai, 2016), 199–203.

12. Yokoi Shōnan, "*Kokuze sanron*: The Three Major Problems of State Policy," annotated translation by D.Y. Miyauchi, *Monumenta Nipponica* 23, nos. 1–2 (1968): 168, modified here by the translator; the Japanese text used here is found in Yamaguchi Muneyuki et al. eds., *Nihon shisō taikei 55: Watanabe Kazan, Takano Chōei, Sakuma Shōzan, Yokoi Shōnan, Hashimoto Sanai* (Iwanami Shoten, 1971), 448–49.

13. Asai Kiyoshi, *Meiji ishin to gunken shisō*, rev. ed (1939; repr. Gannandō Shoten, 1968). See also Maeda Tsutomu, *Edo kōki no shisō kūkan* (Perikansha, 2009).

14. Tsuda Michitarō, ed., *Tsubo no ishibumi* (Aoki Tōsaku, 1917), 24–25.

CHAPTER 11

1. Fukuzawa Yukichi, "Fukuzawa zenshū shogen," in *Fukuzawa Yukichi zenshū*, 5 vols. (Jiji Shinpōsha, 1898).

2. Fukuzawa, *Fukuzawa Yukichi zenshū*, vol. 1 (Iwanami Shoten, 1958), 29.

3. Entry for *keimō*, in *Iwanami tetsugaku, shisō jiten*, ed. Hiromatsu Wataru et al. (Iwanami Shoten, 1998).

4. Fukuzawa, *Fukuzawa Yukichi zenshū*, vol. 1, 33–34.

5. Fukuzawa, *Fukuzawa Yukichi zenshū*, vol. 2 (Iwanami Shoten, 1959), 272.

6. Fukuzawa, *Fukuzawa Yukichi zenshū*, vol. 1, 395.

7. The phrase *kaika bunmei* appears in issue 17 of *Nihon shinbun*, dated Keiō 1.10.15 (1865).

8. Satō Tōru, *Gendai ni ikiru Bakumatsu—Meiji shoki kango jiten* (Meiji Shoin, 2007).

9. Richard Wilhelm and Cary F. Baynes, trans., *The I Ching, or Book of Changes* (Princeton University Press, 1950), 380.

10. Ishida Mizumaro, *Reibun Bukkyōgo Daijiten* (Shōgakukan, 1997).

11. *Meiji bunka zenshū*, reprint, vol. 17 (Nihon Hyōronsha, 1992), 134–35.

12. Mita Munesuke, "Bunmei kaika no shakai shinrigaku," in *Teihon Mita Munesuke chosakushū III: Kindaika Nihon no seishin kōzō* (Iwanami Shoten, 2012), 94.

13. Rutherford B. Alcock, *The Capital of the Tycoon: A Narrative of a Three Years' Residence in Japan*, vol. 2 (London: Longman & Green, 1863), 211.

14. Reprinted in Yamada Hajime, ed., *Zuihitsushū: Meiji no Tōkyō* (Iwanami Shoten, 1989).

15. *Teiken Taguchi Ukichi zenshū*, vol. 2 (Yoshikawa Kōbunkan, 1927), 127.

16. Ōkubo Toshiaki et al., eds. *Tsuda Mamichi zenshū*, vol. 1 (Misuzu Shobō, 2001), 286–300.

17. Kōno Yūri, *Meiroku zasshi no seiji shisō: Sakatani Shiroshi to "dōri" no chōsen* (Tōkyō Daigaku Shuppankai, 2011), 242–43.

18. Narushima Fukusaburō, ed., *Ryūhoku ikō*, vol. 1 (privately printed, 1890), 11–12.

19. Alcock, *The Capital of the Tycoon*, vol. 2, 276.

20. Ibid., 277.

21. Fukuzawa, *Fukuzawa Yukichi zenshū*, vol. 1, 290.

22. Matsuzawa Hiroaki, "Bunmeiron ni okeru 'shizō' to 'dokuritsu': *Bunmeiron no gairyaku* to sono zengo," originally published 1981–82, reprinted as chapter 5 of *Kindai Nihon no keisei to Seiyō keiken* (Iwanami Shoten, 1993).

23. *Fukuzawa Yukichi zenshū*, vol. 4 (Iwanami Shoten, 1959), 25; Fukuzawa Yukichi, *Outline of a Theory of Civilization*, trans. David A. Dilworth and G. Cameron Hurst III (New York: Columbia University Press, 2009), 28.

24. *Fukuzawa Yukichi zenshū*, vol. 4, 4.

25. Tokutomi Sohō, *Shōrai no Nihon*, in Uete Michiari, ed., *Meiji Bungaku zenshū 34: Tokutomi Sohō* (Chikuma Shobō, 1989); *The Future Japan*, trans. and ed. Vinh Sinh (Edmonton: University of Alberta Press, 1989), 154.

26. *Nakae Chōmin zenshū*, vol. 14 (Iwanami Shoten, 1985), 168.

REFERENCES

INTRODUCTION

Braudel, Fernand. *Grammaire des civilisations.* Paris: Flammarion, 1993.

Elias, Norbert. *The Civilizing Process.* 2 vols. Oxford: Blackwell, 1969.

Ferguson, Niall. *Civilization: The West and the Rest.* New York: Penguin Press, 2011.

Huntington, Samuel P. "The Clash of Civilizations?" *Foreign Affairs* 72, no. 3 (Summer 1993): 22–49.

——. *The Clash of Civilizations and the Remaking of World Order.* New York: Simon & Schuster, 1996.

Ignatieff, Michael. *Blood and Belonging: Journeys into the New Nationalism.* London: BBC Books, 1993.

——. "Fault Lines." *New York Times,* 1 December 1996.

——. *The Warrior's Honor: Ethnic War and the Modern Conscience.* London: Chatto & Windus, 1998.

Katsurajima Nobuhiro. *Shisōshi no jūkyū-seiki: Tasha to shiteno Tokugawa Nihon.* Perikansha, 1999.

Mitani Hiroshi and Yamaguchi Teruomi. *Jyūkyū-seiki Nihon no rekishi: Meiji-ishin o kangaeru.* Hōsō Daigaku Kyōiku Shinkōkai, 2000.

Senghaas, Dieter. *The Clash within Civilizations: Coming to Terms with Cultural Conflicts.* London: Routledge, 2002.

Shiota Ryōhei, ed. *Meiji Bungaku zenshū 4: Narushima Ryūhoku, Hattori Bushō, Kurimoto Jōun.* Chikuma Shobō, 1969.

Tōyama Shigeki. "Bakumatsu seiji katei ni okeru kōshitsu." *Rekishi hyōron,* October 1946 (inaugural issue).

——. *Meiji ishin.* Iwanami Shoten, 1951.

——. "Mitogaku no seikaku." In *Kokumin seikatsushi kenkyū: Seikatsu to shisō,* edited by Nakamura Kōya. Shōgakukan, 1944.

Walzer, Michael. *Thick and Thin: Moral Argument at Home and Abroad.* Notre Dame, IN: Notre Dame Press, 1994.

Yamazaki Masakazu. *Kindai no yōgo.* PHP Kenkyūjo, 1994.

CHAPTER 1

Adams, Francis Ottiwell. *The History of Japan.* 2 vols. London: Henry S. King, 1874–75.

Gordon, Andrew. *A Modern History of Japan: From Tokugawa Times to the Present.* New York: Oxford University Press, 2003.

Griffis, William Elliot. *The Mikado's Empire.* New York: Harper & Brothers, 1876. Reprint, Berkeley: Stone Bridge Press, 2006.

Itō Takeo. *Fukko no sekishi, Tamamatsu Misao.* 2 vols. 2nd ed. Kinkei Gakuin, 1934.

Jansen, Marius B. *The Making of Modern Japan.* Cambridge, MA: Harvard University Press, 2000.

Maki Kenji. *Kindai ni okeru seiyōjin no Nihon rekishi kan.* Kōbundō, 1950.

Mitani Hiroshi. "Meiji Revolution." In *Oxford Research Encyclopedia of Asian History.* New York: Oxford University Press, 2017.

Miyachi Masato. *Bakumatsu ishin henkaku shi.* 2 vols. Iwanami Shoten, 2012.

Ōhama Tetsuya. *Tennō to Nihon no kindai.* Dōseisha, 2010.

Ōkubo Toshiaki. *Iwakura Tomomi.* Chūō Kōronsha, 1973.

Sakamoto Takao. *Nihon no kindai 2: Meiji-kokka no kensetsu.* Chūō Kōronsha, 1999.

Sasaki Suguru. *Bakumatsu ishin no kosei 5: Iwakura Tomomi.* Yoshikawa Kōbunkan, 2007.

Takahashi Hidenao. *Bakumatsu ishin no seiji to tennō.* Yoshikawa Kōbunkan, 2007.

Tōyama Shigeki, ed. *Nihon kindai shisō taikei 2: Tennō to kazoku.* Iwanami Shoten, 1988.

Watanabe Hiroshi. *A History of Japanese Political Thought, 1600–1901.* Translated by David Noble. I-House Press, 2012.

CHAPTER 2

Fukuzawa Yukichi. *Fukuzawa Yukichi zenshū.* Vols. 1, 2, 4. Iwanami Shoten, 1958–59.

——. *Outline of a Theory of Civilization.* Translated by David A. Dilworth and G. Cameron Hurst III. Revised translation. New York: Columbia University Press, 2009.

Itō Yahiko. *Ishin-kakumei shakai to Tokutomi Soho.* Kizasu Shobō, 2013.

Kōno Yūri. *Gishi no seijigaku: Shin-Nihon seiji shisōshi.* Hakusuisha, 2017.

Kōsaka Morihiko. *Aru meiji riberarisuto no kiroku: Kokō no sentōsha Takekoshi Yosaburō den.* Chūō Kōronsha, 2002.

Noro Eitarō. *Shohan Nihon shihonshugi hattatsu shi.* 2 vols. Iwanami Shoten, 1983.

Takekoshi Yosaburō. *Shin Nihon shi.* 2 vols. Iwanami Shoten, 2005.

Watanabe Hiroshi. "Anshan rejīmu to Meiji kakumei." In *Tokuviru to demokurasī no genzai*, edited by Matsumoto Reiji et al. Tōkyō Daigaku Shuppankai, 2009.

——. "'Meiji ishin' ron to Fukuzawa Yukichi." *Kindai Nihon kenkyū* 24. Keiō Gijuku Fukuzawa Kenkyū Center, 2008.

Williams, Raymond. *The Long Revolution.* London: Chatto & Windus, 1961.

CHAPTER 3

Hiraishi Naoaki. *Ogyū Sorai nenpu kō.* Heibonsha, 1984.

Kobayashi Noboru. *Chūgoku Nihon ni okeru rekishikan to in'itsu shisō.* Waseda Daigaku Shuppanbu, 1983.

Masubuchi Tatsuo. *Rekishika no dōjidaishiteki kōsatsu ni tsuite.* Iwanami Shoten, 1983.

Minear, Richard H. "Ogyū Sorai's *Instructions for Students*: A Translation and Commentary." *Harvard Journal of Asiatic Studies* 36 (1976): 5–81.

Nishida Taiichirō, ed. *Nihon shisō taikei 36: Ogyū Sorai.* Iwanami Shoten, 1973.

Ōkubo Takeharu. *The Quest for Civilization: Encounters with Dutch Jurisprudence, Political Economy, and Statistics at the Dawn of Modern Japan.* Translated by David Noble. Leiden: Global Oriental, 2014.

Ōkubo Toshiaki, ed. *Meiji Bungaku zenshū 3: Meiji keimō shisō shū.* Chikuma Shobō, 1967.

Sugawara Hikaru. *Nishi Amane no seiji shisō: Kiritsu, kōri, shin.* Perikansha, 2009.

Watanabe Hiroshi. *Kinsei Nihon shakai to Sōgaku.* Revised edition. Tōkyō Daigaku Shuppankai, 2010.

Yoshimi Shun'ya. *Banpaku to sengo Nihon.* Kōdansha, 2011.

CHAPTER 4

Hayami Akira and Miyamoto Matao, eds. *Nihon keizaishi 1: Keizai shakai no seiritsu 17–18 seiki.* Iwanami Shoten, 1988.

Ishihama Juntarō et al., eds. *Nihon koten bungaku taikei 97: Kinsei shisōka bunshū.* Iwanami Shoten, 1966.

Katō Shūichi. "Edo shisō no kanōsei to genjitsu: Kyōhō no nika ni tsuite." In *Nihon no meicho 18: Tominaga Nakamoto, Ishida Baigan.* Chūō Kōronsha, 1972.

——, trans. "*Okina no Fumi*: The Writings of an Old Man, by Tominaga Nakamoto." *Monumenta Nipponica* 22, nos. 1/2 (1967): 204.

Kobori Kazumasa. *Kinsei Ōsaka to chishikijin shakai.* Seibundō Shuppan, 1996.

Lewis, James B. "Beyond *Sakoku*: The Korean Envoy to Edo and the 1719 Diary of Shin Yu-han." *Korea Journal* 25, no. 11 (November 1985): 22–41.

Minamoto Ryōen. *Tokugawa gōri shisō no keifu.* Chūō Kōronsha, 1972.

Miyagawa Yasuko. *Jiyū gakumon toshi Ōsaka: Kaitokudō to Nihonteki risei no tanjō.* Kōdansha, 2002.

——. *Tominaga Nakamoto to Kaitokudō: Shisōshi no zenshō.* Perikansha, 1998.

Miyamoto Matao. *Kinsei Nihon no shijō keizai: Ōsaka komeichiba buneski.* Yūhikaku, 1988.

Mizuta Norihisa and Arisaka Takamichi, eds. *Nihon shisō taikei 43: Tominaga Nakamoto, Yamagata Bantō.* Iwanami Shoten, 1973.

Saitō Osamu. *Edo to Ōsaka: Kindai Nihon no toshi kigen.* NTT Shuppan, 2002.

Shin Yu-han. *Kaiyūroku*. Translated by Kang Jeon. Heibonsha, 1974.

Yoshikawa Kōjirō et al., eds. *Nihon shisō taikei 40: Motoori Norinaga*. Iwanami Shoten, 1978.

CHAPTER 5

Dazai Shundai. "*Keizairoku shūi*: Addendum to 'On the Political Economy.'" In *Tokugawa Political Writings*, edited by Tetsuo Najita, 141–53. Cambridge: Cambridge University Press, 1998.

Gotō Yōichi et al., eds. *Nihon shisō taikei 30: Kumazawa Banzan*. Iwanami Shoten, 1971.

Hiraishi Naoki, ed. *Seidan: Hattori-bon*. Heibonsha, 2011.

Mervart, David. "Keizai no shisō." In *Iwanami kōza Nihon no shisō 6: Chitsujo to kihan*, edited by Karube Tadashi et al. Iwanami Shoten, 2013.

Mizutani Mitsuhiro. *Edo wa yume ka*. Chikuma Shobō, 1992.

Nakamura Yukihiko, ed. *Nihon shisō taikei 59: Kinsei chōnin shisō*. Iwanami Shoten, 1975.

Nomura Kanetarō. *Tokugawa jidai no keizai shisō*. Nihon Hyōronsha, 1939.

Nomura Maki. "Kinsei Nihon ni okeru 'kami no miezaru te'—Dōjima kome sōba no chōnin shisō." In *Hokkaidō Daigaku Hōgakubu Raiburarii 6: Fukusū no kindai*, edited by Ogawa Kōzō. Hokkaidō Daigaku Tosho Kankōkai, 2000.

Rai Tsutomu, ed. *Nihon shisō taikei 37: Sorai gakuha*. Iwanami Shoten, 1972.

Satō Tsuneo et al. *Hinnō shikan o minaosu*. Kōdansha, 1995.

Takei Kōichi. *Edo nihon no tenkanten: Suiden no gekizō wa nani o motarashita ka*. NHK Shuppan, 2015.

CHAPTER 6

Katō Hidetoshi. *Media no tenkai: Jōhōshakaigaku kara mita 'kindai.'* Chūō Kōron Shinsha, 2015.

Kazu Tsuguto. *Tenmon gakusha-tachi no Edo jidai: Koyomi uchū kan no daitenkan*. Chikuma Shobō, 2016.

Kuranami Shōji, ed. *Kaiho Seiryō zenshū*. Yachiyo Shuppan, 1976.

Miyauchi Norio. *Yamagata Bantō: 'Yume no shiro' to shōgai*. Sōgensha, 1984.

Strauss, Leo. "How to Begin to Study Medieval Philosophy." In *The Rebirth of Classical Political Rationalism: An Introduction to the Thought of Leo Strauss*, edited by Thomas L. Pangle. Chicago: University of Chicago Press, 1989.

Tokumori Makoto. *Kaiho Seiryō: Edo no jiyū o ikita jusha*. Asahi Shimbun Shuppan, 2013.

Tsukatani Akihiro and Kuranami Shōji, eds. *Nihon shisō taikei 44: Honda Toshiaki, Kaiho Seiryō*. Iwanami Shoten, 1970.

Wakita Osamu et al. *Kaitokudō to sono hitobito*. Ōsaka Daigaku Shuppankai, 1997.

CHAPTER 7

Hasegawa Ikuo. *Yoshida Ken'ichi*. Shinchōsha, 2014.

Ishikawa Jun, ed. *Nihon no meicho 21: Motoori Norinaga*. Chūō Kōronsha, 1970.

Motoori Norinaga. *Ashiwake obune, Isonokami sasamegoto*. Edited by Koyasu Nobukuni. Iwanami Shoten, 2003.

———. *Shibun yōryō*. Edited by Koyasu Nobukuni. Iwanami Shoten, 2010.

Ōkubo Tadashi et al., ed. *Motoori Norinaga zenshū*. Vols. 1, 8, 14. Chikuma Shobō, 1968–72.

Takayama Daiki. *Kinsei Nihon no 'reigaku' to 'shūji': Ogyū Sorai igo no 'setsujin' no seido kōsō*. Tōkyō Daigaku Shuppankai, 2016.

———. "'Mono no aware o shiru' setsu to 'tsū' dangi—shoki Norinaga no ichi." *Kokugo kokubun* 84, no. 11 (November 2015).

Yoshida Ken'ichi (Kennichi). *Japan Is a Circle: A Tour Round the Mind of Modern Japan*. London: Paul Norbury Publications, 1975.

———. *Yōroppa no Seikimatsu*. Iwanami Shoten, 1994.

CHAPTER 8

Arakawa Hiroshi. *Nihonjin no uchūkan: Asuka kara gendai made*. Kinokuniya Shoten, 2001.

Descartes, René. *The Principles of Philosophy*. Translated by John Veitch. In *The Method, Meditations and Philosophy of Descartes*. Washington and London: M. Walter Dunne, 1901.

Fujita Yūji. *Ajia ni okeru bunmei no taikō: Jōiron to shukyūron ni kansuru Nihon Chōsen Chūgoku no hikaku kenkyū*. Ochanomizu Shobō, 2001.

Kanazawa Hideyuki. *Norinaga to 'Sandaikō': Kinsei Nihon no shinwa teki sekaizō*. Kasama Shoin, 2005.

Kōnoshi Takamitsu and Yamaguchi Yoshinori, eds. *Shinpen Nihon koten bungaku zenshū 1: Kojiki*. Shogakukan, 1997.

Koyré, Alexandre. *From the Closed World to the Infinite Universe*. Baltimore: Johns Hopkins University Press, 1957.

Mitsumatsu Makoto. "'Bankoku kōhō' to 'mikuni' no 'kōhō.'" In *Kinsei Nihon no rekishi jojutsu to taigai ishiki*, edited by Inoue Yasushi. Bensei Shuppan, 2016.

Nishimura Ryō. "Shumisen to chikyūsetsu." In *Iwanami kōza Nihon no shisō 4: Shizen to jin'i*, edited by Karube Tadashi et al. Iwanami Shoten, 2013.

Philippi, Donald L., trans. *Kojiki*. Princeton University Press and University of Tokyo Press, 1969.

Tahara Tsuguo et al., eds. *Nihon shisō taikei 50: Hirata Atsutane, Ban Nobutomo, Ōkuni Takamasa*. Iwanami Shoten, 1973.

Watanabe Toshio. *Kinsei Nihon tenmongakushi*. 2 vols. Kōseisha Kōseikaku, 1986–87.

CHAPTER 9

Asai Kiyoshi. *Meiji ishin to gunken shisō*. Revised edition. Gannandō Shoten, 1968.

Haga Shōji. *Shisekiron: Jūkyū seiki Nihon no chiiki shakai to rekishi ishiki*. Nagoya Daigaku Shuppankai, 1998.

Hamano Seiichirō. *Rai San'yō no shisō: Nihon ni okeru seijigaku no tanjō*. Tōkyō Daigaku Shuppankai, 2014.

Hiraishi Naoaki. Introduction to *Maruyama Masao kōgiroku*. Vol. 6. Tōkyō Daigaku Shuppankai, 2000.

Hirose Yutaka, ed. *Yamaga Sokō zenshū shisōhen 12*. Iwanami Shoten, 1940.

Ito Takayuki, ed. *Chiran no hisutoria: Kai, seitō, sei*. Hōsei Daigaku Shuppankyoku, 2017.

Kizaki Aikichi and Rai Seiichi, eds. *Rai San'yō zensho*. Vol. 2. Rai San'yō Sensei Iseki Kenshō Kai, 1932.

Maeda Tsutomu. *Kinsei Shintō to Kokugaku*. Perikansha, 2002.

Maruyama Masao. "Rekishi ishiki no 'kosō.'" In *Maruyama Masao shū*. Vol. 10. Iwanami Shoten, 1996.

Matsumoto Sannosuke et al., eds. *Nihon shisō taikei 48: Kinsei shironshū*. Iwanami Shoten, 1974.

Ozawa Eiichi. *Kindai Nihon shigakushi no kenkyū: Bakumatsu-hen*. Yoshikawa Kōbunkan, 1966.

Shimada Hideaki. "Keisei no yume, bunshi no yūgi: Rai San'yō ni okeru seiji shisō to shigaku." *Kokka gakkai zasshi* 127, nos. 7–8 (August 2014).

Steben, Barry D. "Rai San'yō's Philosophy of History and the Ideal of Imperial Restoration." *East Asian History* 24 (December 2002).

Tokutomi Sohō. *Rai San'yō*. Min'yūsha, 1926.

Uete Michiari, ed. *Nihon shisō taikei 49: Rai San'yō*. Iwanami Shoten, 1977.

Watanabe Hiroshi. *Higashi ajia no ōken to shisō*. Revised edition. Tōkyō Daigaku Shuppankai, 2016.

Yamamuro Kyōko. *Ōedo akinai hakusho: Sūryō bunseki ga tokiakasu shōnin no shinjitsu*. Kōdansha, 2015.

Zhang Xiang and Sonoda Hidehiro, eds. *'Hōken,' 'gunken' saikō: Higashi ajia shakai taiseiron no shinsō*. Shibunkaku Shuppan, 2006.

CHAPTER 10

Imai Usaburō et al., eds. *Nihon shisō taikei 53: Mitogaku*. Iwanami Shoten, 1973.

Jiang Jianwei. "Aizawa Seishisai no 'kokutai' shisō ni okeru 'minmei.'" *Nihon Chūgoku gakkai hō* 617 (October 2015).

Katsuta Masaharu. *Haihan chiken: Kindai kokka tanjō no butaiura.* Kadokawa, 2014.

Kirihara Kenshin. "*Shinron* teki sekaikan no kōzō to sono shisōshiteki haikei." *Ibaraki kenshi kenkyū* 91 (2007).

Maeda Tsutomu. *Edo kōki no shisō kūkan.* Perikansha, 2009.

Matsuda Kōichirō. *Edo no chisiki kara meiji no seiji e.* Perikansha, 2008.

Ogawa Tsunendo and Tokunaga Haruo, eds. *Maki Izumi no Kami zenshū.* 3 vols. Kurume: Suitengū, 1998.

Takayama Daiki. "Seido: Ogyū Sorai to Aizawa Seishisai." In *Kindai Nihon Seiji Shisōshi: Ogyū Sorai kara Amino Yoshihiko made,* edited by Kōno Yūri. Nakanishiya Shuppan, 2014.

Tsuda Michitarō, ed. *Tsubo no ishibumi.* Private edition. 1917.

Wakabayashi, Bob Tadashi. *Anti-Foreignism and Western Learning in Early-Modern Japan: The* New Theses *of 1825.* Cambridge, MA: Harvard University Press, 1986.

Yamaguchi Muneyuki et al., eds. *Nihon shisō taikei 55: Watanabe Kazan, Takano Chōei, Sakuma Shōzan, Yokoi Shōnan, Hashimoto Sanai.* Iwanami Shoten, 1971.

Yokoi Shōnan. "*Kokuze sanron*: The Three Major Problems of State Policy." Annotated translation by D.Y. Miyauchi. *Monumenta Nipponica* 23, nos. 1–2 (1968): 168.

Yoshida Toshizumi. *Mitogaku to Meiji ishin.* Yoshikawa Kōbunkan, 2003.

CHAPTER 11

Alcock, Rutherford B. *The Capital of the Tycoon: A Narrative of a Three Years' Residence in Japan.* 2 vols. London: Longman & Green, 1863.

Karube Tadashi. "Bunmei kaika no jidai." In *Iwanami Kōza Nihon rekishi* 15, edited by Yoshida Yutaka et al. Iwanami Shoten, 2014.

Kōno Yūri. *Meiroku zasshi no seiji shisō: Sakatani Shiroshi to "dōri" no chosen.* Tōkyō Daigaku Shuppankai, 2011.

——. *Taguchi Ukichi no yume.* Keiō Gijuku Daigaku Shuppankai, 2013.

Matsuda Kōichirō. *Gisei no ronri, jiyū no fuan: Kindai Nihon seiji shisō ron.* Keiō Gijuku Daigaku Shuppankai, 2016.

Matsuzawa Hiroaki. *Kindai Nihon no keisei to Seiyō keiken.* Iwanami Shoten, 1993.

Mita Munesuke. "Bunmei kaika no shakai shinrigaku." In *Teihon Mita Munesuke chosakushū III: Kindaka Nihon no seishin kōzō.* Iwanami Shoten, 2012.

Miyamura Haruo. *Shintei Nihon seiji shisōshi: 'Jiyū' no gainen o jiku nishite.* Hōsō Daigaku Kyōiku Shinkōkai, 2005.

Nakanome Tōru. "Bunmei kaika no jidai." In *Nihon no jidaishi 21: Meiji ishin to bunmei kaika,* edited by Matsuo Masahito. Yoshikawa Kōbunkan, 2004.

Ogawara Masamichi. *Fukuzawa Yukichi: 'Kan' to no tatakai.* Bungei Shunjū, 2011.

Ohara Hiroyuki. *Gunji to kōron: Meiji genrōin no seiji shisō.* Keiō Gijuku Daigaku Shuppankai, 2013.

Ōkubo Toshiaki et al., eds. *Tsuda Mamichi zenshū.* 2 vols. Misuzu Shobō, 2001.

Tokutomi Sohō. *The Future Japan.* Translated and edited by Vinh Sinh. Edmonton: University of Alberta Press, 1989.

Uete Michiari, ed. *Meiji Bungaku zenshū 34: Tokutomi Sohō shū.* Chikuma Shobō, 1989.

Wanatabe Hiroshi. "Yōroppa, moshikuwa 'jiyū bentō' no kanata." *UP* 387 (January 2005).

ILLUSTRATION CREDITS

p. 12   The issue of *Foreign Affairs* (Summer 1993) featuring "The Clash of Civilizations?" by Samuel P. Huntington. Courtesy of Foreign Affairs.

p. 13   Samuel P. Huntington (1927–2008). Photograph courtesy of World Economic Forum. Photo by Peter Lauth.

p. 18   A map from Huntington's 1996 book *The Clash of Civilizations and the Remaking of World Order*. Courtesy of Kyle Cronan at the English Wikipedia.

p. 20   Fukuzawa Yukichi (1835–1901). Photograph courtesy of National Diet Library Digital Collection, *Keiō gijuku souritsu 100nen kinenshi* (1958) (Keiō Gijuku, 1960).

p. 22   Tōyama Shigeki, *Meiji ishin* (1951). Photo courtesy of Shinchōsha Photo Department.

p. 25   Emperor Kōmei (1831–67). Courtesy of *The Sun*, vol. 3, no. 4 (Hakubunkan, 1887).

p. 28   Michael Walzer (b. 1935). Photo courtesy of Wikipedia.

p. 32   Tōshū Shōgetsu, *Samurai of Various Domains Defend the Coast Following the Arrival of the American Ships* (1889). Illustration courtesy of the Historiographical Institute, University of Tokyo.

p. 36   The Kogosho Conference, as portrayed in a mural at the Seitoku Memorial Painting Museum by Shimada Bokusen, entitled *The Restoration of Imperial Rule*. Illustration courtesy of Meiji Jingu Gaien Seitoku Kinen Kaigakan.

p. 37   William Elliot Griffis (1843–1928). Photo courtesy of Fukui City History Museum.

p. 39   Iwakura Tomomi (1825–83). Photo courtesy of National Diet Library Digital Collection, "Kindai Nihonjin no shōzō."

p. 43   King Wen of Zhou. Illustration courtesy of Asahi Shimbun Digital.

p. 44   Emperor Meiji (1852–1912). Photo by Uchida Kuichi.

p. 45   Detail of woodblock print by Hashimoto Chikanobu (Yōshū) celebrating the 1889 proclamation of the Constitution of the Empire of Japan. Illustration courtesy of Kochi Liberty and People's Rights Museum.

p. 50   First edition of Takekoshi Yōsaburō's *Shin Nihon shi* (History of the New Japan, 1891–92). Reprinted from National Diet Library Digital Collection, *Shin Nihon shi* by Takekoshi Yōsaburō (Minyūsha, 1892).

p. 51   Takekoshi Yosaburō (1865–1950). Photo courtesy of National Diet Library Digital Collection, in "Kindai Nihonjin no shōzō."

p. 57   John Hampden (1595–1643). Courtesy of the Japanese Wikipedia.

p. 59   Noro Eitarō (1900–34). Photo courtesy of http://binder.gozaru.jp/noro/index.htm.

p. 60   A page from chapter 5 of Fukuzawa Yukichi's *Bunmeiron no gairyaku* (1875). Reprinted from National Diet Library Digital Collection, *Bunmeiron no gairyaku*, vol. 6, no. 2.

p. 66   Expo '70 in Osaka. Photo courtesy of Marui Takato at Wikipedia Commons.

p. 68   The beginning of chapter 3 of Fukuzawa Yukichi's *Bunmeiron no gairyaku* (1875). Reprinted from National Diet Library Digital Collection, *Bunmeiron no gairyaku*, vol. 6, no. 1.

p. 69   François Guizot (1787–1874). Courtesy of the Kayoko Misaki website.

p. 71   Map of Asia from *Sekai kunizukushi* (1869), a world atlas compiled and translated by Fukuzawa Yukichi. Reprinted from National Diet Library Digital Collection, *Sekai kunizukushi*, vol. 1, no. 2 (Creator: Fukuzawa Yukichi).

p. 74   Ogyū Sorai (1666–1728), from Hara Tokusai, *Sentetsu zōden* (Illustrated Biographies of Great Scholars, 1845). Reprinted from National Diet Library Digital Collection, *Sentetsu zōden*, vol. 1 (Shōka Shobō, 1897).

p. 77   Nishi Amane (1829–97). Photo reprinted from *Nishi Amane zenshū*, vol. 1 (Munetaka Shobō, 1960).

p. 79   Immanuel Kant (1724–1804). Photo courtesy of the Japanese Wikipedia.

p. 82   Hanegawa Tōei, *The Korean Embassy Visits the Capital*, c. 1748. Illustration courtesy of Kobe City Museum Ikenaga Hajime Collection.

p. 86   The Dōjima Rice Market in Osaka (from *Settsu meisho zue*, 1796–98). Reprinted from National Diet Library Digital Collection, *Settsu meisho zue*, vol. 4, no. 1 (Morimoto Tasuke et al., 1798).

p. 89   Entrance to Kaitokudō (computer graphic recreation courtesy of the Kaitokudō Archive, Osaka University).

p. 91   Amemiya Shōteki, c. 1760, Ogyū Sorai (seated at center, top) and his disciples. Drawing reproduced from *Ken'en shogen kaienzu* by Amemiya Shōteki, courtesy of Tamagawa University Museum of Education.

p. 92   A spread from the printed edition of Tominaga Nakamoto's *Okina no fumi* (Writings of an Old Man), 1746. Reprinted from *Okina no fumi*. Courtesy of Osaka Prefectural Library Collection.

p. 94   Statue of Yamagata Bantō in Takasago, Hyōgo prefecture. Photo courtesy of Graduate School of Letters, Center for Kaitokudō Studies, Osaka University.

p. 96   Kamogawa Seitoku, *Portrait of Motoori Norinaga in His Seventy-Second Year*, 1801. Illustration courtesy of Museum of Motoori Norinaga.

p. 98   From a late Tokugawa copy of *Kōka shunjū* (Farmer's Almanac, 1707). Illustration courtesy of Nishio City Iwase Library, Aichi prefecture.

p. 101   Kumazawa Banzan (1619–91). Reprinted from National Diet Library Digital Collection, *Sentetsu zōden*, vol. 1 (Shōka Shobō, 1897).

p. 105   Map of the world by Nishikawa Joken, from *Zōho ka'i tsūshō kō* (An Inquiry into Commerce among the Civilized and Barbarian). Illustration reprinted from National Diet Library Digital Collection, *Zōho ka'i tsūshō kō*, vol. 3.

p. 106   *Chōnin bukuro* (Bagful of Knowledge for Merchants) by Nishikawa Joken. Reprinted from National Diet Library Digital Collection, *Chōnin bukuro, Nishikawa Joken isho*), vol. 7 (Kyūrindo Shorin, 1898).

p. 110   Yamashita Kōnai's petition, as reproduced in *Nihon keizai sōsho* (Library of Japan's Economy), edited by Takimoto Seiichi. Reprinted from National Diet Library Digital Collection, *Nihon keizai sōsho*, vol. 5 (Nihon keizai sōsho kankōkai, 1915).

p. 111   Dazai Shundai, from *Sentetsu zōden* (Illustrated Biographies of the Great Scholars, 1845). Reprinted from National Diet Library Digital Collection, *Sentetsu zōden*, vol. 1 (Shōka Shobō, 1897).

p. 114   *Tōsei meika hyōbanki* (Ranking the Famous People of Our Time, 1835), a guide to scholars and men of letters. Reprinted from National Diet Library Digital Collection, *Tōsei meika hyōbanki*, vol. 1 (1834).

p. 116   "Mount Fuji at Torigoe," from Katsushika Hokusai's *One Hundred Views of Mount Fuji* (c. 1834–40), depicting the astronomical observatory established in Asakusa in 1782. Reprinted from National Diet Library Digital Collection, *One Hundred Views of Mount Fuji*, vol. 3. (1834), http://dl.ndl.go.jp/info:ndljp/pid/8942999.

p. 117   Nakai Chikuzan (left) and Nakai Riken (right). Photo courtesy of Graduate School of Letters, Center for Kaitokudō Studies, Osaka University.

p. 118   Heliocentric astronomical theory is explained and illustrated in the first volume of Yamagata Bantō's *Yume no shiro* (In Place of Dreams, 1820). Illustration reprinted from *Nihon shisōtaikei 43: Tominaga Chuki and Yamagata Bantō* (Iwanami Shoten, 1973).

p. 125   Kaiho Seiryō wrote many policy proposals. This is a page from *Shinkondan* (On Opening New Lands, 1813). Illustration reprinted from *Nihon shisōtaikei 44: Honda Toshiaki and Kaiho Seiryō* (Tokyo: Iwanami Shoten, 1970).

p. 128   Sketch by a Japanese artist of the Russian envoy Adam Laxman after his arrival at Nemuro. Illustration courtesy of the Japanese Wikipedia.

p. 130   Utagawa Hiroshige, *Ise Pilgrimage: Crossing the Miyakawa River* (1855). Drawing courtesy of Kameyama Museum, Mie Prefectural Museum.

p. 132   Yoshida Ken'ichi (1912–77). Photo courtesy of Shinchōsha Publishing Co., Ltd.

p. 135   Motoori Norinaga (1730–1801) at the age of forty-four. Illustration courtesy of Museum of Motoori Norinaga.

p. 137   Former residence of Motoori Norinaga, relocated to the site of Matsusaka Castle. Illustration courtesy of Museum of Motoori Norinaga.

p. 140   Manuscript of *Hihon tamakushige* in Norinaga's own hand. Illustration courtesy of Museum of Motoori Norinaga.

p. 141   Corrected page proofs of Norinaga's *Kojikiden*, his extensive commentary on the *Kojiki* (712). Illustration courtesy of Museum of Motoori Norinaga.

p. 146 A depiction of the universe in Musō Monnō's *Kusen hakkai gechō ron* (1754). Following Buddhist cosmology, it placed at the center of the universe the immense Mount Sumeru, surrounded by an ocean in which floated four continents and above which were layered thirty-three separate heavens. Illustration reprinted from National Diet Library Digital Collection, Musō Monnō, *Kusen hakkai gechō ron*.

p. 150 An illustration in Hattori Nakatsune's *Sandaikō* (Thoughts on the Three Great Realms, 1797), showing the "Imperial Land" of Japan directly connected to Heaven. Illustration reprinted from National Diet Library Digital Collection, *Sandaikō*.

p. 151 A page from the manuscript of *Tamakatsuma* (The Precious Basket), an essay collection by Motoori Norinaga. Reprinted from National Diet Library Digital Collection, *Tamakatsuma*.

p. 153 An illustration in Hattori Nakatsune's *Sandaikō*, depicting the cosmic void with the names of the three primal deities inscribed within it. Illustration reprinted from National Diet Library Digital Collection, *Sandaikō*.

p. 154 Illustrations 3 (right) and 10 (left) from Hattori Nakatsune's *Sandaikō*. Illustration reprinted from National Diet Library Digital Collection, *Sandaikō*.

p. 156 René Descartes (1596–1650). Courtesy of the Japanese Wikipedia.

p. 158 World map based on a Western source, published in Japan in 1783. Map courtesy of the Museum of Motoori Norinaga.

p. 164 The opening passage of the *Nihon shoki,* from a 1610 edition printed with wooden movable type, preserved in Jingū Bunko, the archives of Ise Grand Shrine. Reprinted from National Diet Library Digital Collection, *Nihon shoki hennsan 1200nen kinen tenrankai mokuroku.*

p. 167 Maruyama Masao (1914–96). Photo courtesy of Asahi Shinbun/Jiji Press.

p. 168 Rai San'yō (1780–1832). Reprinted from National Diet Library Digital Collection.

p. 170 Opening page of Rai San'yō's *Tsūgi* (Historiographical Reflections, posthumously published in 1840). Reprinted from National Diet Library Digital Collection, *Tsūgi*, vol. 1.

p. 172 First page of the "Hōken saku" section in Rai San'yō's *Shinsaku* (New Policies, 1806). Reprinted from National Diet Library Digital Collection, *Shinsaku*, vol. 1.

p. 175 Title page of Asai Kiyoshi's *Meiji ishin to gunken shisō* (The Meiji Revolution and the Concept of Centralization, 1939). Reprinted from National Diet Library Digital Collection.

p. 177 From Rai San'yō's *Nihon gaishi* (An Unofficial History of Japan, completed in 1826). Reprinted from National Diet Library Digital Collection, *Nihon gaishi*.

p. 180 Title page of Date Chihiro's *Taisei santen kō* (A Study of Three Changes in the Momentum of History, 1848). Reprinted from National Diet Library Digital Collection, *Taisei santen kō*, vol. 1.

p. 186   The edict proclaiming the restoration of imperial rule, issued in January 1868. Reprinted from National Diet Library Digital Collection, *Hōreizensho*.

p. 188   The ceremony proclaiming the abolition of the domains and creation of prefectures. Mural by Kobori Tomoto in the Meiji Memorial Picture Gallery, Tokyo. Illustration courtesy of Meiji Jingu Gaien Seitoku Kinen Kaigakan, *Haihanchiken*.

p. 191   Henry Thomas Buckle (1821–1862). Courtesy of the Japanese Wikipedia.

p. 192   Maki Yasuomi (1813–64). Photo courtesy of http://showman.jp/makiizuminokami/makiizuminokami_01.html.

p. 194   Aizawa Seishisai (1782–1863). Photo courtesy of https://bakumatsu.org/photos/view/364.

p. 195   Title page of Aizawa Seishisai's *Shinron*. Reprinted from National Diet Library Digital Collection, *Shinron*.

p. 199   Commemorative postage stamp for the enthronement of Emperor Shōwa in 1928, depicting the Daijōkyū, a structure specially built for the Daijōsai. Courtesy of the Japanese Wikipedia.

p. 203   Yokoi Shōnan (1809–69). Reprinted from National Diet Library Digital Collection, *Yokoi Shōnan den*, vol. 1 (Nisshin Shoin, 1942).

p. 208   *Famous Places of Tokyo: Horse-Drawn Trams on the Streets of Ginza*, woodblock print by Utagawa Hiroshige III, 1882. Illustration courtesy of National Diet Library Digital Collection.

p. 210   Cover and title page of a pirated edition of Fukuzawa Yukichi's *Seiyō jijō* that was published, with unauthorized revisions, by Kuroda Kōjirō in 1868. Reprinted from National Diet Library Digital Collection, *Seiyō jijō*.

p. 212   Page from *Kunmō kyūri zukai* (Illustrated Course in Science, 1868) by Fukuzawa Yukichi. Reprinted from National Diet Library Digital Collection, *Kunmō kyūri zukai*.

p. 217   Inaugural issue of *Meiji gekkan*, a monthly journal published by the Osaka Prefectural Government beginning in 1868.

p. 219   Rutherford Alcock (1809–97). Courtesy of the Japanese Wikipedia.

p. 221   Taguchi Ukichi (1855–1905). Courtesy of Wikipedia.

p. 222   Tsuda Mamichi (1829–1903). Photo courtesy of National Diet Library Digital Collection, *Bunkyū nenkan Oranda ryūgakusei ikkō no shashin*.

p. 223   Narushima Ryūhoku (1837–84). Courtesy of the Japanese Wikipedia.

p. 225   Illustration from Alcock's *The Capital of the Tycoon* (1863). Illustration courtesy of International Research Center for Japanese Studies, *Images of Japan in Non-Japanese Sources*.

p. 229   Tokutomi Sohō (1863–1957). Courtesy of the Japanese Wikipedia.

p. 230   Nakae Chōmin (1847–1901). Courtesy of Asahi Shimbun Digital.

Karube Tadashi (b. 1965) is a professor in the School of Legal and Political Studies at the University of Tokyo, where he earned his Doctor of Laws (LL.D.). He is a specialist in the history of Japanese political thought, and his published works include *Hikari no ryōkoku: Watsuji Tetsurō* [Domain of Light: Watsuji Tetsurō]; *Utsuriyuku "kyōyō"* [Cultivation of Humanity and Its Changing Forms]; *Kagami no naka no hakumei* [Through a Glass Darkly], winner of the Mainichi Book Review Prize; *Rekishi to iu hifu* [The Membrane of History]; *Seijigaku (Hyūmanitīzu)* [Political Theory (Humanities)]; *Abe Kōbō no toshi* [The City in Abe Kōbō]; *Chitsujo no yume: Seiji shisō ronshū* [The Dream of Order: Essays on Political Thought]; and *Monogatari Iwanami Shoten hyakunen-shi 3: Sengō kara hanarete* [A Narrative Centennial History of Iwanami Books 3: Farewell to the Postwar Era]. *Maruyama Masao: Riberaristuto no shōzō,* winner of the Suntory Prize for Social Sciences and the Humanities, was published in English as *Maruyama Masao and the Fate of Liberalism in Twentieth-Century Japan.*

ABOUT THE TRANSLATOR

David Noble is a prize-winning translator currently living on the Olympic Peninsula in the state of Washington. Originally from Nashville, he completed his undergraduate degree at Vanderbilt University, followed by graduate work in Japanese language, history, and literature at the University of Chicago and Princeton University. He served as executive editor of *Japan: An Illustrated Encyclopedia* (Kodansha, 1993) and worked for five years at Weatherhill, Inc., before establishing an independent practice as a translator, editor, and book designer. He has translated more than a dozen books, with a focus on history, political science, and the humanities.

（英文版）「維新革命」への道　「文明」を求めた十九世紀日本

Toward the Meiji Revolution: The Search for "Civilization" in Nineteenth-Century Japan

2019年3月27日　第1刷発行

著　者　　苅部 直

訳　者　　ディビッド・ノーブル

発行所　　一般財団法人出版文化産業振興財団
　　　　　〒101-0051 東京都千代田区神田神保町3-12-3
　　　　　電話　03-5211-7282(代)

ホームページ　http://www.jpic.or.jp/

印刷・製本所　　大日本印刷株式会社